From Darkness
to Light

ISEAS–Yusof Ishak Institute (formerly the Institute of Southeast Asian Studies) was established as an autonomous organization in 1968. It is a regional centre dedicated to the study of socio-political, security and economic trends and developments in Southeast Asia and its wider geostrategic and economic environment.

The Institute's research programmes are the Regional Economic Studies (RES, including ASEAN and APEC), Regional Strategic and Political Studies (RSPS), and Regional Social and Cultural Studies (RSCS).

ISEAS Publishing, an established academic press, has issued more than 2,000 books and journals. It is the largest scholarly publisher of research about Southeast Asia from within the region. ISEAS Publications works with many other academic and trade publishers and distributors to disseminate important research and analyses from and about Southeast Asia to the rest of the world.

From Darkness to Light

Energy Security Assessment
in Indonesia's Power Sector

MAXENSIUS TRI SAMBODO

ISEAS YUSOF ISHAK INSTITUTE

First published in Singapore in 2016 by
ISEAS Publishing
30 Heng Mui Keng Terrace
Singapore 119614

E-mail: publish@iseas.edu.sg
Website: bookshop.iseas.edu.sg

The responsibility for facts and opinions in this publication rests exclusively with the author and his interpretations do not necessarily reflect the views or the policy of the publisher or its supporters.

ISEAS Library Cataloguing-in-Publication Data

Tri Sambodo, Maxensius.
   From Darkness to Light : Energy Security Assessment in Indonesia's Power Sector.
   1. Energy industries—Indonesia
   2. Power resources—Indonesia
   3. Electric industries—Indonesia
   I. Title.
   II. Title: Energy Security Assessment in Indonesia's Power Sector
HD9502 I52T81   2016

ISBN 978-981-4695-47-3 (soft cover)
ISBN 978-981-4695-48-0 (E-book PDF)

Cover photo: Wind Power, Pandansimo Beach, Yogyakarta, 2014. Photo taken by Felix Wisnu Handoyo.

Typeset by International Typesetters Pte Ltd
Printed in Singapore by Markono Print Media Pte Ltd

*F*or my fellow travellers —
Fransiska, Clara, and Megumi

CONTENTS

LIST OF TABLES

LIST OF FIGURES

LIST OF ABBREVIATIONS

ADB	Asian Development Bank
AF	Availability Factor
AFD	Agence Française Développement
AFNEI	Allied Forces Netherlands East Indies
AGECC	Advisory Group on Energy and Climate Change
AMD	*ABRI Masuk Desa* [Armed Forces Rural Operation]
ANIEM	*Algemeene Nederlandsch Indische Electriciteit Maatschappij* [Netherlands Indies General Electricity Company]
APLN	*Pendanaan Interal dari PLN* [Self-Financing from PLN]
ASEAN	Association of Southeast Asian Nations
ASTAE	Asia Sustainable and Alternative Energy Program
ATA	Automatic Tariff Adjustment
AusAID	Australian government overseas aid program
BANAS	*Badan Nasionalisasi Perusahaan Belanda* [Board for Nationalization of Dutch Enterprises]
BANI	*Badan Arbitrase Nasional Indonesia* [Indonesian Arbitrage National Agency]
BPM	*Bataafche Petroleum Maatschappij* [Batavian Oil Company]
BPPT	*Badan Pengkajian dan Penerapan Teknologi* [Technology Assessment and Application Agency]
BPPTL	*Badan Pengawas Pasar Tenaga Listrik* [Monitoring Agency for the Electricity Market]
BPS	*Badan Pusat Statistik* [Statistics Indonesia]
BPU-PLN	*Badan Pimpinan Umum Perusahaan Listrik Negara* [State Electricity Company Management Agency]

BRIC   Brazil, Russia, India and China
BSM   *Bantuan Siswa Miskin* [Student Assistance for the Poor]
CDM   Clean Development Mechanism
CGI   Consultative Group on Indonesia
COD   Commercial Operation Date
COP   Conference of Parties
CO_2 carbon dioxide
CSD   Commission on Sustainable Development
DAK   *Dana Alokasi Khusus* [Special Allocation Fund]
DDPLN   *Dewan Direktur Perusahaan Listrik Negara* [Board of
              Director Electricity State Company]
Dirjen   *Direktur Jenderal* [Directorate General]
DKI   *Daerah Khusus Ibu Kota* [Special Capital Region of
              Jakarta]
DME   *Departemen Mineral dan Energi* [Department of Mining
              and Energy]
DME   *Desa Mandiri Energi* [Energy Self-Sufficient on Village
              Programme]
DPE   *Departemen Pertambangan dan Energi* [Department of
              Mining and Energy]
DPR   *Dewan Perwakilan Rakyat* [House of Representatives]
DPRD   *Dewan Perwakilan Rakyat Daerah* [Regional Legislative
              Assembly]
DSM   Demand Side Management
ECM   Error Correction Model
ECT   Error Correction Term
EMM   *Electriciteits Maatschappij Medan* [Medan Electricity
              Company]
EMS   *Electriciteits Maatschappij Sumatra* [Sumatra Electricity
              Company]
ERPA   Emissions Reduction Purchase Agreements
ESDM   *Energi dan Sumber daya Mineral* [Energy and Mineral
              Resources]
ESMAP   Energy Sector Management Assistance Program
Finec   *Financieel-Economische Overeenkomst* [Financial
              Economic Agreement]
FIT   Feed-in Tariff
GDP   Gross Domestic Product

GEBEO	*Gemeenschapp-Elijk Electriciteitsbedrijf Bandoeng en Omstreken* [Municipal Electricity Works for Bandung and District]
GHGs	greenhouse gases
GOLKAR	*Golongan Karya* [The Party of the Functional Groups]
GW	gigawatt
GWh	gigawatt hour
HPAEs	High Performing Asian Economies
HSD	High Speed Diesel
IBRD	International Bank for Reconstruction and Development
IBW	*Indische Bedrijven Wet* [Indies Enterprises Law]
ICP	Indonesia Crude Oil Price
IEA	International Energy Agency
IGGI	Inter-Governmental Group on Indonesia
IMF	International Monetary Fund
IPP	Independent Power Producer
ISAK	*Interpretasi Standar Akuntansi Keuangan* [Interpretation on Financial Accounting Standards]
IUKS	*Izin Usaha Kelistrikan Untuk Kepentingan Sendiri* [Private Utilities Licence for Electricity]
IUKU	*Izin Usaha Kelistrikan Untuk Kepentingan Umum* [Public Utilities Licence for Electricity]
JICA	Japan International Cooperation Agency
JTM	*Jaringan Tegangan Menengah* [Medium Transmission Network]
JTR	*Jaringan Tegangan Rendah* [Low Transmission Network]
KBC	Karaha Bodas Company
KL	kiloliters
KLP	*Koperasi Listrik Perdesaan* [Rural Electricity Cooperatives]
Kmc	kilometer circuit
KNIL	*Koningklijke Netherlands Indische Leger* [Royal Netherlands Indies Army]
KORBI	*Kantor Urusan barang-barang Republik Indonesia* [Office to Manage the Properties of the Republic of Indonesia]
KPDT	*Kementerian Pembangunan Daerah Tertinggal* [Ministry of Less Developed Areas]

KUD	*Koperasi Unit Desa* [Village Cooperative Unit]
KUR	*Kredit Usaha Rakyat* [Micro Credit Loan]
kWh	kilowatt-hour
LPG	Liquefied Petroleum Gas
LUCF	Forestry and Land Use Changes
LWB	*Lands Waterkracht Bedrijven* [State Water Power Enterprise]
MDGs	Millennium Development Goals
MEMR	Ministry of Energy and Mineral Resources
MIGA	Multilateral Investment Guarantee Agency
MME	Ministry of Mines and Energy
MSA	Management Service Arrangement
$MtCO_2$	metric ton CO_2
MVA	mega volt ampere
MW	mega watt
NAP	National Action Plan
NICA	Netherland Indies Civil Administration
NIEM	*Netherlandsch-Indisch Electriciteit Maatschappij* [Netherlands Indies Electricity Company]
NIGM	*Nederlandsch-Indische Gas-Maatschappij* [Netherlands Indies Gas Company]
NIWEM	*Nederlandsch-Indisch Waterkracht Exploitatie Maatschappij* [Netherlands Indies Hydropower Exploitation Company]
NTB	*Nusa Tenggara Barat* [West Nusa Tenggara]
NTT	*Nusa Tenggara Timur* [East Nusa Tenggara]
NV. EBALOM	NV. Electriciteits Maatschappij Bali en Lombok
NV. MEPB	NV. Maatschappij tot Exploitatie van Plaatselijke Bedrijven
OECD	Overseas Economic Cooperation and Development
OECF	Overseas Economic Cooperation Fund
OGEM	*Overzeese Gas-en Electriciteits-Maatschappij* [Overseas Gas and Electricity Company]
OP	Operating Permit
OPIC	Overseas Private Investment Corporation
P3LG	*Pusat* or *Penguasa Perusahaan Listrik dan Gas Pusat* [Central Administering Board for Electricity and Gas Enterprises]

PENUDITEL	*Perusahaan Negara untuk Pendistribusian Tenaga Listrik* [State Company for Electric Power Distribution]
PENUPETEL	*Perusahaan Negara Untuk Pembangkit Tenaga Listrik* [State Company for Electric Power Generation]
Perum	*Perusahaan Umum*
PGN	*Perusahaan Gas Negara* [National Gas Company]
PISA	Purchase and Instalment Sales Agreement
PKH	*Program Keluarga Harapan* [Family Hope Programme]
PKI	*Partai Komunis Indonesia* [Communist Party of Indonesia]
PLN	*PT Perusahaan Listrik Negara (Pesero)* [The National Power Company]
PLTA	*Pembangkit Listrik Tenaga Air* [Hydropower Plants]
PLTU	*Pembangkit Listrik Tenaga Uap* [Steam Power Plants]
PNI	*Partai Nasional Indonesia* [Indonesia Nationalist Party]
PNMP-MP	*Program Nasional Pemberdayaan Masyarakat–Mandiri Perdesaan* [National Program on Community Empowerment of Rural Independency]
PNPM	*Program Nasional Pemberdayaan Masyarakat* [National Program for People Empowerment]
PNSB	*Pembangunan Nasional Semesta Berencana* [Planned Overall National Development]
PPA	Power Purchase Agreement
PPP	Public Private Partnership
PPU	Private Power Utility
PSAK	*Pernyataan Standar Akuntansi Keuangan* [Standard Statement on Financial Accounting]
PSO	Public Service Obligation
PV	photovoltaics
RDI	*Rekening Dana Investasi* [Investment Fund Account]
Repelita	*Rencana Pembangunan Lima Tahun* [Five-Year Development Plans]
RIS	*Republik Indonesia Serikat* [Federal Republic of Indonesia]
Rp	Rupiah
RPJM	*Rencana Pembangunan Jangka Menengah Nasional* [National Medium Term Development Planning]

RPLN	*Rupiah Pinjaman Luar Negeri* [Rupiah from Foreign Loan]
RTC	Round Table Conference
RUKN	*Rencana Umum Ketenagalistrikan Nasional* [Public Plans for National Electric Power]
SA	sectoral approach
SARBUMUSI	*Serikat Buruh Muslimin Indonesia* [Muslim Labour Unions]
SBII	*Serikat Buruh Islam Indonesia* [Islamic Labour Unions]
SBLGI	*Serikat Buruh Listrik dan Gas Indonesia* [Electricity and Gas Labour Unions]
SBLGI KBM	*Serikat Buruh Listrik dan Gas Indonesia – Kesatuan Buruh Marhaenisme* [Electricity and Gas Labour Unions – Marhaenisme Labour Union]
SEHEN	*Super Ekstra Hemat Energi* [Super Extra Energy Saving]
SHS	Solar Home System
SLI	*Standar Listrik Indonesia* [Indonesia Electricity Standards]
SOBSI	*Sentral Organisasi Buruh Seluruh Indonesia* [All Indonesia Centre of Labour Organizations]
SSS	*Sumatera Staats Spoorwegen* [Sumatra Train Company]
SUSENAS	*Survey Sosial Ekonomi Nasional* [National Socioeconomic Survey]
TPES	Total Primary Energy Supply
TPPI	Trans Pacific Petrochemical Indotama
UN	United Nations
UNDP	United Nations Development Programme
USAID	United States Agency for International Development
USDEK	*U.U.D. '45 Sosialisme Indonesia, Demokrasi Terpimpin, Ekonomi Terpimpin dan Kepribadian Indonesia* [Constitution 1945, Socialism Indonesia, Leaded Democracy, Leaded Economy and Indonesian Personality]
UUD	*Undang Undang Dasar* [National Constitution]
VA	volt ampere
VAR	Vector Autoregressive Model
VCM	Voluntary Carbon Mechanism
WEC	World Energy Council

ACKNOWLEDGEMENTS

It would have been impossible for me to complete this book without the support, encouragement and inspiration from many individuals and organizations. I would like to express my deepest appreciation for all their efforts.

Firstly, some parts of this book were derived from my PhD dissertation entitled, "Mathematical Modeling Analyses for Investigating the Future Expansion of the Electric Power System in Indonesia", which was completed during 2009–12 when I studied at the National Graduate Institute for Policy Studies (GRIPS) in Japan. I would like to express my gratitude to Professor Tatsuo Oyama, my main advisor who guided and helped me in numerous ways. I am also very grateful to my PhD committee members: Professor Morohosi Hozumi, Professor Roberto Leon Gonzales, Professor Takashi Tsuchiya, and Professor Masanori Fushimi.

Secondly, I would like to document my deep appreciation to Mr Tan Chin Tiong, Director of ISEAS–Yusof Ishak Institute, Singapore, for supporting this book project. I would also like to thank Dr Hui Yew-Foong who, as the coordinator of the Indonesia Studies Group, has provided me with ample opportunities and support in finalizing my book at the Institute. My gratitude also goes to Foo Shu Tieng, Kathleen Mariska Azali, and Sheryl Sin Bing Peng from the Institute who meticulously edited and reviewed the drafts of this book. I would also like to thank two anonymous reviewers for their insightful and constructive advices.

I would like to extend sincere thanks to Darwin Syamsulbahri, Head of the Economic Research Center at the Indonesian Institute of Sciences (P2E-LIPI), Jakarta, for his substantial support which allowed me to pursue a visiting fellowship at ISEAS–Yusof Ishak Institute. During the preparation of this book, I have also obtained support from Professor Lukman Hakim, Professor Iskandar Zulkarnain, Professor Aswatini, Latif Adam, Siwage Dharma Negara, Agus Eko Nugroho, Syarif Hidyat, Ahmad Helmy Fuady, M. Soekarni, Agus Syarip Hidayat, and my younger colleagues in the energy study project who have helped me to manage my research on energy at LIPI.

Special thanks also goes to all my friends in the Indonesia Studies Programme at ISEAS–Yusof Ishak Institute, especially Leo Suryadinata, Aris Ananta, Evi Nurfidya Arifin, Ulla Fionna, Alexander Arifianto, Gwenael Njoto-Feillard, Deasy Simandjuntak and other fellows, especially Ooi Kee Beng, Cassey Lee, Francis Hutchinson, Zhao Hong, Tang Siew Mun, Lee Poh Onn, Malcolm Cook, Jason Morris-Jung, Huong Le Thu, Mustafa Izzuddin, Oh Su Ann, Moe Thuzar, Sanchita Basu Das, and Lee Yongwoo who have made my life in Singapore more cheerful.

Preparation for this book took me more than five years and it led me from Indonesia, Japan to Singapore. I was fortunate to have the constant companionship and support of my wife, Fransiska and my daughters, Clara and Megumi. We had experienced the 11 March 2011 earthquake in Japan, just a day before we skied at the Gala Yuzawa Snow Resort. On that quake day, I had to stay in the campus while they were at the school camp. I also remember a great moment when we cycled, had dinner and ate durians at the East Coast Park of Singapore. Thank you for being there and sharing the journey with me.

Finally, I would like to delicate this book to my guru, Dr Thee Kian Wie, senior researcher at P2E-LIPI, who passed away on 8 February 2014 at the age of seventy-eight. He inspired me to devote my life to academia. Without his support, this book would never have materialized.

Maxensius Tri Sambodo

1

INTRODUCTION

After seventy years of Independence, Indonesia still struggles to solve four main challenges. Firstly, Indonesia has the highest number of people without electricity access in the Asian region, after India (IEA 2013). Secondly, out of the ten Southeast Asian countries, Indonesia has the lowest electrification rate, after Cambodia, Myanmar, and the Philippines (IEA 2013). Thirdly, in terms of electricity consumption per capita, out of 135 countries, Indonesia ranked 28th from the bottom in 2011, after the Philippines and before India.[1] Fourthly, in terms of carbon dioxide emissions from electricity and heat production, Indonesia was one of the top emitters, placed at 16th out of 133 countries in 2011. The emissions will increase if Indonesia becomes more dependent on coal power plants in the future. As the demand for electricity in Indonesia is expected to rise, this has consequences not only in terms of the provision of primary energy supply for power generation, but also in terms of electricity transmission and distribution, intended improvements regarding the quality of electricity supply, the maintenance and sustainability of power supply, the reduction of electricity poverty, and finally, the creation of a green (more environmentally sustainable) power system.

Table 1.1
Electricity Access, 2012

Region	Population without Electricity in Millions	Electrification Rate (%)	Urban Electrification Rate (%)	Rural Electrification Rate (%)
China	3	100	100	100
India	204	75	94	67
Southeast Asia	140	77	92	65
Brunei Darussalam	0	100	100	99
Cambodia	10	34	97	18
Indonesia	60	76	92	59
Laos	1	78	93	70
Malaysia	0	100	100	99
Myanmar	36	32	60	18
Philippines	29	70	89	52
Singapore	0	100	100	100
Thailand	1	99	100	99
Vietnam	4	96	100	94
Rest of Developing Asia	175	61	82	52
Bangladesh	62	60	90	48
DPR Korea	18	26	36	11
Mongolia	0	90	98	73
Nepal	7	76	97	72
Pakistan	56	69	88	57
Sri Lanka	2	89	97	88
Other Asia	29	32	59	23
Developing Asia	620	83	95	74

Source: IEA (2014).

Nowadays, the challenges of the power sector can be quite complex and decision-makers would need to take multidimensional objectives into consideration. These include the economic, environmental, social, and human (safety) factors. Further, there is also the trade-offs for some criteria. For example, from an economic perspective, the power system would need to be developed using the least cost principle and following the structure of current generating cost in Indonesia, coal power plants have the lowest cost. However, from the environmental perspective, this policy is not strongly advisable as the coal-based power plants emit more carbon dioxide compared to gas- or oil-based plants. In addition, the power system planning would need to address issues such as reducing energy poverty, regional disparity, and income inequality in order to meet social objectives. Considering the challenges on the geographical and topography situation, and varieties in the population density, there is a need to combine both on-grid and off-grid connection to electrify the most remote parts of Indonesia. The power system would need to have a high degree of resistance in protecting human beings from any disaster, both expected and unexpected. In short, the power system development planning would need to improve people's welfare for both the current as well as future generations.

I argue that as electricity is a vital part of modern-day energy utility services, one can use the analytical framework for energy security to discuss electricity security. The analytical framework of this book follows Savacool (2011), which break down energy security into five dimensions, namely, regulation and governance, availability, technology development and efficiency, environmental sustainability, and affordability. It is important to note that all these dimensions are interconnected and keeping them in balance will determine energy sustainability.

The World Energy Council (WEC) provides the Energy Sustainability Index (WEC 2013) which covers two major elements — energy performance and contextual performance. In terms of energy performance, this consists of energy security, energy equity, and environmental sustainability; while on the contextual performance, this includes political strength, societal strength, and economic strength. Energy performance reflects the trilemma and the score indicates how well the country fares in pursuing the balance score among the three dimensions. WEC (2013) indicated that in 2013, Indonesia had relatively high score in terms of energy security compared to other

ASEAN countries, but it scored lower in terms of energy equity and environmental sustainability. This means that Indonesia needs to take on a more balanced approach in pursuing energy security, energy equity, and environmental sustainability. The trend on political strength and economic strength decreased between 2012 and 2013, while societal strength remained constant (WEC 2013).

Comparing Savacool's dimension and the Energy Sustainability Index, I conclude that they are similar. For example, availability is reflected in energy security dimension; affordability is linked to energy equity; technology development and efficiency and renewable energy is referred to environmental sustainability; and finally, regulation and governance is connected to contextual performance.

This book is organized into five main chapters, in accordance with the five dimensions of energy security. Chapter 2 begins by investigating the regulation and governance dimension. The institutional and organizational developments from the pre-Independence period to the current organizational and institutional setting was evaluated. This chapter broadly captures the history of the electricity sector in Indonesia. Thus far there have only been a few works that have tried to employ a long-term perspective in analysing the Indonesian electricity sector. Thus this chapter is useful for readers as it aims to link the state of the electricity sector with the economic background. It is necessary to broaden the time horison for analysis in order to have a better understanding of the institutional and organizational changes that have occurred in the Indonesian electricity sector and to draw on the lessons that one can learn from the past.

Chapter 3 addresses the availability dimension. It analyses the supply and demand conditions of the electricity sector from the early Soeharto era to the present. The supply side covers the generating, transmission, and distribution sectors, while the demand side covers sectoral consumption. It also investigates the convergence index in three specific areas: the capacity across the big islands, the electrification ratio, and electricity consumption per capita.

Chapter 4 is the extension of Chapter 3. It aims to investigate the 1997/98 economic crisis and its implications on the national power company (PLN). The crisis has huge impact on PLN in terms of financial difficulties and it affected not only PLN, but also the electricity sector in general. The crisis led to an increase in electricity subsidy in the following years. It underlined the importance of good governance and good corporate governance in managing the power sector. Following the under-supply of electricity and the economic crisis, Chapter 5 focuses on whether there is a causality link between economic growth and electricity consumption in Indonesia. This chapter provides an understanding of the consequences of associating economic growth with electricity consumption. Chapter 5 also lays the foundation in understanding the policy setting between availability and environmental sustainability in Chapter 6.

Technological development and efficiency, and renewable energy dimensions are discussed in Chapter 6. This chapter highlights the main problem that Indonesia needs to address of why development of renewable energy lacks behind that of fossil-based fuels. It emphasizes the important role Indonesia will play in pursuing a "green path" (more environmentally sustainable) power system. Finally, Chapter 7 addresses a critical problem of Indonesia's energy poverty by focusing on electricity accessibility. This chapter focuses on three major issues: affordability of electricity; identifying electricity-poor households in terms of housing conditions, social protection, information and communication access; and the rural electrification programme. It suggests that in order to improve the rural electrification ratio, Indonesia will need to take on a more robust, comprehensive, and sustainable approach.

While some parts of this book consist of technical analyses involving econometrics, the general arguments and implications are relevant to the general public and policymakers. It is hoped that this book will provide a better understanding of the problems of the electricity sector in Indonesia and offer some viable directions to pursue sustainable development in providing electricity.

Note

1. <http://databank.worldbank.org/data/views/variableSelection/selectvariables. aspx?source=world-development-indicators#> (accessed 14 February 2014).

References

International Energy Agency (IEA). *World Energy Outlook 2013*. Paris: IEA, 2013.
————. *World Energy Outlook 2014*. Paris: IEA, 2014.
Savacool, Benjamin K. "Evaluating Energy Security in the Asia Pacific: Towards a More Comprehensive Approach". *Energy Policy* 39 (2011): 7472–79.
World Energy Council (WEC). *World Energy Trilemma: 2013 Energy Sustainability Index*. London: WEC, 2013.

2

A HISTORICAL OVERVIEW OF THE ELECTRICITY SECTOR

Since the past influences the institutional setting of the power sector in Indonesia, understanding the history of the electricity sector will help us understand the current situation and analyse the future path. This chapter briefly describes the conditions of organizational and institutional settings of the electricity sector in Indonesia, starting from before the Independence to the present. The pre-Independence period, before the Second World War, and the Japanese Occupation will be discussed. After the Independence period, there are three important periods in the electricity sector, according to the Ministry of Energy and Mineral Resources (DPE 2000): (i) 1945–50 (the formation of electricity and gas department); (ii) 1951–67 (the nationalization and organizational growth of Dutch electricity companies); and (iii) 1968–2014. In addition, between 1961 and now, there are three important organizational changes that need to be discussed: (i) the formation of State Electricity Company Management Agency (*Badan Pimpinan Umum Perusahaan Listrik Negara*/BPU-PLN) in 1961; (ii) the formation of *Perusahaan Umum Listrik Negara* in June

1972; and (iii) the formation of PT. PLN (Persero) (limited company) in June 1994. This chapter analysed the critical elements from each of these episodes of history.

THE PRE-INDEPENDENCE PERIOD

The first electricity trading company in Indonesia (Netherlands East Indies) was established in May 1897 by the Netherlands Indies Electricity Company (*Netherlandsch-Indisch Electriciteit Maatschappij/NIEM*) in Batavia. However, according to McCawley (1971, p. 1), the Dutch plantation companies had developed power generation for their own use even before that time. Developing power generation was important for Dutch companies to run businesses such as sugar factories, tea factories, and other plantations (DPE 2000). Most of these commodities were intended for the export market (see Table 2.1). Hydropower was an important source of power supply for Dutch companies because it required the least cost based on the state of technology at that time and there were abundant supplies of water.

Following the 1890 Ordinance No. 190 dated 13 September 1890, Dutch private sector companies could operate electricity business for public utilities (DPE 2000). There were three most important private utility companies (McCawley 1971): (i) NIGM (*Nederlandsch-Indische*

Table 2.1
Composition of Indonesia's Exports, 1900–29
(average % shares per decade)

Commodity	1900–9	1910–19	1920–29
Sugar	35	32	28
Coffee, tobacco, tea	23	17	14
Rubber, copra	7	16	24
Oil, tin	12	20	18
Other	23	15	16
Total	100	100	100

Source: Lindblad (1994), Table II, p. 97.

Gas-Maatschappij or Netherlands Indies Gas Company);[1] (ii) GEBEO (*Gemeenschapp-Elijk Electriciteitsbedrijf Bandoeng en Omstreken* / Municipal Electricity Works for Bandung and District); and (iii) ANIEM (*Algemeene Nederlandsch Indische Electriciteit Maatschappij* / Netherlands Indies General Electricity Company).[2] The right to run businesses in electricity was given in the form of electricity licences, issued as local and regional concessions.

The private sector had played an important role from the early stages of power development in Indonesia. Even as early as 1928, the installed capacity of the private sector was higher than that of government utilities (see Figure 2.1). The Dutch East Indies government was interested in developing hydropower plants to electrify the state railways, radio stations, industries, plantations, and for domestic consumers (McCawley 1971). The Dutch government took a special interest in hydropower as indicated by the establishment of its independent subdivision, the Service for Water, Power and Electricity, under the Department of Government Enterprises, in August 1917 (McCawley 1971). This

Figure 2.1
Installed Capacity in Private and Government Utilities, 1914–40 (MW)

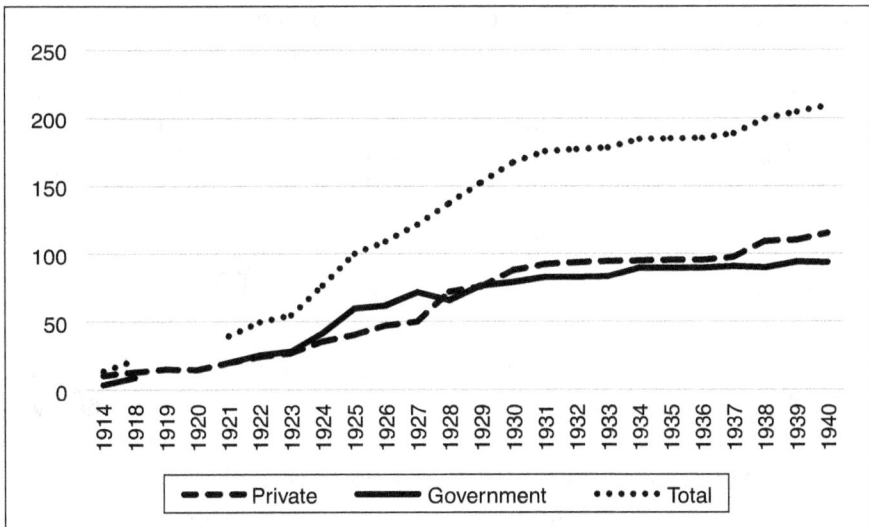

Source: McCawley (1971).

subdivision issued water concession permits for both small power plants (less than 75 kW) with time period undefined until further notice, and large power plants (above 75 kW), which were granted a fixed period (forty years). The small-scale permits were further divided into two types: one for European plantations, and the other for the indigenous sector. The average permit of European plantations was about 37.5 kW while for the indigenous sector, it was about 4.5 kW. By issuing these permits, it is clear that the government intended to control the development of small scale hydropower (McCawley 1971).

The Dutch colonial government also issued *Staatsblad* (Statesheet) 1927 No. 419 for the establishment of the State Water Power Enterprise (*Lands Waterkracht Bedrijven*/LWB) (DPE 2000). This company managed several hydropower plants (*Pembangkit Listrik Tenaga Air*/PLTA). In West Java, there were several PLTA, such as: PLTA Plengan, PLTA Lamajang, PLTA Bengkok-Dago, PLTA Ubrug, and PLTA Kraca. PLTA Giringan was located in Madiun and PLTA Tonsea Lama in North Sulawesi. The company also managed a steam power plant (*Pembangkit Listrik Tenaga Uap*/PLTU) in Jakarta.

The power system in Java depended on hydropower with the system in West Java being supported by Batavia and Bandung. The power distribution system in Batavia was conducted by private companies. In central Java, the development of the power sector was conducted by the private sector company, ANIEM, and Tuntang hydropower plant became the source of electric power in the Semarang area. The development of power supply in East Java lagged slightly behind that of other Java regions. As a result, the government planned to construct a hydropower plant near Malang and this plant (Mendalan hydropower plant) would support the grid connection for Surabaya, Kediri, Pasuruan and other nearby towns. Mendalan was economically very feasible and it could replace thermal plants that had been used by ANIEM (McCawley 1971).

While Java had an integrated system, outside Java, the system was dispersed, with no transmission sector and only a modest distribution system (McCawley 1971). In North Sumatra, there were several private companies that supplied electricity, such as NIGM (*Nederlandsch Indische Gas Electriciteits Maatschappij*), EMM (*Electriciteits Maatschappij*

Medan), EMS (*Electriciteits Maatschappij Sumatra*), and BPM (*Bataafche Petroleum Maatschappij*). NIGM obtained a concession from Medan municipality in 1920 and the company constructed diesel power and hydroelectric power plants. In West Sumatra, the railway company SSS (*Sumatera Staats Spoorwegen*) built a steam power plant in 1912 which used coal from Ombilin Sawah Lunto. In Kalimantan, NV. West Borneo Electriciteit Maatschappij obtained a concession in 1920. Diesel engine was the prime mover. In Sulawesi, NV. NIGM operated in 1920 in Makassar city, while NV. MEPB (NV. Maatschappij tot Exploitatie van Plaatselijke Bedrijven) operated in 1930 in Parepare city. In Bali, electricity was controlled by NV. EBALOM (NV. Electriciteits Maatschappij Bali en Lombok) in 1927/28. Thus, outside Java, the power system was not wholly supported by hydropower, but instead utilized several sources such as hydropower, diesel power (gasoline), and steam coal.

McCawley (1971) provided useful information regarding the power sector in Indonesia during the pre-Second World War expansion (1914–40). First, the government aimed to control the development of hydro capacity. Second, although the growth in power capacity was not spectacular, the electricity capacity increased at a healthy average growth rate. The growth was also equally shared between the public and private sectors and between Java and the outer islands, although the share of capacity in Java was constant at 70 per cent. Third, the growth in hydropower (50 per cent) was slightly higher than that of thermal (30 per cent) and diesel (20 per cent) power plants. Fourth, by international standards, the electricity consumption rate was very low. In 1938, there were only 4.2 consumers per 1,000 population, with the average consumption per capita of 5.1 kWh — a very low amount. Average consumption per inhabitant was 6.2 kWh in Java and 2.7 kWh in the outer islands and in terms of average consumption per consumer, 1,255 kWh in Java and 975 kWh in outer islands. Finally, there were two characteristics of consumption patterns across the regions: (i) concentration of consumption, and (ii) wide variations in average consumption.

There are three conclusions that we can draw about electricity in pre-Independence Indonesia. First, the power system was then dominated by renewable energy (hydropower). Second, running a business in electricity was profitable as seen from the participation of both public and private companies. Third, the substantial gap in electricity access between Java and other regions has existed even then.

During the Japanese invasion, all the generating plants and electricity companies owned by the central government, municipal councils and private owned utilities were merged into a single company called Djawa Denki Djigyo Kosha (Java Electricity Company) (McCawley 1971). This electricity company was under the Army (*Riku Gan*) control in Java, and under the Navy (*Kai Gun*) outside of Java. In Java, the management of the power system was divided into three regions: West Java, Central Java, and East Java. All employees were not only responsible for their daily routine tasks but also for military training (PLN 1995).

Through forced labour called *Romusha*, the Japanese developed some electricity infrastructure projects in Indonesia, such as: (i) the construction of 30 kV transmission lines Ketenger-Tegal; (ii) the construction of a water tunnel in Baturaden, Purwokerto that aimed to add power capacity to the Ketenger hydropower plant; (iii) the Cilaki water project at Pangalengan, West Java, that aimed to increase the capacity of Lamajang and Plengan hydropower plants; (iv) Tulungagung-Indian Ocean Tunnel Project or Neyama Project that attempted to prepare for the construction of the Tulungagung hydropower plant; and (v) the reconstruction project on Mendalan and Siman hydropower plants that were damaged due to the Allied Forces bombing in February 1945 (PLN 1995).

The Japanese government imposed strict restrictions for electricity utilization especially after the Japanese were defeated by the Alliance Forces. At that time, there was a shortage of light bulbs and people needed to queue very long to buy them (PLN 1995). The Japanese government also turned off street lights and allowed any lighting to cover around 75 cm square of table area for fear of military attack from the Alliance Air Force (PLN 1995).

McCawley (1971) highlighted three important points during the Japanese invasion. First, Japan took control and replaced the management and personnel to Japanese civilian administration. Second, Japan merged all entities of power administrative (central government, municipal councils, and privately owned utilities) into the control of one organization. Third, although Japan could finish building the transmission line between Bandung and Cirebon, Yogyakarta to Solo, and the unfinished hydropower project in North Sumatra, maintenance procedures were not conducted properly. The total power capacity in 1945 decreased due to plant damages and lack of maintenance.

THE INDEPENDENCE PERIOD

In May 1945, youth leaders and employees of Honsha Djawa Denki Djigyo Sha attempted to take action when Indonesia proclaimed its independence.[3] They formed a "Committee for taking over electricity and gas company from the Japanese", and conducted several meetings and discussed issues such as the position of the head of Electricity and Gas Company of Java and Madura, method for takeover, and a negotiation delegation (PLN 1995). On 15 August 1945, Hirohito announced Japan's surrender. Two days later, Indonesia declared its independence and the first cabinet was formed on 19 August 1945, but the department under which the Electricity and Gas Company should be positioned was not decided yet. Three possible positions were under the Ministry of Welfare, Ministry of Communications, or Ministry of Public Works (DPE 2000). After the delegation of Electricity and Gas workers led by Kobarsjih met with the Chairman of the Central National Committee of Indonesia (*Komite Nasional Indonesia Pusat*) and President Sukarno, on 27 October 1945, the government decided that the Electricity and Gas Company was to be under the Ministry of Public Works. On the same day, the Office of Electricity and Gas (*Jawatan Listrik dan Gas*) was established with a head office in Bandung. On 23 and 24 November 1945, the workers' organization namely the Office of Electricity and Gas Labour Front (*Barisan Buruh Jawatan Listrik dan Gas*) conducted its first conference in Jakarta. A shortage of trained manpower was an acute problem at that time (McCawley 1971).

Nationalistic sentiment was high at that time and before the allied soldiers arrived, Indonesian political leaders aimed to take control of a number of industries (McCawley 1971). Labour union movements succeeded in taking over some unions from the Japanese authority

— for example, *Laskar Buruh Listrik dan Gas Indonesia* (Indonesian Electricity and Gas Workers Militia) and *Angkatan Muda Listrik dan Gas Indonesia* (Indonesia Electricity and Gas Youth Force) under the leadership of Banoearli Mangkoesoejanto. Indonesian personnel started to seize electricity and gas installations on 29 September 1945 (McCawley 1971), when Allied Forces Netherlands East Indies (AFNEI) landed in Jakarta.

As a member of AFNEI, the Dutch established Netherland Indies Civil Administration (NICA) and armed former soldiers of Royal Netherlands Indies Army (*Koningklijke Netherlands Indische Leger*/KNIL). Terror occurred frequently at that time because the Dutch tried to re-establish their colonial rule. In order to avoid attacks from NICA, the management of republican electricity moved their offices and electricity facilities to the hinterland (PLN 1995). The government of the Republic of Indonesia instructed that vital installations must not fall under the control of NICA. Some operations were prepared to demolish power infrastructures such as Lamajang hydropower plant, central Java transmissions poles, substations at Kanigaran, Mendalan hydropower plant, and Siman hydropower plant.

Until end-1950s, the situation of the power sector remained uncertain. The Office of Electricity and Gas was dissolved into the Office to Manage the Properties of the Republic of Indonesia (*Kantor Urusan barang-barang Republik Indonesia*/KORBI). KORBI became the Logistics Department (*Jawatan Perlengkapan*) of the Ministry of Communications. After the Federal Republic of Indonesia (*Republic Indonesia Serikat*/RIS) was removed in September 1951, *Jawatan Perlengkapan* was abolished and the Electricity Department was again re-established under the Power Department (*Jawatan Tenaga*) within the Ministry of Public Works and Power (DPE 2000). The Department of Power was upgraded and became the Directorate of Power that managed four units (PLN 1995): (i) PENUPETEL (State Company for Electric Power Generation); (ii) PENUDITEL (State Company for Electric Power Distribution); (iii) Directorate of Construction; and (iv) Administration and Finance Department.[4]

There was a dispute between the Indonesian and the Dutch governments on the ownership of utilities companies of railways, trams, gas and electricity (McCawley 1971). The Dutch government attempted to regain its power. The Linggarjati Agreement in March 1947 was followed by the Dutch Military Aggression I in July 1947. The situation between 1945 and the Renville Agreement in January 1948 was also followed by the Dutch Military Aggression II in December 1948. The Indonesian government attempted to manage the power sector businesses and Indonesian nationalists tried to move the electricity office in Surabaya, that had been occupied by British troops, to Mojokerto and Kediri in 1945. In mid-1946, it was moved to Yogyakarta and finally after the head of government moved from Yogyakarta to Jakarta, the Office of Electricity and Gas also shifted to Jakarta and it became the Office of Power (*Jawatan Tenaga*) (McCawley 1971). This demonstrated the long struggle by the Indonesian nationalist workers to gain control of the electricity sector. The third congress of the Labour Front of the Indonesian Electricity and Gas Office (*Barisan Buruh Jawatan Listrik dan Gas*) demanded that the government nationalize all important services, including the Office of Electricity and Gas. Similarly, the Youth Group of the Indonesian Electricity and Gas Office (*Angkatan Muda Jawatan Listrik dan Gas*) also asked for the nationalization of electricity and gas companies (McCawley 1971).

After the Round Table Conference (RTC) in November 1949, the Dutch recognized Indonesia's independence, but the RTC came with two political and two economic agreements (Thee 2012). The political agreements stated that: (1) the Dutch agreed to the transfer of sovereignty from the Netherlands to the Republic of the United States of Indonesia (*Republik Indonesia Serikat*/RIS); but (2) the Dutch refused to transfer the sovereignty of West New Guinea (named West Irian by the Indonesian nationalists, today's Papua) to Indonesia. The economic agreements indicated that (Thee 2012): (1) Indonesia would take over the foreign debts incurred by the Netherlands Indies government and was also obliged to take over the rights and liabilities of the colonial government's external floating debt; and (2) Indonesia guaranteed that Dutch economic and business interests would be allowed to continue to operate in Indonesia without any interference, just like during the colonial times.

As part of the RTC in the Hague (23 August–2 November 1949), Indonesia and Dutch delegations also reached an agreement formalized in the so-called Finec (*Financieel-Economische Overeenkomst*). The Finec had two important components (Thee 2012). Firstly, private Dutch businesses in Indonesia had the highest protection, so they could provide the greatest possible economic and financial benefits for the Netherlands. Secondly, Finec also included a clause to the effect that nationalization would only be permitted if it was in Indonesia's national interest and if both parties agreed. According to Meijer (1994, pp. 46–47), as cited in Thee (2012, p. 6), "a judge would then decide on the amount of compensation to the owners on the basis of the real value and nationalised enterprise".

Electricity management was temporarily returned to Dutch companies and in December 1951, the government set up an Electric and Gas Companies Nationalisation Commission. After the Commission took a year to evaluate, it recommended that all electricity companies should be nationalized (McCawley 1971). In November 1951, a committee in Parliament proposed that all public utilities be nationalized, starting with the Overseas Gas and Electricity Company (*Overzeese Gas-en Electriciteits-Maatschappij*/OGEM). On the matter of acquisition of OGEM's assets, the Dutch owner asked for Rp 52 million but eventually received Rp 15 million that reflected the present condition of the properties, according to observers. Similarly, in the case of the nationalization of ANIEM, 300 Dutch employees working in Central Java and East Java were dismissed (Lindblad 2008).

Due to the state budget constraint, it was decided that nationalization would begin with the expropriation of entirely privately owned companies in accordance with the terms of their concession licences (McCawley 1971). Between 1956 and 1957, due to shortages of funds, further nationalization was postponed (Lindblad 2008). The total cost of acquiring the remaining privately owned electricity and gas firms was estimated at Rp 300 million, at a time when the government budget deficit was increasing from Rp 2.3 billion to Rp 5.3 billion (Antara 15 Agustus 1957; Bank Indonesia 1958, p. 82, as cited in Lindblad 2008).

There were two pertinent issues regarding nationalization, namely compensation and timing (McCawley 1971). Basically, on the issue of compensation, all major political parties agreed to the principle of fair compensation, but some of the ultra-Marxist group advocated for low compensation for nationalization. On the issue of timing, the ultra-Marxist group preferred to obtain nationalization at once without considering the source of funds for maintenance and development.[5] The opposite group (the moderate religious, nationalist, and socialist parties) argued that nationalization should be given priority only after the country's limited resources had been put into productive undertakings. Following the Presidential Decree No. 163 on October 1953, nationalization of foreign owned electricity companies proceed when their concessions were terminated. The Government of Indonesia issued Law No. 86/1958 for the nationalization of all Dutch companies, and Government Regulation No. 18/1958 to deal with the takeover of Dutch owned electricity and gas companies (DPE 2000).[6]

Until 1957, the establishment of electricity enterprises was classified as *Indische Bedrijven Wet* (Indies Enterprises Law/IBW) and under the control of the Department of Public Works (McCawley 1971). In the mid-1950s, relationship between Indonesia and the Netherlands deteriorated due to unsettled discussions on the status of West Irian (Papua). The militant labour unions that were affiliated with the Indonesia Nationalist Party (PNI) started to take over Dutch enterprises and business offices on 3 December 1957 (Meier 1994, p. 584, as cited in Thee 2012, p. 13). On 5 December 1957, the Department of Foreign Affairs urged all Dutch citizens to leave Indonesia as soon as possible. Unauthorized takeovers on Dutch enterprises were happening all over the country.

On 13 December 1957, the Army Chief of Staff, Major General A.H. Nasution, in his capacity as Central War Administrator, issued an order to all local war administrators to take over all Dutch enterprises immediately. In January 1958, Nasution issued a decree which transferred the control of the administration of Dutch-owned electricity and gas enterprises to the Minister of Public Affairs and appointed an Enterprises Administrator responsible to the Minister (McCawley 1971). Because the terms of the position of the Central War Administrator expired in mid-April 1958, the President issued Regulation No. 23/1958 that stated that all Dutch enterprises were now under Indonesian administration.

In order to coordinate the electricity and gas companies, the government set up a Central Administering Board for Electricity and Gas Enterprises (*Pusat* or *Penguasa Perusahaan Listrik dan Gas Pusat*/P3LG) in January 1958. P3LG was responsible to the Ministry for Public Works and Power, as well as three regional Electricity and Gas Boards in Surabaya, Bandung, and Jakarta. The board consisted of several members and was responsible for operating the facilities of a number of Dutch electricity enterprises (McCawley 1971). Based on the Minister of Public Works and Power Decision No. P.25/45/17 dated 23 September 1958, the Power Department (*Jawatan Tenaga*) was converted into the State Electricity Company (*Perusahaan Listrik Negara*) (DPE 2000). Following the Junior Minister of Public Works and Power Decision No. Ment.1/7/20 dated 25 August 1958, P3LG was dissolved and PLN Board of Director (DDPLN) was established.[7]

A nationalization bill was passed as Act No. 86/1958 and promulgated on 31 December 1958. The government issued Regulation No. 3/1959 on the establishment of the Board for Nationalization of Dutch Enterprises (BANAS). On 20 May 1959, the government promulgated Government Regulation No. 18/1959 dealing with the nationalization of Dutch-owned electricity and gas enterprises. However, the regulation did not affect the organization and operation of companies already in de facto existence (McCawley 1971). In June 1959, a Board of Directors for a New State Electricity Corporation (PLN) was established, under the responsibility of the Ministry of Public Works. With the new arrangement, PLN had objectives not only to make profit, but also to carry out new tasks such as implementing regulations, development of electricity infrastructure, supervision of electricity infrastructure projects and power planning. These responsibilities were previously under the authority of the Director General of Electricity and Power.

THE ECONOMIC DIMENSION IN THE INDEPENDENCE AND THE LATE SUKARNO ERA

Although on 27 December 1949, the Netherlands transferred the sovereignty to Indonesia, the Dutch still dominated the Indonesian economy. Political independency did not necessarily be accompanied by economic independency. Indonesia had a huge burden from the debt obligation of the Dutch, and many senior positions in the public service were still occupied by Dutch officials. Indonesia did not even have the authority to conduct monetary policy since the Java Bank that controlled the circulation of money and credit only became nationalized as Bank Indonesia in December 1951. In order to enhance the participation of the indigenous Indonesia business class and to fight the "Big Five",[8] the government launched the *Banteng* (fortress) programme in 1950. The Indonesian government also implemented a quota on work permit for Dutch employees — from free, unlimited entry permit to only 1,000 work permits in 1953 — to limit the role of the Dutch and to enhance the position of Indonesian personnel in Dutch companies (Thee 2012).

In the early 1950s, real GDP per capita was declining, from US$1,252 before the Pacific War (at 1990 prices) to US$840 in 1950 (Thee 2012). Thus, improving the standard of living was the main goal of the new cabinet. Physical infrastructures (irrigation networks and power stations) were in poor conditions due to the Japanese occupation and the subsequent Indonesia Revolution. Reconstruction of the severely damaged physical infrastructure needed funds and in 1950, the government budget was in deficit.[9] By mid-1952, Indonesia was facing a serious financial crisis (Thee 2012, p. 41):

> This brief survey underscores the enormous challenges the Indonesian government faced in the early 1950s in both maintaining macroeconomic stability (by restraining inflationary pressures and reducing balance of payments deficits) and rehabilitating the badly damaged physical infrastructure and production apparatus whilst attempting to raise standards of living and repaying a large foreign debt.

Thee (2012) also said that "Indonesia only embarked in earnest upon a path of independent economic development after 1966, seventeen years after the transfer of sovereignty."

The economic policy during that time was driven by two main groups (Higgins 1957, as cited in Thee 2012): (i) the "economics minded" group (who were more concerned about Indonesia's economic and social development), and (ii) the "history minded" group (who were more radical, nationalistic, and often isolationist). The former group was able to cooperate with Western countries in terms of receiving investment capital and technical assistance. The highest priority of the latter group was to "complete national revolution" that aims to eliminate foreign control over Indonesian economic resources. President Sukarno belongs to this group.

It seems that the economics minded became less influential in the decision-making process (Glassburner 1971, as cited in Thee 2012):

> From the point of view of economic policy, the years 1950 to 1957 in Indonesia are best understood as years of a hopeless losing battle on the part of a very small group of pragmatically conservative political leaders against an increasingly powerful political opposition of generally radical orientation.

Thee (2012) also said that,

> By late 1957 and early 1958, the pragmatic political leaders had not only lost the political battle, but had either withdrawn from political life (in December 1956 Hatta had resigned as Vice President) or had joined the PRRI rebellion in West Sumatera (Sjafruddin and Sumitro) and/or the Permesta rebellion in North Sulawesi (Sumitro).

As seen in Figure 2.2, although the trend of GDP was increasing, the annual growth tended to decline, especially after 1957. In 1962 and 1963, there were negative economic growth of 0.1 per cent and 4 per cent respectively, while in 1965 and 1966 the economic growth was about 1 per cent and 0.02 per cent respectively. Inflation showed an increasing trend after the 1960s and it reached a peak in 1965. Macroeconomic indicators also gave gloomy facts.[10] Rapid growth in inflation contributed to the rapid increase in money supply that reached 763 per cent in 1966 while in early 1951, it grew by about 16 per cent. Inflation also caused depreciation of Rupiah against the US dollar from Rp/USD 3.8 to Rp/USD 10,000 between 1951 and 1965, while in the black market the exchange rate could reach even Rp 36,000 in 1965. A huge depreciation of Rupiah also led to the rapid decline in foreign reserves from US$511 million to about US$23 million in 1966. Furthermore, between 1960 and 1967, GDP per capita showed a decreasing trend from about Rp 2,441 to about Rp 2,141.

The larger problem, however, was inflation which became progressively worse after 1960. The effect of inflation was that Rupiah budgets were often exhausted well before the end of the financial year. To make matters worse, the administrative machinery that arranged

Figure 2.2
Gross Value Added and Retail Price Index

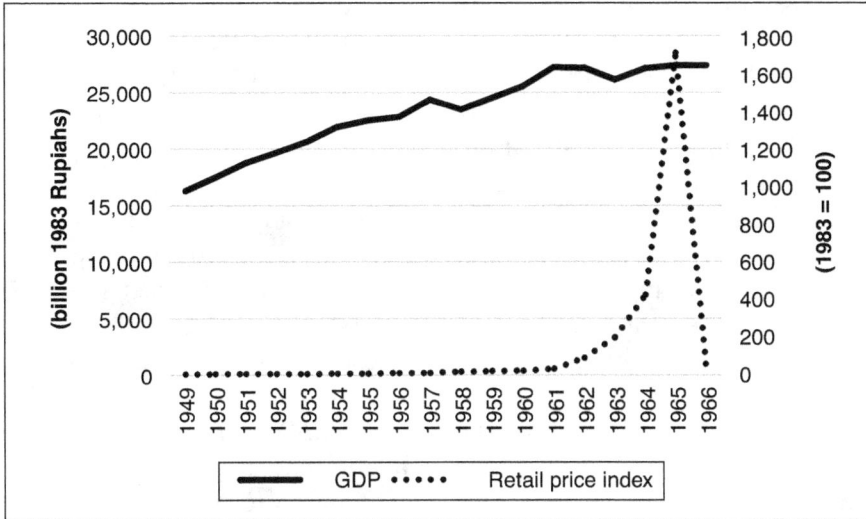

Source: van der Eng (2002), Table A7.1

the necessary revisions for budget projection was poorly developed (McCawley 1971, p. 282).

Paauw (1963, pp. 186–87) as cited in Thee (2003) said that the rapid increase in government expenditure was largely caused by an increase in government payroll for expanding military personnel and bureaucracy. Between mid-1952 and mid-1954, the exchange reserves declined rapidly. The government attempted to protect the reserves by implementing import restrictions, but this gave rise to black markets for several goods and foreign exchange (Thee 2003). Thus, by the end of President Sukarno's reign, the economic condition was in chaos.

AFTER NATIONALIZATION: FROM BPU-PLN TO PT PLN (PERSERO)

The first law on state enterprises was Act No. 19/1960 and following that the Government Regulation No. 67/1961 State Electricity Company

Management Agency (*Badan Pimpinan Umum Perusahaan Listrik Negara/* BPU-PLN). BPU-PLN was a corporate body and the management was expected to be relatively powerful. BPU-PLN operated under several conditions (McCawley 1971): (1) to support economic development by producing and distributing electricity and gas; (2) to obtain surplus of revenue over expenditure combined with reasonably efficient operation; and (3) to make electricity affordable a priority.

As a large state enterprise that needed to coordinate operations over a huge area with a great number of employees or about 15,000–20,000 people employed in 1961 (McCawley 1971), there were three reasons in selecting a centralized rather than decentralized mode on power management (McCawley 1971). Firstly, the political situation at that time allowed the government to closely monitor the performance of state enterprises. For example, the Sukarno's Independence Day Speech in August 1959 announced Manipol USDEK. It consisted of four ideas: the 1945 constitution, socialism a la Indonesia, guided democracy, and Indonesia Personality. This legated a state control over vital production sectors such as electricity. Secondly, although the electricity sector has been nationalized in the early 1950s, the specific form of the state enterprises was still unclear. The industry needed to move forward as soon as possible. Thus the public works department and PLN wanted the form decided quickly. Thirdly, the financial condition of each unit was different with some units making profits while others suffered losses. Further, there was a scarcity of experienced managers. Thus, by having a centralized enterprise, it would be easier to pool resources and expertise together.

There were five bodies in BPU-PLN: (1) long-term planning and construction; (2) engineering; (3) trade; (4) finance and supplies; and (5) general affairs. There were also several PLN Development (*PLN Pembangunan*) and fourteen PLN Exploitation (*PLN Ekspoitasi*). The objectives of BPU-PLN were to obtain profit combined with reasonably efficient operation. However, the regulation emphasized that the tariff needed to be low so that people could afford electricity. As a corporate body, BPU-PLN needed to coordinate with all areas of operations but this was difficult due to poor communication infrastructure. BPU-PLN also had a larger number of employees compared to other state enterprises.

In less than five years since BPU-PLN was established, it became increasingly clear that the organization was an unsuccessful venture, for four reasons (McCawley 1971). First, financial problems were becoming worse with escalating financial losses, budget deficits, and disorderly accounting practices (that mismatch gas and electricity, or funds for investment used for expenditure). Second, BPU-PLN had a complicated relationship with the public works department as the President Director of BPU-PLN was also the Secretary General to the Ministry of Public Works. There was a conflict of interest between the two positions but there was no measure of checks and balances between the two roles. There was also no screening body within or outside the public works department and no officer to examine BPU-PLN's claims critically. Third, there was regionalization within the industry. Many of BPU-PLN's units were located outside Jakarta, and due to poor communication facilities, there were delays in information while urgent decisions needed to be made. Fights and personality clashes between party members were common. Note that there were different historical background and practices deriving from the origins of the BPU-PLN in different Dutch private firms, and the different operating conditions that various regional boards faced. Fourth, there were internal difficulties due to weak coordination among the directors that led to contradicting directions among them.

The Board of Director of BPU-PLN coordinated both PLN (electricity) and PGN (gas), but the Minister of Public Works and Power by Regulation No. 9/PRT/1964 dated 28 December 1964, divided BPU-PLN into two boards of director — PLN and PGN. Because BPU-PLN had no further functions, it was abolished by the Government Regulation PP No. 19/1965 dated 13 May 1965. BPU-PLN thus managed the electricity and gas sectors in Indonesia for only four years. The government also attempted to upgrade the Department of Public Works and Power by issuing the Presidential Decree No. 64/1966 dated 27 March 1966. Four departments were formed within this compartment: Department of Electricity and Power, Department of Irrigation, Department of Road Construction (*Bina Marga*), and Department of Planning and Construction (*Ciptakarya*). However, by Presidential Decree No. 163/1966 dated 25 July 1966 to Presidential Decree No. 170/1966 dated 1 August 1966, PLN was placed under the Directorate General of Electric Power within the Department of Basic and Light Industries and Power. It was then believed that having one department would be more efficient and that it was better to place the power sector under the industry department rather than the more construction-oriented public works department (McCawley 1971).

Yet later, the government transferred the Directorate General of Power and Electricity from the Ministry of Basic and Light Industries and Power back to the Ministry of Public Works and Power by the Presidential Decree No. 183/1968 dated 6 June 1968 and Presidential Decree No. 184/1968 dated 7 June 1968. In 1970, the Minister of Public Works and Power Regulation formed the Director General of Electricity and Power (*Ditjen Gatrik*). All the time, relations between PLN and its parent directorate had remained substantially intact. The main function of the Directorate General was to oversee large scale investment, to advise the Minister on tariff matters, and to supervise the activities of PLN (McCawley 1971).

Ideological factors significantly affected labour organizations in PLN. It was publicly noticeable that PLN and the Directorate General of Power and Electricity were the bases of the Communist Party of Indonesia (*Partai Komunis Indonesia*/PKI). Faktur Hadi formed the Electricity and Gas Labour Organization (SBLG) under the auspices of the All Indonesia Centre of Labour Organizations (*Sentral Organisasi Buruh Seluruh Indonesia*/SOBSI) that was closely linked to PKI. There were four non-SOBSI/PKI organizations in PLN, namely SBLGI (*Serikat Buruh Listrik dan Gas Indonesia*) non-vaksentral/PKI, SBLGI KBM (*Serikat Buruh Listrik dan Gas Indonesia — Kesatuan Buruh Marhaenisme*), Nadhatul Ulama-oriented SARBUMUSI (*Serikat Buruh Muslimin Indonesia*), and SBII (*Serikat Buruh Islam Indonesia*, affiliated with the Masyumi Party). Because there were two ideological labour unions under the PLN, there were many frictions and conflicts among the workers. After the PKI coup in September 1965, PLN begun to clean up its organization and during its first screening, 3,265 employees were acted upon. The screening was also extended to the Ministry of Public Works and Electric Power and 8,549 employees were found to be involved in the coup (PLN 1995). By 1975, the cleaning-up process was completed.

ELECTRICITY PERFORMANCE: BEFORE THE NEW ORDER REGIME

As seen in Figure 2.3, between 1921 and 1940, electric power capacity grew by 6.8 per cent, while between 1944 and 1969 the capacity grew by 6.67 per cent. Thus after Independence, the power capacity had actually lower growth than before. The analysis from the previous section showed that after Independence, the political situation was unstable which affected the investment capacity of PLN. In 1964, the new power capacity increased by 156 MW, the highest during the 1914–69 period. The rapid increase in capacity during that time was attributed to the thermal and hydropower plants that had both increased by 75 MW (calculated from Table 2.2). However, it seems that after 1964, the additional capacity showed a decreasing trend. McCawley (1971) even said that the rapid expansion during the 1960–64 period was mainly the result of investment agreement in the late 1950s, while the decrease in additional capacity in the mid-1960s was due to a failure to finalize a new project agreement in the early 1960s. Looking

Figure 2.3
Capacity in the Public Electricity Industry (MW)

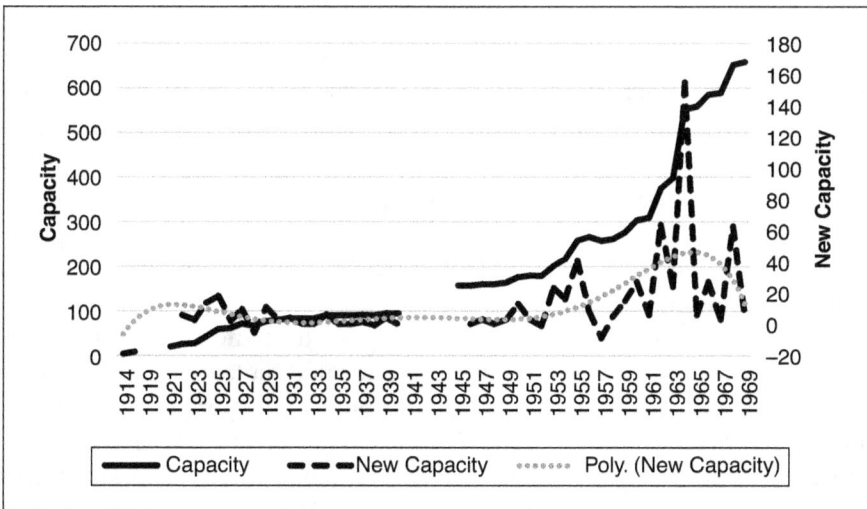

Source: Calculated from McCawley (1971).

Table 2.2
Total Installed Capacity by Prime Mover

	Diesel		Thermal		Hydro		Gas		Total
Year	MW	%	MW	%	MW	%	MW	%	MW
1952	56	30.9	24	13.3	101	55.8	—	—	181
1953	78	35.6	32	14.6	109	49.8	—	—	219
1954	90	41.9	22	10.2	103	47.9	—	—	215
1955	89	36.8	20	8.3	133	55.0	—	—	242
1956	100	39.1	30	11.7	126	49.2	—	—	256
1957	106	39.8	29	10.9	131	49.2	—	—	266
1958	109	41.0	25	9.4	132	49.6	—	—	266
1959	107	38.8	26	9.4	143	51.8	—	—	276
1960	115	38.0	25	8.3	163	53.8	—	—	303
1961	125	39.9	25	8.0	163	52.1	—	—	313
1962	149	39.8	50	13.4	175	46.8	—	—	374
1963	165	41.5	50	12.6	183	46.0	—	—	398
1964	171	30.9	125	22.6	258	46.6	—	—	554
1965	177	31.6	125	22.3	258	46.1	—	—	560
1966	178	30.4	125	21.3	283	48.3	—	—	586
1967	182	30.8	125	21.2	283	48.0	—	—	590
1968	192	29.4	109	16.7	310	47.5	42	6.4	653
1969	193	29.3	113	17.2	310	47.1	42	6.3	658

Source: McCawley (1971).

at these polynomial trends, it seems that between the early 1930s and the early 1950s, or for more than two decades, there was no substantial increase in new capacity. The long dormant period indicated that war and political instability had substantially affected the development of the power sector in Indonesia.

As seen in Table 2.2, hydropower became the main source of power generating, followed by diesel and thermal. Most of the existing hydropower plants were developed during the Dutch colonial period. Most of the diesel power plants were located outside Java, while in Java, hydro and thermal power dominated the generating system. Because power generating was dominated by renewable hydropower, it seems that in the 1950s and 1960s, carbon dioxide emissions was not an issue. However, between 1952 and 1969, the capacity growth of diesel, thermal and hydro were 6.49 per cent, 11.96 per cent,

Table 2.3
Electricity Production by Area (million kWh)

Year	Java		Sumatra		Other		Total
	Production	%	Production	%	Production	%	
1952	565	81.3	79	11.4	51	7.3	695
1953	593	78.5	102	13.5	60	7.9	755
1954	641	80.6	91	11.4	63	7.9	795
1955	686	79.4	106	12.3	72	8.3	864
1956	681	76.2	133	14.9	80	8.9	894
1957	766	77.8	145	14.7	73	7.4	984
1958	805	80.2	133	13.2	66	6.6	1,004
1959	842	77.8	146	13.5	94	8.7	1,082
1960	909	78.3	153	13.2	99	8.5	1,161
1961	872	80.6	145	13.4	65	6.0	1,082
1962	1,004	80.9	159	12.8	78	6.3	1,241
1963	1,026	79.3	180	13.9	88	6.8	1,294
1964	1,121	79.7	182	12.9	104	7.4	1,407
1965	1,229	81.2	182	12.0	103	6.8	1,514
1966	1,297	83.0	176	11.3	89	5.7	1,562
1967	1,346	83.7	169	10.5	93	5.8	1,608
1968	1,452	82.7	200	11.4	104	5.9	1,756
1969	1,515	81.7	220	11.9	119	6.4	1,854

Source: McCawley (1971).

and 7.2 per cent respectively, indicating that thermal power plants showed the highest growth. This was mainly driven by the increasing capacity in steam coal and gas. If this pattern continues in the long term, carbon dioxide emissions from the power sector will increase.

Between 1952 and 1969, the average electricity production was about 5.55 per cent. Java dominated electricity production with the average share between 1952 and 1969 at about 80.2 per cent, while the share of Sumatra and other islands were about 12.7 per cent and 7.2 per cent respectively (see Table 2.3). The imbalance in electricity production indicated that the development of power capacity was concentrated in Java. This was mainly due to the concentration of population and industries in Java, causing higher electricity demand in Java than in other islands.[11]

Figure 2.4
Sales of Electricity in the Public Sector

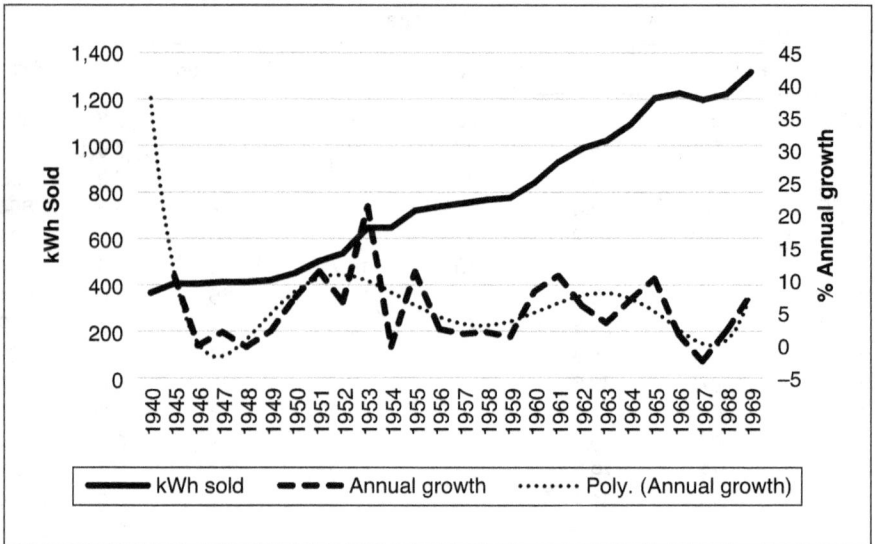

Source: Calculated from McCawley (1971).

Between 1940 and 1969, the annual growth of electricity sales was about 5.49 per cent. This growth was slightly lower than electricity production. In 1967, electricity sales decreased by –2.45 per cent compared to the previous year. It seems that the growth of electricity sales was followed by six order polynomial trend lines. Between 1954 and 1959, electricity sold tended to decrease. This indicated that the financial difficulties of the state affected the amount of electricity sold in the mid-1950s to the early 1960s. Further decline in electricity production happened between 1964 and 1967, in relation to the political instability of PKI's coup and the regime change in 1965. However, in 1968, both electricity consumption and production tended to increase.

LESSONS LEARNED: BEFORE THE NEW ORDER REGIME

Before Independence, Indonesia had modern electricity companies that were managed by the Dutch government. Three types of companies based on their ownership were identified: state companies, private companies, and regional government-owned electricity companies.[12] Until 1969, hydropower had the highest share of installed capacity. This indicated that for more than five decades, renewable energy was the backbone of the power generating system. Later in Chapter 6, the declining share of renewable energy to the total electricity production was discussed. This indicated that the electricity sector had became less environmentally friendly. Because the return on investment in the power sector was economically sound, the role of the private sector was important during the Dutch colonial period. This happened because the Dutch government offered the economic opportunity or profit to the private sector. In contrast, in Chapter 4, PLN had faced financial difficulties and asked for subsidies. Further, there were also possibilities for joint partnership between the government and the private sector. For example, due to the shortage of personnel and financial resources in constructing Mendalan power station, government commissions were set up to prepare for collaboration between the government and NIWEM (*Nederlandsch-Indisch Waterkracht Exploitatie Maatschappij* or the Netherlands Indies Hydropower Exploitation Company) (McCawley 1971). This mechanism has been continued till today through private participation in power generating, while transmission and distribution are still monopolized by PLN.

However, during the Japanese invasion, the power sector shifted completely from a decentralized system that allowed active participation of the private sector to a more centralized system. This style is continued until now. Due to war and the unstable situation at that time, the power sector during the Japanese invasion could not be well developed and maintained. Further, using ANIEM as a case study, McCawley (1971) showed that the installed capacity declined by 25 per cent, from 209 MW in 1940 to about 157 MW in 1945. It seems that the gradual increases in capacity happened during the 1950s. That was consistent with the economic situation during the rehabilitation period (Dick 2002).

In the early stages of the Independence period, the government attempted to gain sovereignty on the electricity sector and selected the Ministry of Public Works as the main agency to handle the power sector. However, this was hampered by the Dutch military invasion, which led to the demolition of many power infrastructures, affecting organizational structures, electricity services, and infrastructure development of the power sector in Indonesia. Thus the turbulent situation during the Japanese occupation and a decade after Independence indicated that the electricity sector in Indonesia was in a difficult situation.

Two approaches were used to nationalize Dutch companies — gradual approach and "big bang" approach. The former approach means to wait until the concession is terminated before taking any action to nationalize the Dutch companies while the latter approach means to nationalize the Dutch companies immediately. The Indonesian government had pursued a gradual approach due to financial difficulties.

In the early 1960s, it has been decided that the electricity sector should be handled by one state company which controlled two areas of electricity — within Java and outside Java. This was similar to the situation during the Japanese occupation. Thus, there was one single state company for the electricity sector. However, after nationalization, BPU-PLN failed to develop a solid management and to make profit. In fact, BPU-PLN became dependent on government financial support. There were indications that from the mid-1960s to the early 1970s, PLN had internal organizational problems. This was due to mistrust on PLN management and board of directors, ideological disputes among the workers, and too close a relationship between PLN and Ditjen Gatrik that prevented any checks and balances.

Development of the power sector was not only affected by the political situation but also by the economic conditions. The economic situation, especially in the 1960s, was not favourable for creating a sound investment climate in the power sector. PLN needed financial support from the government to mitigate financial loss, at a time when deficit in government budget tended to increase. As a result, government capacity to assist PLN financial difficulties was also limited. The shortage of foreign reserves also led to difficulties in obtaining imported spare parts or other capital goods that were needed to replace and repair electrical equipment, forcing PLN to buy them from the black market at unfavourable exchange rates. Finally, hyperinflation affected PLN business planning in managing expenditure and revenue.

Following the history of the electricity sector in Indonesia, for more than two decades (1940s–60s), no substantial achievement has been found. In fact the situation became even worse compared to pre-1940s. Struggling with organizational and institutional setting led to unresolved challenges on good governance and good corporate governance. Indonesia did not have independent and professional business entities to manage the power sector. The government was too dominant in handling matters in the power sector and this created high dependency between the government and the state electricity company. Thus conflict of interest between the two agencies became difficult to resolve.

THE DYNAMICS OF INSTITUTIONS AND ORGANIZATIONS: POST-OLD ORDER REGIME

After the nationalization or in late 1968, there was internal dispute in PLN triggered by the misuse of medical benefits scheme among the employees. The way in which the case, which was obtained by the PLN board of directors, was investigated was challenged by some employee organizations. Three organizations (KASI-Gatrik/PLN, SARBUMUSI, and SBLGI non-vaksentral) sent a letter directly to the Minister for Public Works and Electric Power on 8 September 1968 to address their objections (McCawley 1971). On 8 October 1968, the letter that was signed by forty senior employees was sent to the Board of Directors. The letter was concerned about the medical benefits scheme and a need to return to normal procedure. There were important messages from Ir Sutami, the Minister for Public Works on the Day of Electricity and Gas on 28 October 1968, that noted the importance of unifying PLN and to encourage initiatives for free discussion.

A week later on 5 November 1968, a letter (or known as "77" letter) that expressed dissatisfaction with the management practices was sent to Hoesni (Ditjen Gatrik) and PLN's directors, and copies were also sent to Ir Sutami, and the Inspector General and Secretary General of the department. The close relationship between Ditjen Gatrik and PLN was perceived negatively and the newspaper alleged that the PLN-Gatrik complex was run by a "power hungry clique" (McCawley 1971). Criticisms of top managers of PLN rose on issues such as incapability to conduct administrative matters, centralistic in decision-making processes, a lack of trust on the lower managers, unclear criteria for job promotion, and exclusivity within PLN-Gatrik (private empire) (McCawley 1971). This created a lack of trust in organizational relationship.

The lack in mutual trust among PLN employees and between the employees and the managers on the one hand, and the suspiciously close relationship between PLN and Gatrik that shed some doubts on the integrity of these two organizations on the other, indicating that PLN had serious internal organizational problems. According to McCawley (1971), while initially the dispute was driven by administrative issues, it escalated to political and criminal aspects. The political aspect of the dispute was related to mitigating the influence of old order and communism in PLN while the criminal aspect was related to corruption by top PLN officials. In 1973, by Presidential Decree No. 9/1973, Gatrik was removed from his position and PLN was positioned directly under the control of the Minister for Public Works and Electric Power. Gatrik's functions were then transferred to PLN.

Based on Government Regulation No. 18/1972 dated 3 June 1972, the status of PLN was raised to *Perusahaan Umum Listrik Negara* or *Perum Listrik Negara* (State Electricity Corporation). This implied that the government delegated the tasks of electric power regulation, development, supervision, and power planning to Perum PLN. This authority was held by the Directorate General of Electricity and Power. Then, Presidential Decree No. 9/1973 dated 23 March 1973 had abolished the Directorate General of Electricity and Power. With the Minister of Public Works and Power Regulation No. 13/PRT/1975, it was again stated that *Perum Listrik Negara*, in addition to its function as a commercial enterprise, was also entrusted with some government tasks and functions to support national development. Further, with the Minister of Public Works and Power Regulation No. 16/PRT/1976, *Perum Listrik Negara* was given an additional task in rural electrification programme. According to Presidential Decree No. 15/1978 dated 29 March 1978, PLN and PGN were transferred from the Ministry of Public Works and Power to the new Ministry of Mines and Energy.

In the early 1980s, in order to execute government functions concerning electricity as well as new energy, the government set up the Directorate General of Energy and some of PLN functions such as issuing licences, preparing regulation and standards, supervision, and general policy planning were transferred to the Directorate General of Energy. According to Government Regulation No. 36/1979 dated 17 December 1979, the government allowed private companies and cooperatives to operate in commercial electricity businesses beside PLN, and by the Minister of Mines and Energy Regulation No. 11/PM/Pertamben/1981 dated 5 November 1981, the government transferred the task of issuing electricity business licences (*izin usaha kelistrikan*) from PLN to the Directorate General of Energy. Regulation on electricity for public utility and for business use was also issued by the Directorate General of Energy in January 1983. Regulation concerning Indonesia Electricity Standards (SLI) and requirements in electricity connection were issued in November 1983 and June 1984. Thus the Directorate General of Energy took over the functions of development, supervision, and general policy planning that were previously held by PLN. By Presidential Decree No. 15/1984 dated 6 March 1984, the title of Directorate General of Energy was changed to Directorate General of Electricity and New Energy.

On 30 December 1985, Law No. 15/1985 on Electricity was issued as a reference for *Perum Listrik Negara* in conducting electricity activities. Following Presidential Decree No. 67/1992, the title of Directorate General of Electricity and New Energy was changed to Directorate General of Electricity and Energy Development. By the authority of Government Regulation No. 23/1994 dated 16 June 1994, the status of PLN was changed from State Electricity Enterprise to PT. PLN (Persero) (limited company).

As a limited company, PLN has four main objectives (PLN 1995): (i) to provide electric power for public utilities and to make profit based on good business management principles; (ii) to supply electric power at an appropriate quantity and quality; (iii) to pioneer activities of providing electric power; and (iv) to carry out miscellaneous activities in support of electricity provision in line with existing laws and regulations.

Electricity Law No. 15/1985 gave the state the authority to provide electricity utilities, while the central government delegated the task to the state electricity company, *PT Perusahaan Listrik Negara* (PT PLN), to provide electricity to the public. The government also offered business opportunities to cooperatives and the private sector to provide and support electricity utilities, both for the needs of the public and for the goverment's own needs. By definition, providing electricity involves the generation, transmission, and distribution of electricity to the public, the government, and the private sector. Operating electricity utilities refers to any activities that are related to consulting, developing and installing, maintaining, and developing technology. Business permission for electricity utilities is given based on the relevant government regulations.

After more than a decade, there was a need for a new law in response to the rapid development in the power sector, as well as the changing political landscape and other external factors such as the economic crisis of 1997/98. Only in 2002 did the government issued a new law on the electricity sector, although the trigger for revision had started in 1997/98. The white paper on the new law, titled "Restructuring Policy for Electricity Sector", was drafted in August 1998 by the Department of Mining and Energy (DME), and signed by Mr Kuntoro Mangkusubroto, then the Minister of DME. After the 1997/98 economic crisis, the Indonesian government applied for financial assistance from the International Monetary Fund (IMF). In return for a standby loan from IMF, World Bank, Asian Development Bank (ADB), and contingency loans from individual countries such as Japan and Singapore, the Indonesian government promised to implement comprehensive reform programmes, including sound macroeconomic policies, financial sector restructuring, and structural reforms (Soesastro and Basri 1998, p. 16, as cited in Thee 2002).

According to the letter of intent of the Indonesian government to the IMF dated 31 October 1997, the government planned to conduct structural reforms by pursuing deregulation and privatization. The government agreed to promote domestic competition and efficient use of government resources in state-owned enterprises by conducting a public sector expenditure and investment review.[13] This process was undertaken in collaboration with the World Bank.[14] Public enterprises were also required to establish a clear profit and performance target. It was also stated that by the end of March 1998, the electricity price needed to increase by 30 per cent. The letter of intent on 13 November 1998 mentioned that the state-owned electricity enterprises and the national airlines need to be restructured for privatization later in 1999 and 2001.[15] Thus, it was clear that the restructuring of public enterprises was one of the government's plans in requesting financial support from the IMF.

This situation was noticed by non-government organizations. Tumiwa (2002) argued that the drafting of the new electricity law did not undergo a proper procedure. There was a lack of transparency and accountability in the process, without any substantial public consultancy and academic papers for review. Instead of preparing a completely new law on electricity, the working group on the power sector sent a letter to the Commission VIII of the House of Representatives (DPR) on 11 February 2002.[16] The letter argued that the government needed to carefully evaluate the preconditions before implementing a fully competitive electricity market; to develop a credible regulatory institution; to set the electricity price using the marginal cost principle; to improve the reserve margin; and to focus on a single market buyer policy.

Finally, Electricity Law No. 20/2002 was signed by then President Megawati Soekarnoputri on 23 September 2002. The new law aimed to create a more competitive environment for the power-generating businesses in the short term and in the selling areas or areas of services in the long term. Thus consumers have the choice as to which electricity sellers to buy from. Based on Electricity Law No. 20/2002, competition and transparency will improve efficiency in the electricity industry. Thus, there is a need to provide equal opportunities for all parties to participate in providing electricity utilities. Supporting electricity utilities means any activities that are related to consultation, development and installation, testing, installation operation, research and development, education and training, and any activities that are directly related to electricity.

Based on Electricity Law No. 20/2002, the government categorized the electricity business into two areas, namely the competitive and non-competitive areas.[17] In the competitive area, the Monitoring Agency for the Electricity Market (*Badan Pengawas Pasar Tenaga Listrik*/BPPTL) provides entry permits for new players. In the non-competitive area, permission to provide electricity utilities depends on the head of the central or local governments where the project is implemented, whether it is at a district, municipality, or province. Operating permission is related to the personal use of electricity utilities, and permission is given based on the area of jurisdiction, such as the whole country, the province, district, or municipality.

Electricity Law No. 20/2002 provides a broad definition of the business of electricity utilities that consist of generating, transmitting, and distributing electricity, sales, sales agents, market organizers, and system organizers. There is no competition in transmission and distribution, and priority to start businesses in these areas is given to PLN. Similarly, it is possible to have three different business units in a single state-owned company, as long as they are managed by different divisions, for example, in the area of electricity transmission, a market organizer and a system organizer. It is also possible to have two different business units, namely a market organizer and a system organizer, in one state-owned company. On the other hand, in a non-competitive region, market integration is allowed.

Under Electricity Law No. 20/2002, the Supervisory Agency for the Electricity Market (*Badan Pengawas Pasar Tenaga Listrik*/BPPTL) has an important role. BPPTL is a government agency appointed by the President and approved by Parliament. BPPTL's membership consists of five to eleven people, who can hold their positions for up to five years and can be re-elected for the next five. BPPTL is directly responsible to the President. It is assigned to regulate and monitor the electricity market, to determine the competitive and non-competitive market for the distribution, transmission and sale of electricity, and to determine the market prices in a competitive market.

However, three parties have appealed to the Constitutional Court to review the new law.[18] On 15 December 2004, Electricity Law No. 20/2002 was voided by the Constitutional Court on the ground of violation of the Constitution. Electricity is very important for achieving national goals, thus it should be controlled by the state and cannot be liberalized. Electricity was legally regulated again by Electricity Law No. 15/1985. On 16 January 2005, the government issued Government Regulation No. 3/2005 that replaced Government Regulation No. 10/1989.

Generally speaking, there are two reasons for the issue of Government Regulation No. 3/2005. First, Government Regulation No. 10/1989 was based on Electricity Law No. 15/1985, in which authority was very centralized. On the other hand, in 2004, the government issued Law No. 32/2004 on the local government. The new law allocated six areas — foreign policy, national defence, national security, justice, monetary and fiscal policy, and religion — to come under the authority of the central government. Thus, there is a demand for decentralizing electricity authority to the local governments. Second, the government needs to enhance the participation of cooperatives, state-owned enterprises, local government-owned enterprises and the private sector to supply electricity.

On 23 September 2009, the government issued Electricity Law No. 30/2009. Generally speaking, the new law has the same spirit as Government Regulation No. 3/2005. Although the state has the highest authority to provide electricity, the government needs to supply electricity based on the decentralization principle. The law also explicitly mentions the authorities of the central, provincial, district and municipality governments in the provision of electricity. The central and local governments have the authorities to set the price and the network renting cost. To set the electricity price, the central government needs to obtain approval from Parliament (*Dewan Perwakilan Rakyat/DPR*), while the local government needs to get approval from the regional parliament (*Dewan Perwakilan Rakyat Daerah/DPRD*). Electricity Law No. 30/2009 defines the government in terms of central, provincial and city/district, with the service area or operational unit of the power utility of PLN covering at least one province, though most of them consist of more than two provinces. Thus, to improve the existing capacity requires a collaboration or a joint agreement between the provinces and the national government.

It seems that appeals against Electricity Law No. 30/2009 are still coming in. By the end of 2009, representatives of PLN labour union, Ahmad Daryoko and Sumadi, sent an appeal to the Constitutional Court, arguing that Electricity Law No. 30/2009 had violated the National Constitution (UUD 1945).[19] However, by the end of 2010, the Constitutional Court rejected the appeal. The court argued that compared to Electricity Law No. 20/2002, Electricity Law No. 30/2009 had clear standing position on the role of the state and the state-owned company (in this case, PLN) has an important role in conducting electricity business in Indonesia. The Indonesian government (or the State) still has "five veto power" in designing policy (*beleid*), regulation (*regelendaad*), administrative (*bestuursdad*), management (*beheersdaad*), and monitoring (*toezichthoudensdaad*) aspects of the electricity sector.[20]

The "five veto power" are distributed under government, house of representative, and PLN. The court also argued that the basic constitution does not cancel out privatization or competition as long as the "veto power" of the state still exists.[21]

Interestingly, Electricity Law No. 30/2009 provides the space to unbundle electricity businesses (including generating, transmission, distribution, and selling). Article 10 Part 2 of Electricity Law No. 30/2009 states that "business on electricity supply for public *can be* done by integrated way". Because the words "can be" connote an option rather than an imperative, this article "can be" interpreted in different ways such as saying that generating, transmission, distribution and selling can also be done in a non-integrated way. This is one of the reasons why the Head of National Unified Confederation (*Dewan Pimpinan Pusat Konfederasi Serikat Nasional*) on 29 January 2014, sent an appeal to the Constitutional Court, arguing that there was no strong legal force in Electricity Law No. 30/2009.[22] On the other hand, based on the previous appeal addressed by Ahmad Daryoko and Sumadi, the court argued that the role of the state was stronger in Electricity Law No. 30/2009 than in Electricity Law No. 20/2002 because the state could influence pricing policy and the first priority to conduct electricity business was given to PLN.

Similarly, the Head of District (*Bupati*) Tanah Bumbu, Mardani H. Maming, also sent an appeal to the Constitutional Court,[23] arguing that Electricity Law No. 30/2009 has hindered his job to better serve his people. He challenged Article 10 Part 3 that states that the electricity business for public needs must be conducted by one business entity within one business area; and Part 4 for setting the limitation on business area (stated in Part 3) is also valid for other electricity business (for example, in distribution and/or selling).[24] The Constitution Court rejected the appeal on the ground that a business area did not necessarily coincide with an administrative area.[25]

This analysis on the dynamics of electricity institutions shows that it is possible to challenge existing laws by appealing to the Constitutional Court. The court will then evaluate the appeals by investigating their relevance to the "five veto power" of the state. Ultimately, the role of the state in pricing policy and giving priority to PLN are the two main indicators of the power of the state.

To some extent, Electricity Law No. 30/2009 has adopted the decentralization principle although the set administrative area does not necessarily correspond to a business area. State-owned companies and the local government need to cooperate to optimize comparative and competitive advantages for both sides.

POSTSCRIPT: CENTRALIZATION, DECENTRALIZATION, AND COMPETITION

In the early years of the New Order regime, PLN had internal problems and these affected the solidarity, cohesiveness, and sense of unity among the employees. Until the mid-1990s, the government attempted to separate regulatory authority of the government from the business operation of PLN. The government restructured PLN to become more business oriented. However, an attempt to liberalize PLN by creating a more competitive environment was unsuccessful, especially in the Java region. This indicated that the commanding power for providing electricity still falls under PLN. However, the centralized structure of the power sector is likely to change after the Electricity Law No. 30/2009 adopted decentralization as one of its principles.

Electricity Law No. 30/2009 may pose a potential challenge to the existence of PLN in the future, especially in bridging the gap between the expectation of the local governments to electrify their regions quickly and the lack of resources to do so. Chapters 3 and 4 discuss that although the private sector can participate in the power generating sector, PLN is still the single buyer (monopsony) of electricity in Indonesia. This implies that PLN has both monopoly and monopsony powers.

There are two main challenges to the monopoly and monopsony powers of PLN. Firstly, the challenge on PLN's monopoly power comes from the local governments due to the persistence of a power crisis. A rapid growth in electricity demand and a lack in power supply resulted in a power crisis in many parts of Indonesia. In March 2015, the government mentioned that 6 out of 22 power systems in Indonesia had reserved capacity above 20 per cent, while 11 were in a standby position and 5 systems were in deficit.[26]

This means that 80 per cent of the existing power system needs to be upgraded.

Lack of power supply outside Java has increased unhappinessness over the performance of PLN. The preference for nuclear power plants has become a real threat in addressing the lack of progress in developing the power infrastructure. Dissenting opinions at the national level for promoting nuclear power plants have been used to attack the central government and PLN. According to the Minister of Science and Technology, the three provinces (Bangka Belitung, East Kalimantan, and Central Kalimantan) are ready to develop nuclear power plants.[27] Experts said that Kalimantan is the best place for developing nuclear power plants, although Kalimantan and Sumatra Island are the centres of coal production. As of January 2012, 56.43 per cent of coal reserves were located in Kalimantan, mainly in the East, South and Central Kalimantan Provinces.[28]

Similarly, the Governor of West Kalimantan Province said that due to a power deficit, West Kalimantan needs to import electricity from Malaysia, and so it is time for Indonesia to develop its own nuclear power.[29] In contrast, Mr Jusuf Kalla, Vice President of Indonesia, argued that developing nuclear power should be the last priority,[30] although Mr Sudirman Said, Minister of Energy and Mineral Resources, disagreed. According to the National Medium Term Development Planning (*Rencana Pembangunan Jangka Menengah Nasional*/RPJM) 2015–19, the government will build a small-scale nuclear power plant with a capacity of about 100 kW–5 MW. However, based on PLN's business plan for 2015–24, there is no intention to construct such a nuclear power plant. PLN (2014) argued that from the economic point of view, there is still a lot of uncertainties surrounding developing nuclear power plants, in terms of capital cost, waste management and decommissioning, and nuclear liability. Furthermore, due to the multidimensional aspects of nuclear power, especially the safety factor, the decision to develop nuclear power plant falls within the government's domain.

However, the main challenge for a more decentralized power system in Indonesia is in the area of business operation. PLN business operations are not compatible with its administrative boundary. Although PT PLN Business Plan for Electricity Utility has been designed at the province level, the power system is connected through the provinces, districts and cities. Further, the primary energy sources — both fossil and non-fossil — are unequally distributed across the provinces, even among the islands. These issues make decentralizing the role of PLN to the provinces, or even to the island level, even more complicated.

In addition, developing the electricity sector needs both skilled labour and huge investment. The local governments lack such capacities. Most of the funds from the central government is spent on routine expenditure and only a small portion is left for capital outlay. Thus the best strategy to strengthening the role of the local governments to provide electricity is by constructing local government enterprises and collaborating with reputable investors. Unfortunately, six years after Law No. 30/2009 on electricity has been implemented, we have yet to hear any success stories.

According to PLN's business plan for 2015–24, to implement its projects, PLN needs US$69.4 billion for investment with the composition for generating, transmitting, and distributing electricity at approximately 49 per cent, 30 per cent and 21 per cent respectively (PLN 2014). PLN still lacks in financial capacity to develop power infrastructure (detailed discussion on the impact of the financial crisis in 1997/98 on the power sector is discussed in Chapter 4). Thus to finance the projects, PLN needs to issue obligations and borrow from multilateral donors such as IBRD (International Bank for Reconstruction and Development), ADB (Asian Development Bank), JICA (Japan International Cooperation Agency), and AFD (Agence Francaise Developpment).

It seems that PLN is more dependent on private financing. Between 2010 and 2019, PLN estimated that about US$35.8 billion of its new investments will be financed by the private sector, but from 2015 to 2024, it expects that the private sector will contribute US$62.8 billion or 47 per cent of the total investment requirements. Further, it is highly likely that PLN needs to compete to buy electricity or the trading system will move from a single buyer to a wholesale competition. In early January 2015, the Ministry of Energy and Mineral Resources issued a regulation on cooperation in supplying electricity and common use of electricity networks. This regulation was issued in response to Government Regulation No. 12/2012 on Business in Providing Electricity. The regulation highlighted the importance of open access on transmission for public interest through a rental network. Then Regulation No. 12/2012 was revised into Government Regulation No. 14/2014. The new regulation pointed out that rental network needs to follow the business plan for electricity utility.

Finally, regulations in the electricity sector need to encourage competition among producers. This will bring about greater efficiency and eliminate rent-seeking (see Chapter 4).

Notes

1. The Dutch private sector company, namely NV NIGM (*Netherlands Indische Gas Maatschappij*/Netherlands Indies Gas Company), expanded its business from a gas company to supplying electricity to the public.
2. ANIEM was the largest private utilities. In 1938, it served almost 45 per cent of all subscribers and distributed more than 35 per cent of electricity sold by the utilities (McCawley 1971).
3. Honsha Djawa Denki Djigyo was the sister organization of Djawa Denki Djigyo Kosha. The latter was controlled by the military while the former by the civilians.
4. In the early years of PENUPETEL's establishment, the director of PENUPETEL was involved in improper behaviour towards his staff and was discharged from his position (PLN 1995).
5. Kobarsjih (radical Nationalist and ultra-Marxist), the electricity trade union leader and also a member of Parliament, asked the government to nationalize all electricity and gas utilities before 1954, otherwise the Indonesian Electricity and Gas Labor Union (*Serikat Buruh Listrik dan Gas Indonesia*/SBLGI) will go on strike (McCawley 1971).
6. There were some stages of nationalization: NV EMA in Ambon (September 1953), NV EMBP in Balikpapan (November 1953), NV OGEM in Jakarta, Tanggerang, and Cirebon (January 1954), and NV ANIEM in East Java and Central Java (November 1954).
7. DDPLN had four divisions: planning service, engineering service, trade service, and administration service.
8. "Big Five" were the five leading Dutch trading companies that had monopoly power in the trading sector. They were Borsumij, Jacobson van den Berg, Geo Wehry, Internatio, and Lindeteves. In fact, the Banteng programme was primarily aimed at countering both Dutch and Chinese economic domination (Thee 2012).

9. In 1951, there was an unexpected increase in export revenues that resulted in an increase in balance of payment surplus and budget surplus. This was due to the "Korea boom", or the period of a rapid increase in demand for raw materials by the American government during the Korean War (Thee 2003).

10. Description of macroeconomic indicators is obtained by interpreting Table 6.3 of Dick (2002).

11. Between 1941 and 1967, the percentage of the population living in Java island was about 66 per cent; the share of employment in the industrial sector in Java was about 11.6 per cent (in 1930) and this decreased to about 9.1 per cent (in 1961), while in the outer islands, the share in employment was about 9.6 per cent and 5.3 per cent respectively for the same period. (Note: this data is interpreted from van der Eng (2002), Tables 7.3 and 7.4.)

12. Owned by private electricity companies such as NV. EMTO, S.W. YOUNGE, NV. PRAPAT, NV. MEPB; NV. KEM, NV. STEM, NV. EMA, NV. EMBP, and NV. Maatschappij ter Exploitatie van Openbare Werken (PLN 1995). Owned by regional governments such as Regentschaps Electriciteits Bedrijf (which handled electricity in the districts of Lamongan, Trenggalek, Kandangan, and Barabai); Gemeentelijk Electriciteits Bedrijf (which handled electricity in the cities of Padang, Jambi, Pematang Siantar, Prapat, Tanjung balai, Tarutung, Madiun, etc.); Zelfbestuurders Electriciteits Bedrijf (which handled electricity in Sanggau, Mempawah, Malino, and Karangasem); and SSS (*Sumatera Staats Spoorwegen* — railway company handling Kampungdurian Padang Steam Power Plant to serve Teluk Bayur Harbour and coal transportation) (PLN 1995).

13. Letter of Intent of the Government of Indonesia, 31 October 1997, <https://www.imf.org/external/np/loi/103197.htm> (accessed 15 April 2014).

14. Ibid.

15. Letter of Intent of the Government of Indonesia, 13 November 1998, <https://www.imf.org/external/np/loi/1113a98.htm#matrix> (accessed 15 April 2014).

16. The NGO Working Group on Power Sector Restructuring consists of several organizations, such as International NGO Forum on Indonesia Development (INFID), Yayasan Gei Nastiti (GENI), Lembaga Bantuan Hukum Jakarta (LBH Jakarta), Indonesia Corruption Watch (ICW), Wahana Lingkungan Hidup Indonesia (WALHI), and Bank Information Center (BIC). During the meeting in Jakarta in September 2001, the aim of the working group was to advocate for better transparency, public accountability, and encouraging public participation in electricity restructuring in Indonesia.

17. According to Electricity Law No. 20/2002, Article 15, a competitive area is determined by government regulations. There are eight conditions for setting up a competitive area: the electricity price achieved economic price; there is competition in primary energy supplies; there is a Supervisory Agency for the Electricity Market (*Badan Pengawas Pasar Tenaga Listrik*); the competition regulation is ready for implementation; the infrastructure, software and hardware have to be ready; the system is ready for competition; the players have to have relatively the same power; and other requirements as determined by the *Badan Pengawas Pasar Tenaga Listrik*.

18. The three parties were: (i) APHI (Asosiasi Penasehat Hukum dan Hak Asasi Manusia Indonesia), PBHI (Perhimpunan Bantuan Hukum dan Hak Asasi Manusia Indonesia), and Yayasan 324; (ii) PLN Labour Union; (iii) Ir. Januar Muin and Ir. David Tombeng.

19. <http://www.mahkamahkonstitusi.go.id/Sinopsis/sinopsis_Ikhtisar%20 Putusan%20MK%20(SINOPSIS).pdf> (accessed 15 April 2014).

20. Ibid.

21. Ibid.

22. <http://www.mahkamahkonstitusi.go.id/Risalah/risalah_sidang_5857_ PERKARA%20NOMOR%20106.PUU-XI.2013%20%208%20JANUARI%20 2014%20by%20lindy.pdf> (accessed 16 April 2014).

23. <http://www.mahkamahkonstitusi.go.id/putusan/putusan_sidang_1661_9- PUU-2013_26Maret2014%20.pdf> (accessed 16 April 2014).

24. According to Electricity Law No. 30/2009, a business area is an area that is stated by the government (central government) as a place for distributing and/or selling entities to supply electricity.

25. <http://www.mahkamahkonstitusi.go.id/putusan/putusan_sidang_1661_9- PUU-2013_26Maret2014%20.pdf> (accessed 16 April 2014).

26. <http://www.cnnindonesia.com/ekonomi/20150330115044-85-42906/ menteri-esdm-5-dari-22-sistem-listrik-nasional-masih-defisit/> (accessed 30 March 2015).

27. <http://www.batan.go.id/gunber/2012/2012-04-22%20www.bisnis-jabar. com_Nuklir-3%20Provinsi%20di%20Indonesia%20Siap%20Kembangkan%20 PLTN.PDF> (accessed 13 May 2015).

28. <http://prokum.esdm.go.id/Publikasi/Statistik/Statistik%20Batubara.pdf> (accessed 13 May 2015).

29. <http://finance.detik.com/read/2015/05/12/103756/2912664/1034/7-tahun- impor-listrik-dari-malaysia-gubernur-kalbar-kami-ingin-pltn> (accessed 13 May 2015).

30. <http://www.energitoday.com/2015/04/15/jk-nuklir-jadi-opsi-terakhir-atasi- krisis-listrik/> (accessed 13 May 2015).

References

Departemen Pertambangan dan Energi (DPE). *55 Years of Mining and Energy Development*. Jakarta: DPE 2000.

Dick, Howard. "Formation of Nation-State, 1930s-1966". In *The Emergence of a National Economy: An Economic History of Indonesia, 1800-2000*. NSW: Allen & Unwin, 2002.

Lindblad, J. Thomas. "The Contribution of Foreign Trade to Colonial State Formation in Indonesia, 1900-1930". In *The Late Colonial State in Indonesia: Political and Economic Foundations of the Netherlands Indies 1880-1941*, edited by Robert Cribb. Leiden: KITLV Press, 1994.

————. *Bridges to New Business: The Economic Decolonization of Indonesia*. Leiden: KITLV Press, 2008.

McCawley, Peter. "The Indonesian Electric Supply Industry". PhD dissertation, Australian National University, 1971.

PT PLN (Persero). *50 Years of PLN Dedication*. Jakarta: PT PLN (Persero), 1995.

————. *Rencana Usaha Penyediaan Tenaga Listrik PT PLN (Persero) 2015–2024* [PT PLN Business Plan for Electricity Utility 2015–2024]. Jakarta: PT PLN (Persero), 2014.

Thee Kian Wie. "Introduction". In *Recollections the Indonesia Economy 1950s-1990s*, edited by Thee Kian Wie. Singapore: Institute of Southeast Asian Studies, 2003.

————. *Indonesia's Economy since Independence*. Singapore: Institute of Southeast Asian Studies, 2012.

Tumiwa, F. *Listrik yang Menyengat Rakyat: Menggugat Peran Bank-Bank Pembangunan Multilateral*. Jakarta: WGPSR, 2002.

van der Eng, Pierre. "Indonesia's Growth Performance in the Twentieth Century". In *The Asian Economies in the Twentieth Century*, edited by Angus Maddison, D.S. Prasada Rao, and William F. Shepherd. Cheltenham: Edward Elgar, 2002.

3

ELECTRICITY PRODUCTION AND CONSUMPTION
Boom and Bust

THE PRODUCTION SIDE

This chapter investigates electricity production and consumption in Indonesia since the First Five-Year Development Plan (*Rencana Pembangunan Lima Tahun Repelita I*) which began in April 1969. An analysis of the production process involves the development of electrical generation, transmission, and distribution, whereas a study of the consumption pattern involves the sectorial and regional dimensions. Electricity consumption is represented by the amount of electrical energy sold at any one time. As seen in Figure 3.1, between 1969 and 2012, electricity production and sales increased more than a hundred times. Electricity production is still predominantly generated by PLN. However, PLN can also purchase electricity from captive power plants and independent power producers (IPP).[1] Between 1968 and 2012, the average growth of electricity production was about 11.3 per cent, whereas the growth of electricity consumption was about 11.7 per cent.[2] Before the 1998 economic crisis, electricity

Figure 3.1
Electricity Energy Production and Sales

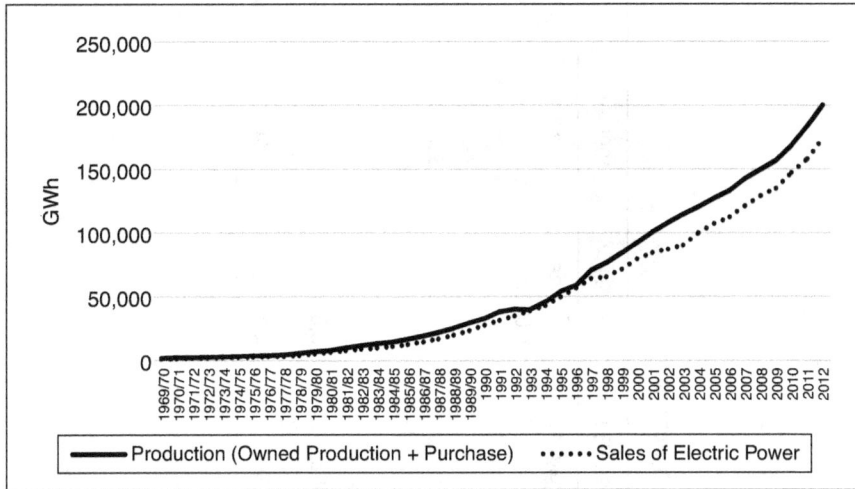

Sources: PLN (1995) for 1969/70–1993/94 data; ESDM (2006) for 1994–2003 data; and PLN (2012) for 2004–12 data.

production increased by 13.3 per cent; however, after the crisis, it was about 6.3 per cent. The growth rates in electricity consumption before and after the economic crisis were about 14.1 per cent and 6.6 per cent respectively. This chapter analyses how the 1997/98 economic crisis had substantially affected the development of the power sector in Indonesia as the growth of electricity production and consumption had decreased from double-digit to single-digit growth. A detail analysis of the impact of the economic crisis on PLN is discussed in Chapter 4.

As mentioned in the previous chapter, the private sector had played an important role in the early stages of the development of the energy sector in Indonesia. After Indonesia gained its independence, the new government had adopted a gradual nationalization of the electricity sector; by the early 1960s, the entire electricity sector was under state control. As seen in Table 3.1, in 1973/74 or at the end of the first five years of development planning, hydropower made up a capacity of about 278.7 MW, or about 35 per cent of the total installed capacity (that was owned by PLN). As discussed in Chapter 2, in the early 1970s, the contribution of hydropower was about 30 per cent.

Table 3.1
Installed Capacity by Type of Power Plant

Type of power plant	1973/74	1978/79	1983/84	1988/89	1993/94	1998	2014
Hydropower	278.77	349.67	536.44	1,969.57	2,178.75	3,006.76	3,526.86
Steam-coal	225.00	556.25	1,556.25	3,416.95	4,690.60	6,770.60	20,451.67
Steam-gas	42.00	882.07	1,027.92	1,233.68	995.92	1,347.41	3,012.10
Steam-gas-coal	–	–	–	–	3,411.31	6,560.97	8,886.11
Geothermal	–	–	30.00	140.00	195.00	360.00	537.00
Diesel	230.31	500.40	784.39	1,769.02	2,128.46	2,535.02	2,798.55
Wind	–	–	–	–	–	–	0.47
Solar panel	–	–	–	–	–	–	8.73
Total-PLN	776.08	2,288.38	3,934.99	8529.22	13,600.05	20,580.76	39,257.53
Private + Captive Power	NI	NI	NI	833.52	1,178.16	2,893.88	11,442.47
Total National	–	–	–	9,362.74	14,778.21	23,474.64	50,700.00*

Note: NI = No information;
   * It is obtained from the Medium-Term National Development Planning 2015–2019.
Source: PLN (2014*b*) and ESDM (2006).

However, by 1978/79, the installed capacity of steam coal, steam gas, and diesel were higher than that of hydropower. In 1983/84, geothermal was produced and it added to the national installed capacity. Further, the contribution of the private sector and captive power to the total national installed capacity increased from about 833.5 MW in 1988/89 to about 11,442 MW in 2014, or its share to the total national installed capacity increased from about 9 per cent to about 22.5 per cent.

However, the private sector was allowed to sell electricity to PLN. Since the early 1970s, the PLN had purchased electricity from captive power sources. As seen in Figure 3.2, captive power sources made up a quarter of all electricity purchases. Until the Asian financial crisis in 1998, the proportion of PLN's own electricity power generation gradually increased from 75 per cent to more than 97 per cent. However, after the 1997/98 Asian Financial Crisis, the proportion of PLN's own electricity production decreased gradually to about 77 per cent in 2012, even as the share of purchased electricity increased from 2.2 per cent in 1991/92 to about 20 per cent in 2012. The same figure also indicated that the share of electricity production from rented generators increased to about 9 per cent between 1998 and 2012.

It is useful to investigate why the share of electricity purchased from captive power sources decreased gradually, and why PLN's electricity production increased until the late 1990s. Firstly, PLN's installed capacity increased rapidly between 1972/73 and 1993/94; the average growth reached 16 per cent per annum. This amount was the highest average growth after independence. Secondly, there was a rapid increase in electricity demand from the industrial sector; thus, rather than selling electricity to PLN, the private sector had incentives to produce electricity for their own needs, so much so that even the PLN provided special facilities to procure the required power plant machinery (DPE 2000). Thirdly, there was a lack of incentives in selling electricity to PLN because the rates at which PLN set for their purchases were too low compared to the prices offered by the private sector. It should be noted, however, that after the 1997/98 Asian Financial Crisis, electricity purchases had increased due to electricity purchases from the IPP segment.

The private sector was initially encouraged to provide electricity for public utilities companies, which was accommodated by the 1985 Electricity Law No. 15. The central government would issue Public

Figure 3.2
Electricity Production (%)

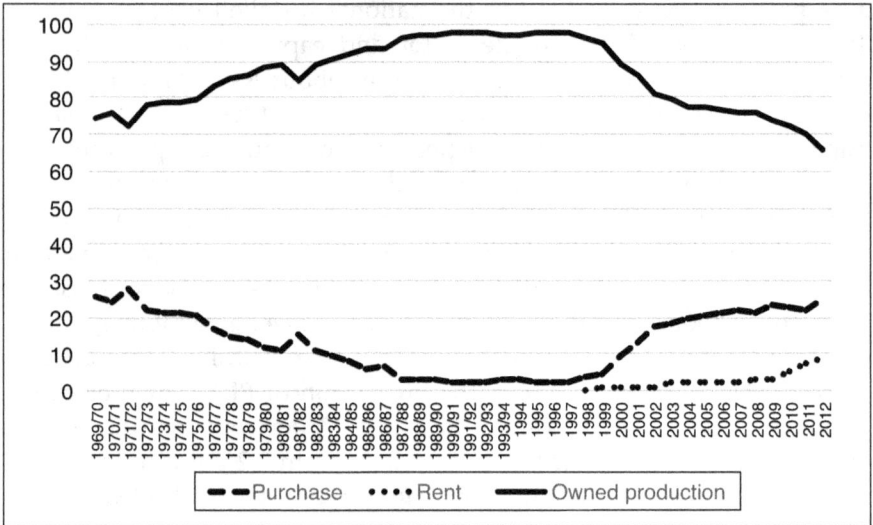

Sources: DPE (2000) for 1969/70–1993/94 data; ESDM (2006) for 1994–2003 data; PLN (2012) for 2004–12 data.

Utilities Licences (*Izin Usaha Kelistrikan Untuk Kepentingan Umum/* IUKU) to the private sector companies that participated in the energy generation sector (DPE 2000). There are two models for IUKU: solicited projects and unsolicited projects.[3] As holders of IUKU, the scope of the projects for the private sector was based on the following criteria (DPE 2000):

1. IUKU holders could operate in areas where electric power service provided by PLN existed but could not meet the demand for electric power. Private electricity companies could then supply its electric power for the PLN network.
2. IUKU holders could operate in areas where no electric power service were provided by PLN. The private sector could therefore generate electric power for their own use (on the basis of IUKS) or supply it to other parties (on the basis of IUKU).

It can be observed that there are five ways for private involvement in the electricity business:

1. In order to generate electricity for one's own use, an Operating Permit (OP) is required. However, OP holders can sell any excess power to any parties who own electricity permits, such as businesses or laymen. The permit lasts for ten years and is extendable.[4]

2. The private power utility (PPU) aims to serve a specific geographic area. The PPU model has the rights to generate, transmit, and distribute power. The PPU may or may not be affiliated to PLN, but its primary activity is to supply electricity directly to customers within its operating area (Kristov 1995). Examples of the PPU model are: PT Cikarang Listrindo in Bekasi, West Java; PT Kariangau Power in Balikpapan, East Kalimantan; PT Bekasi Power in Bekasi, West Java; PT Karakatau Daya Listrik in Cilegon, Banten; PT Pelayanan Listrik Nasional Batam in Batam, Kepuluan Riau; PT Tata Jabar Sejahtera in Karawang, West Java; and PT Makmur Sejahtera Wisesa in Tabalong, West Kalimantan.[5] Business licences can be provided for thirty years and are renewable.

3. The independent power producer (IPP) model allows producers to develop and operate their own power generating plants and sell electricity to PLN. The first IPP project was the Paiton I project in East Java which managed to achieve financial closure in March 1995.

4. PLN can also rent generators for generating power. This meant that PLN would be responsible for the costs and payment of the generator leases, fuel and land acquisitions, while private companies would provide the generators. This policy of generator renting is generally only utilized as a temporary measure during an energy crisis.

5. Public private partnership (PPP) has been introduced by Presidential Regulation No. 67/2005.[6] PLN (2014a) indicated that there are four projects under the PPP scheme and they are steam coal Central Java (2 × 1,000 MW), steam coal Sumsel-9 (2 × 600 MW), steam coal Sumsel-10 (1 × 600 MW), and Hydro Karama (450 MW) in West Sulawesi.

As seen in Table 3.2, in 2013, the total electricity generating capacity in Indonesia was about 43.5 GW and it increased by about 44 per cent compared to the 2007 level.[7] The IPP sector contributed between 14.7 and 14.9 per cent of the total electricity generating capacity.

Table 3.2
Current Condition of Power Generating in Indonesia

Indicators	IPP	PLN	Rent	Total
Year 2007 (MW)	4,441	24,764	1,073	30,278
Year 2013 (MW)	6,496	34,037	2,933	43,466
Growth 2007–13 (%)	46	37	173	44
Share in 2007 (%)	14.7	81.8	3.5	100
Share in 2013 (%)	14.9	78.3	6.7	100

Note: In 2013, more than 75 per cent of rented power generation was based on diesel power plants.
Sources: PLN (2009, 2013).

These numbers remained stable and are in contrast to PLN's share of the total electricity generating capacity, which shrank from 82 per cent to about 78 per cent. Meanwhile, the proportion of rented power generation had a tendency to increase from 3.5 per cent to about 6.7 per cent. Rented power generation also showed the highest growth when one compares those rates to other types of ownership. These results could be due to PLN having to rent generators from both the private sector as well as in collaboration with the local government districts. There are three main objectives of rented power generation (PLN 2013): (i) as a temporary measure during a power deficit before the non-oil generating power plants can begin to operate; (ii) as a temporary measure during the transitory period where the existing diesel-based power generation plants are replaced with more efficient plants that have better fuel consumption rates; (iii) as a measure which can increase the electrification ratio, especially for regions that do not have renewable energy resources.

Electricity production is dependent on the total capacity for power generation. The development of power generation can be captured by investigating the growth rates for installed capacity. As seen in Figure 3.3, PLN's installed capacity had increased by more than sixty times between 1968 and 2012; it increased from 536 MW in 1968 to about 33 GW in 2012. Although the installed capacity showed a tendency to increase, the annual growth rates indicated a declining trend (see Figure 3.3). This implies that growth of new capacity also had a tendency to reduce substantial fluctuations. During that period, PLN's annual growth capacity was about 9.87 per cent. However, if we calculate

Figure 3.3
Installed Capacity of PLN

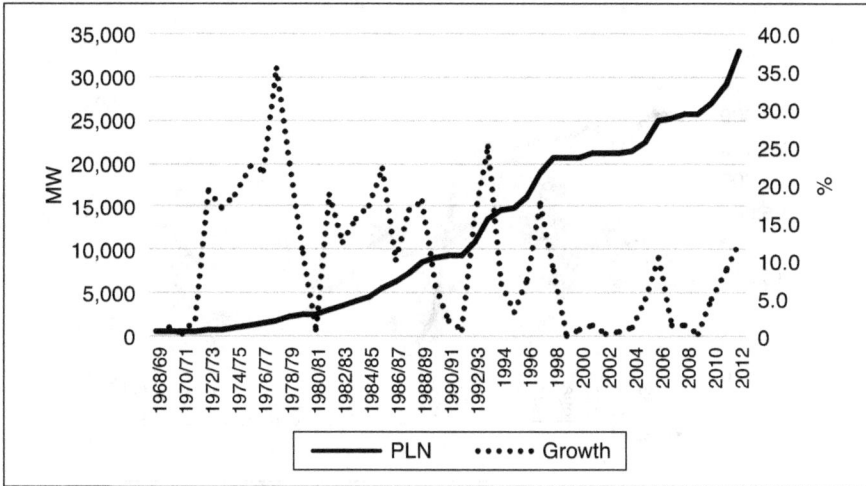

Sources: PLN (1995) for 1968/69–1993/94 data; ESDM (2006) for 1994–2003 data; PLN (2012) for 2004–12 data.

the capacity for growth before and after the Asian financial crisis in 1998, it was about 13.4 per cent and 3.1 per cent respectively. Thus the 1997/98 Asian Financial Crisis substantially affected the development of power generation in Indonesia. Chapter 4 provides an analysis on why the 1997/98 Asian Financial Crisis contributed negatively to the performance of PLN and the power sector in Indonesia. The decline in capacity growth is due to a lack of investment in power infrastructure. Another consideration is that additional electrical generation capacity is subject to investment phases, while the scale of electricity generation, types of power generation, and technical and non-technical factors would determine the rates at which such additional capacities can support the existing power generation system.

There is a lack of reliable data for captive power generation of the private sector before the 1990s (see Box 3.1 for updated information on captive power). Therefore, in order to properly investigate the role of the private sector, the period between 1990/91 and 2012 was selected. During this period, PLN was not the sole electricity producer. As seen in Figure 3.4, in the early 1990s, the proportion of privately installed

Figure 3.4
National, PLN, and Private Installed Capacity

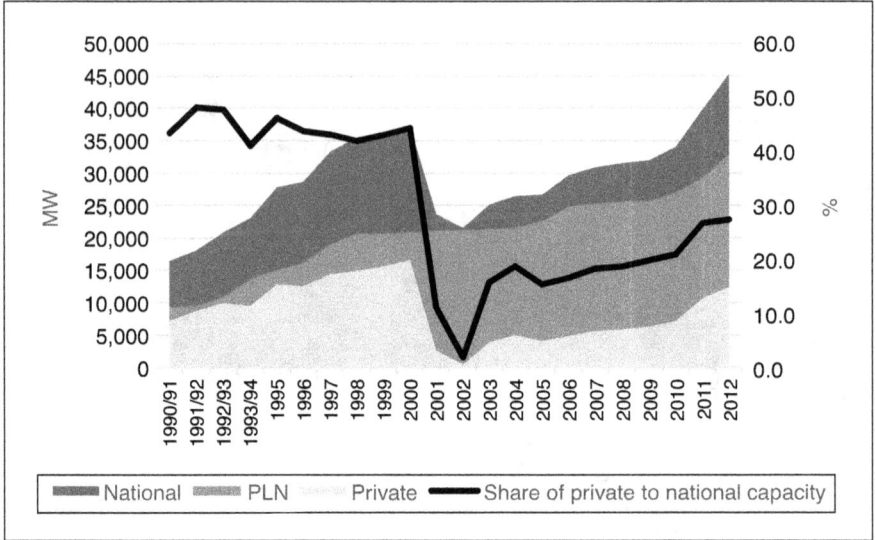

Sources: PLN (1995) for 1968/69–1993/94 data; ESDM (2006) for 1994–2003 data; PLN (2012) for 2004–12 data.

Box 3.1
Captive Power in Indonesia

According to the latest survey from Statistics Indonesia (*Badan Pusat Statistik/* BPS 2011) on 22,999 firms, there are three important points with regards to captive power. Firstly, more than 83 per cent of the firms operate on captive power; that is, they produce electricity for their own consumption. There are two main businesses that depend on captive power and they are banking and mini/supermarket. These businesses made up approximately 49 per cent and 44 per cent respectively of the total captive power. Secondly, most of the captive power depends on diesel power plants and 96.5 per cent of all businesses utilize a power capacity of less than 500 kW. In 2010, the total electricity production from captive power amounted to about 7,839 GWh (3 per cent of PLN's total electricity production). Thirdly, captive power from diesel power plants consume both HSD (high speed diesel) and gasoline. The total consumption for these plants are about 61.4 million litres and 1.8

Box 3.1 (*continued*)

million litres respectively. Captive power's HSD consumption is less than 1 per cent of PLN's. Thus, following the latest figures on captive power, one may argue that in comparison to PLN, the size of captive power is relatively small. This may be true for two reasons. Firstly, the size of the sample firms is relatively small. Secondly, the unit sampling only covers service sectors such as banking, mini/supermarket, television and radio, and train stations. These units consume less energy compared to the industrial sector.

Next, data from large and medium manufacturing indicators was collected from various issues of BPS. There is information on electricity production as well as sales and purchase prices of each industry. The electricity production and selling prices to represent captive power are included. Figure 3.5 shows that between 2002 and 2005, the proportion of captive power to the total electricity sold by PLN increased and it reached a peak of 25 per cent in 2005. This indicates that during this period, the manufacturing sector developed their own power generators. This is due to a slow growth in national electricity production and as a measure to mitigate the risk for possible rising energy cost in the future (some companies, such as Pan Asia Indosyntec, developed coal steam power plants instead of diesel-oil power plants). However, in 2009, the proportion of captive power to the total PLN power sold was about 5 per cent. As the rate of electricity sold also had a tendency to decrease, it can be argued that many industries have reduced their electricity production. However, there was no substantial increase in electricity purchase even though it also had a tendency to decrease. Therefore, the author argues that many industries (especially energy-intensive industries) collapsed due to the rapid increase in energy prices (especially companies that have used oil instead of coal power plants). On 1 October 2005, the fuel prices were raised by a weighted average of 114 per cent (Sen and Steer 2005). Kerosene had the highest increase, followed by gasoline and automotive diesel. As most of the captive power plants were diesel based, it became very costly to produce electricity after the energy price increase.

According to PLN (2009), between 2002 and 2009, the rate of electricity sold to the industrial sector increased from 36,831 GWh to 46,204 GWh, or by 3.6 per cent per year. Thus, one may argue that even though electricity purchases showed a declining trend based on the manufacturing survey, at the national level (industrial level), the electricity purchased rates had a tendency to increase. However, one might also argue that the decline in captive power is due to increases in oil price and PLN power production, improvement in the efficiency of energy usage, decline in industrial output, and the collapse of many industries.

Box 3.1   (*continued*)

Figure 3.5
Captive Power in Indonesia

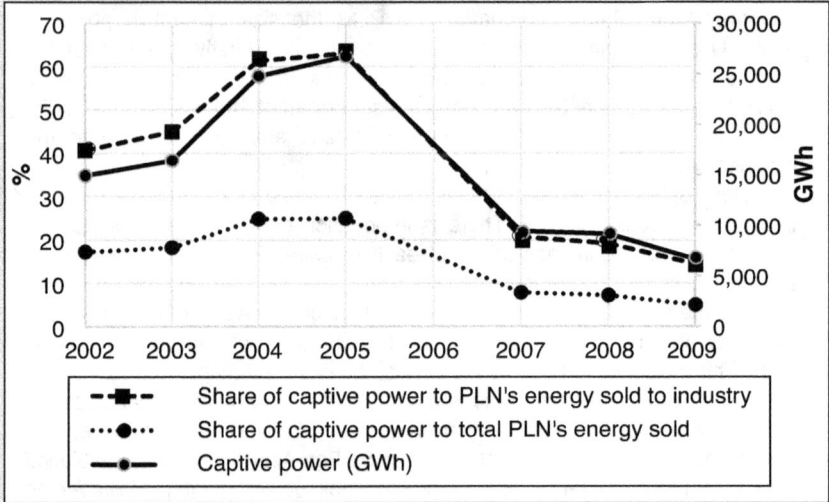

Note: Data in 2001 does not include captive power.
Sources: ESDM (2012) and PLN (2012).

capacity to the national installed capacity was about 43.4 per cent. The privately installed capacity at that time was about 7.1 GW while the capacity of PLN was about 9.3 GW. The private sector's proportion to the national installed capacity was relatively stable at 44 per cent until 2000. However, in 2001, the data indicated that the national installed capacity decreased to about 23 GW. This discrepancy was mainly due to unreported data on captive power and private power producers. The decrease was quite substantial, but an interesting factor to take note of here is how the capacity of the private sector increased gradually. In 2012, the proportion of private sector to the national installed capacity was about 27.3 per cent. A later section confirms that this figure is consistent with power purchased from the private sector.

Although the national installed capacity decreased between 2000 and 2001, the national electricity production rates increased by

8.9 per cent from 92,639 GWh to about 100,883 GWh (ESDM 2006). As seen in Figure 3.6, in 2001, the national capacity declined to about 36 per cent, and as indicated previously, this is due to a lack of available data for captive power sources and private power. Most power plant categories showed a decline in capacity and the category which had decreased the most was the diesel power plant. Thus, it can be argued that the proportion of privately owned diesel power plants was relatively high. This led to a significant decline in the proportion of the private sector's contributions to the nation's overall capacity. Although the author contends that the growth rate of the private sector in relation to the total national capacity had a tendency to decline in 2001 and 2002, it did not reach pre-2000 levels. There must have been extenuating circumstances as to why the government did not give any figures for captive power and private power for that period. A substantial increase in the world oil prices could have been the main reason as to why the proportion of installed capacity of diesel power plants decreased substantially. In 1999, the Indonesia

Figure 3.6
National Installed Capacity between 2000 and 2001

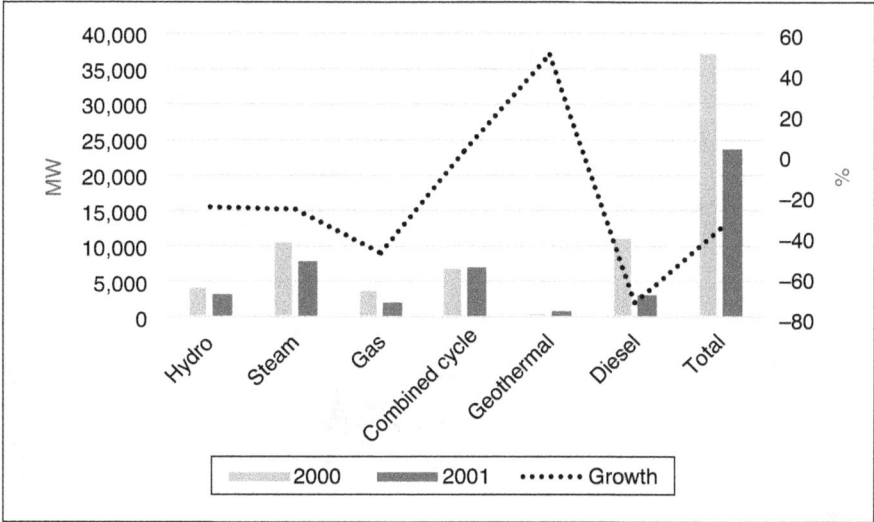

Note: Data in 2001 does not include captive power.
Sources: ESDM (2012) and PLN (2012).

Crude Oil Price (ICP) was about US$17.52 per barrel, but it increased to about US$28.39 per barrel in 2000. On average, between 2001 and 2005, the oil prices stood at US$32 per barrel.[8]

As power generation costs from diesel power plants increased substantially due to the increase in world oil prices, the central government would need to reduce electricity production from diesel power plants. It is then that we see how steam power plants became an important factor that would offset the decline in electricity production from diesel power plants. As seen in Figure 3.7, the steam power plant (steam coal) category was the major source of power for PLN power plants and this category had the second highest growth after the gas category; this would indicate that steam coal power plants would become an important future energy supply. Geothermal power plants also showed the third highest growth, even though it made up the lowest proportion of the total market share in 2012. The growth rates between hydroelectric plants and diesel

Figure 3.7
Share and Growth of PLN Power Plants

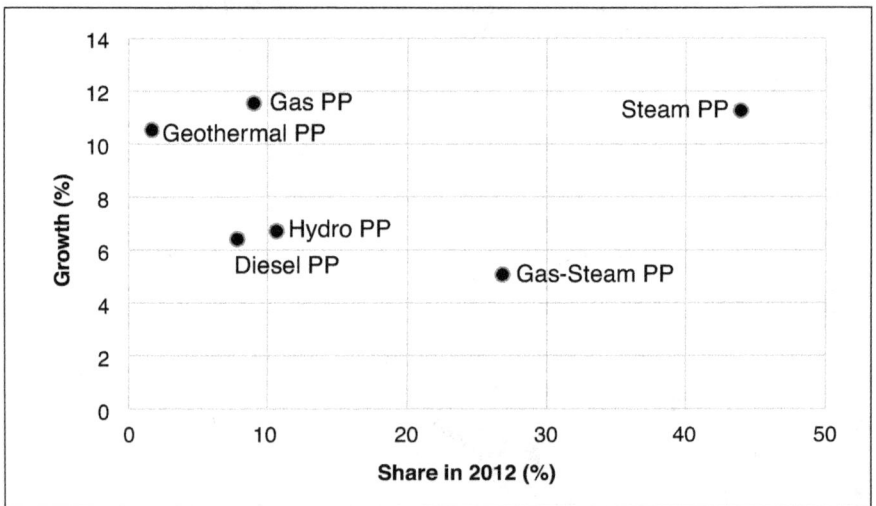

Note: 1973–2012 growth included data for steam power plants (PP), hydroelectric power, gas, and diesel; meanwhile, steam gas only involved during the 1993–2012 period. Geothermal was for the 1983–2012 period.
Source: Calculated from PLN (2012).

power plants were comparable, but the share of hydroelectric power in relation to the total installed capacity was higher than that of diesel power plants. It seems likely that hydroelectric power plants will become more important in the future as compared to diesel power plants.

In order to account for better service and quality of power supply, the growth in capacity would need to be followed by increases in transmission lines, distribution lines, and other supporting infrastructure. Between 1978 and 2012, the growth of transmission lines was at about 4.86 per cent, whereas the expansion of substations was at 8.8 per cent in total (see Figure 3.8). Furthermore, if one compares the conditions which existed prior to and after the 1997/98 economic crisis, it seems that prior to the crisis, the rates of transmission and the expansion of substations were at about 6.1 per cent and 12.8 per cent respectively; after the crisis, they were at about 3.45 per cent and 3.3 per cent respectively. This indicates that the rates of transmission, power distribution, and expansion of electrical substations were negatively affected by the economic crisis.

Figure 3.8
Transmission Facilities

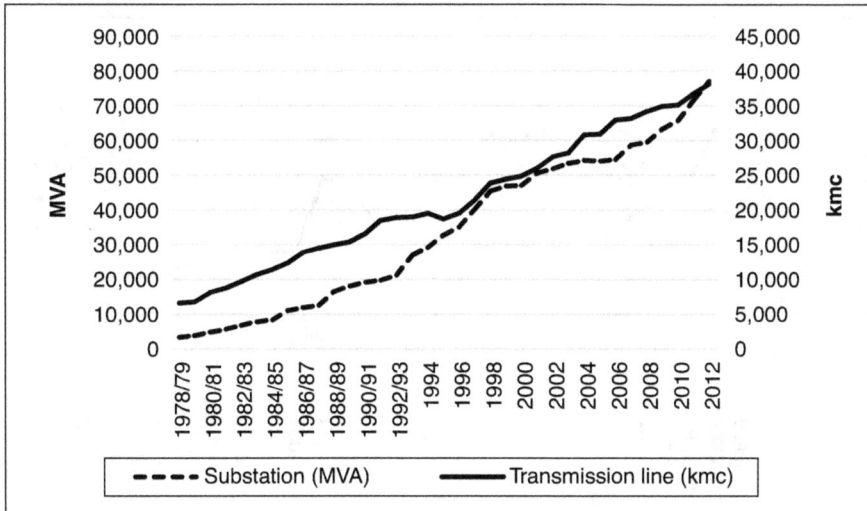

Sources: PLN (1995) for 1978/79–1993/94 data; ESDM (2006) for 1994–2003 data; PLN (2012) for for 2004–12 data.

As power infrastructure develops (this would include power generation, electrical transmissions, electrical distribution, and increases in electrical substations), electrical transmission and distribution losses can be reduced. As seen in Figure 3.9, electrical transmission and distribution losses decreased rapidly from about 23.8 per cent in the mid-1970s to about 12.8 per cent in the early 1990s. Between the 1990s and 2012, the transmission and distribution losses decreased gradually at a marginal level, but in 2000 it had a tendency to increase, reaching a peak of 16.9 per cent in 2003. Furthermore, the author argues that the slight decrease in transmission and distribution losses since the last decade is due to a decrease in investments on new transmission lines and substations as compared to the conditions prior to the 1997/98 economic crisis.

Electric power losses occur due to two main reasons: technical losses and non-technical losses. Technical losses can be reduced by improving maintenance regimes and constructing more efficient networks of distribution. While, for non-technical losses, such as

Figure 3.9
Distribution and Transmission Losses (%)

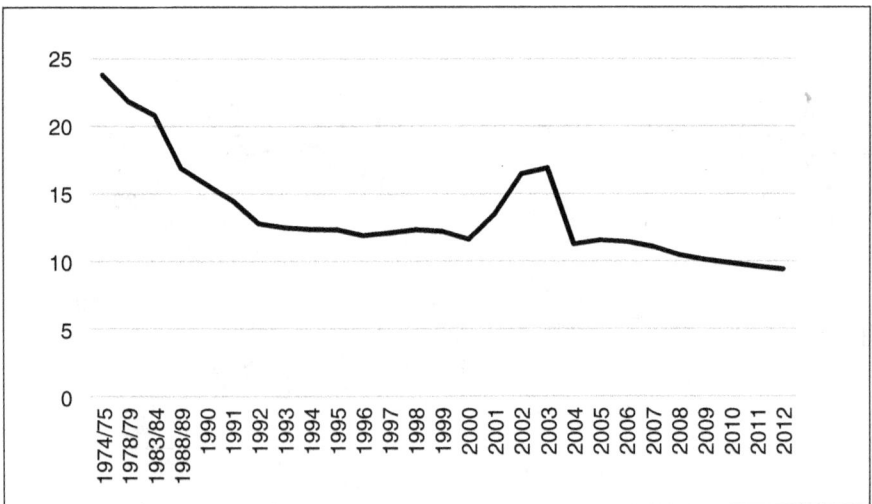

Sources: PLN (1995) for 1974/75–1993/94 data; ESDM (2006) for 1994–2003 data; PLN (2012) for 2004–12 data.

electricity theft, they can be minimized by improving monitoring procedures and by enforcing stricter laws. Increases in network distribution losses between 2001 and 2003 were mainly due to increasing rates of electricity theft.[9] The author argues that the increase in electricity tariffs between April 2000 and January 2002 contributed to the escalation of such electricity theft. From a technical point of view, it can also be said that network capacity was lacking (PLN 2002).

Table 3.3 gives the average figures for electrical transmission and distribution losses in several Asian countries. It indicates that in the 1970s, the transmission and distribution losses for Indonesia was relatively low; Indonesia had the second lowest reading among the stated Asian countries after the Philippines. In the 1980s, China and Vietnam showed a decreasing trend, with China showing consistent results until 2011. It seems that all countries depicted showed decreasing network losses except India, while the Philippines has shown decreasing trends since the 1980s. In Indonesia, the average transmission and distribution losses between 2000 and 2011 was higher than that in the 1990s. This indicates that Indonesia still needs to improve its efficiency in electrical transmission and distribution networks. A single-digit target needs to be set for the medium term, while a target of less than 5 per cent can be set for the long term.

Table 3.3
Average Electrical Transmission and Distribution Losses
(% of Output)

Country	1970s	1980s	1990s	2000–11
Indonesia	7.14	13.47	11.43	11.76
Malaysia	9.77	11.34	9.57	7.56
India	17.23	18.57	20.32	24.52
Philippines	4.91	13.92	15.16	12.38
Thailand	9.42	10.37	9.17	7.29
China	8.11	7.60	7.05	6.46
Vietnam	22.00	18.83	21.33	11.80

Source: Calculated from World Development Indicators.

THE DEMAND SIDE

The current supply of electricity cannot fulfil the demand for power in Indonesia. This demand can be seen by looking at three main indicators. Firstly, the electrification ratio in Indonesia is about 73.4 per cent; this means that 26.6 per cent of all households do not have access to electricity. Secondly, more than 1 million people were on the waiting list for electricity connection in 2014 (PLN 2014*b*). Thirdly, the electricity consumption per capita is still relatively low in comparison to other countries that have a lower income per capita than Indonesia, such as India, Vietnam, Moldova, Uzbekistan, Kyrgyz Rep., and Tajikistan. This indicates that the demand side situation does not fully capture the real conditions.

The rates for electricity demand or consumption can be captured from the total rates of electricity sold and can be divided into four sectors: households, commercial, industry and hotels, and the public sector. As seen in Figure 3.10, the household sector dominated the national figures for electricity consumption at about 56 per cent in the early

Figure 3.10
Share of Energy Sales by Sector

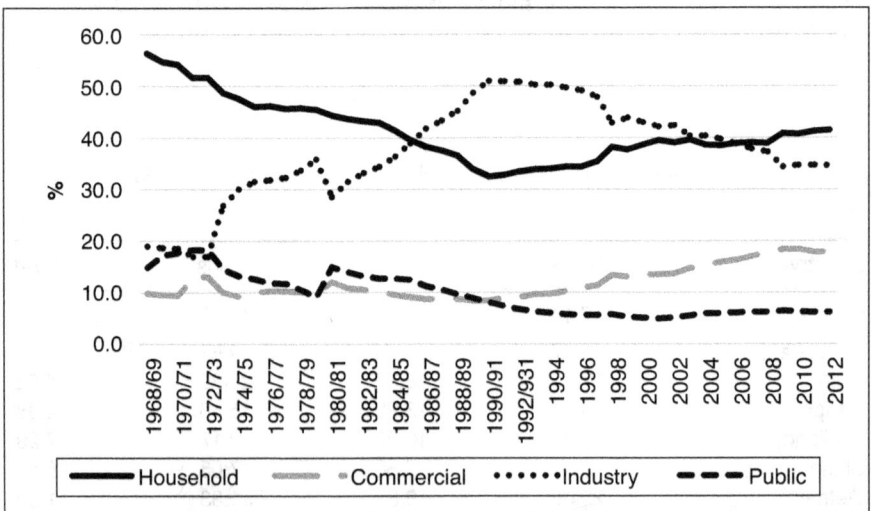

Sources: PLN (1995) for 1968/69–1993/94 data; ESDM (2006) for 1994–2003 data; PLN (2012) for 2004–12 data.

1970s. However, within two decades, the proportion for the household sector had decreased, reaching 32.5 per cent in the early 1990s. On the other hand, the share of energy sales to the industrial sector increased rapidly from 19 per cent in the early 1970s to about 51 per cent of the national electricity consumption rates in mid-1990s. Electricity consumption for each sector can be further divided into subsectors based on the connected voltage of customers. As seen in Table 3.4, at the household level, most electricity was sold to 450 VA and 900 VA customers that mostly represent the lower and medium income households.

Indonesia's rapid industrial growth and transformation during the Soeharto era contributed to rapid increases in electricity consumption from the industrial sector. The industrial sector grew by about 12.6 per cent during the 1980–90 period; this rate was much faster than

Table 3.4
Electricity Sold and Total Revenue by Group of Customers in 2007

Category	Electricity sold (TWh)		Revenue	
	TWh	%	Billion IDR	%
Social	2,909	24	1,664	2.2
Household	47,116	39.1	26,770	35.6
R1 up to 450 VA	16,776	13.9	6,811	9.1
R1 900 VA	14,701	12.2	8,824	11.7
R1 1300 VA	6,558	5.4	4,424	5.9
R1 2200 VA	4,341	3.6	2,906	3.9
R2 + R3 (>2200 VA)	4,740	3.9	3,805	5.1
Commercial	19,176	15.9	14,374	19.1
B1 up to 2200VA	2,319	1.9	1,489	2
B2 – B3 (>2200 VA)	16,857	14	12,885	17.1
Industry	45,493	37.7	28,220	37.5
I1 up to 14 kVA	0.126	0	103	0.1
I2 up to 200 kVA	3,284	2.7	2,594	3.4
I3 + I4 (>200 kVA)	42,209	35	25,523	33.9
Public	4,605	3.8	3,127	4.2
P1 – P3	4,605	3.8	3,127	4.2
Multipurpose (T/C/M)	1,071	0.9	1,045	1.4
Total	120,529	100	75,204	100

Source: Sambodo (2009).

that of the agricultural and services sector, which grew at the rates of 3.4 per cent and 7.0 per cent respectively (Thee 2012). This situation led to positive outcomes, such as a rapid and generally sustainable economic growth of around 7 per cent per year during the thirty-two years of the Soeharto era (Thee 2012). As a result, Indonesia increased its status from a poor country to one of the eight High Performing Asian Economies (HPAEs) by the early 1990s.

However, as seen in Figure 3.10, the share of the industrial sector has declined since the mid-1990s. Interestingly, the share of the household and commercial sectors have increased since the early 1990s. In fact, the share of the household sector has surpassed the industrial sector since 2006. The economic crisis which hurt Indonesia significantly in 1998 caused a 13.1 per cent economic contraction, whereas the manufacturing sector shrank by 11.4 per cent (Thee 2012). The post-economic crisis growth rates for the manufacturing sector never reached the double digits experienced during the Soeharto era (Thee 2012). As seen in Figure 3.11, the

Figure 3.11
Annual Growth of Electricity Sold by Sector

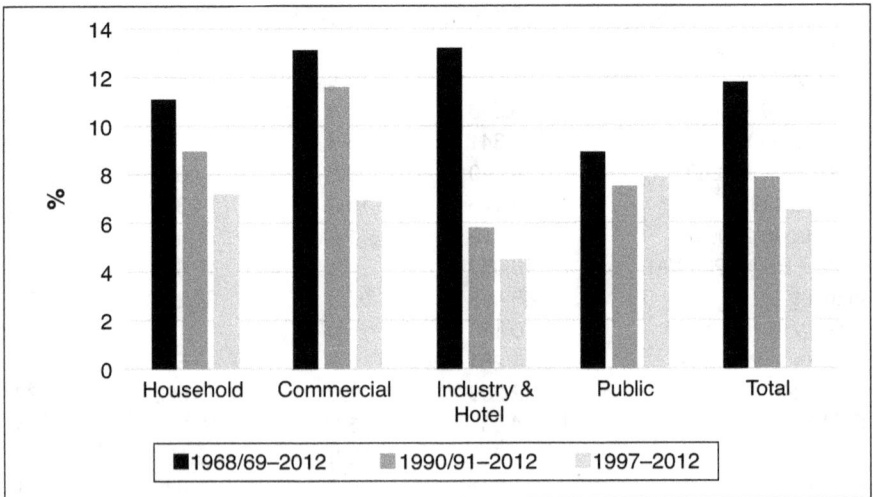

Sources: PLN (1995) for 1968/69–1993/94 data; ESDM (2006) for 1994–2003 data; PLN (2012) for 2004–12 data.

economic crisis had severely affected the growth of electricity consumption for all sectors with the exception of the public sector, which showed a slight increase during the 1997–2012 period. Between 1997 and 1998, the rate of electricity sold only increased by 1 per cent, which was the lowest rate of growth in comparison to other years. Between 1997 and 1998, the industrial sector experienced a 9 per cent contraction.[10] Sambodo (2009) pointed out the power deficit in 2008, which led the government to implement higher electricity tariff during the peak load (between 5.00 p.m. and 10.00 p.m.). As a result, some industries shifted one of their working days to a weekend. This affected especially the business and commercial sector which needs to use the generator twice a week. The policies caused an extra cost to the companies and made them adjust their electricity consumption. Many big companies developed their own power supplies while others attempted to improve their efficiency in electricity consumption.

Table 3.5 shows the share of electricity sold of the seven major Indonesian islands. The table indicated that the island of Java dominated the market for sold power. In 1973, Java made up 82.3 per cent of the total electricity sold by PLN. However, even though Java still dominated the power purchases, the proportion of its electricity sold decreased to about 73.9 per cent in 2012. This implies that other islands, such as Sumatra, Kalimantan, Sulawesi, Bali-NTB-NTT, had increased their shares of electricity sold, with

Table 3.5
Share of Electricity Sold (%)

Island	1973	2012	Change 1973–2012
Sumatra	10.40	14.86	4.45
Kalimantan	1.90	3.76	1.87
Sulawesi	2.99	3.69	0.70
Maluku	0.45	0.36	−0.09
Papua	0.74	0.54	−0.20
Bali-NTB-NTT	1.24	2.93	1.68
Java	82.28	73.86	−8.41
Total (GWh)	2,175	173,991	

Source: BPS, various years.

the exception of Papua and Maluku, the islands which indicated decreasing proportions of electricity purchases. In 2012, Java's share of electricity consumption from the industrial and business sector consisted of 58 per cent of the total electricity sold, while for regions outside Java, it was at about 36 per cent. On the other hand, the proportion of residential consumption was approximately 36.5 per cent in Java; outside of Java, the residential consumption rates amounted to 55.4 per cent. The reason why Java's electricity purchases were so high compared to the rest of the nation was because the island of Java alone contributed 58 per cent of the national GDP in 2013, and 57.5 per cent of Indonesians live on the island of Java. In terms of economic activities, Java still plays an important role in Indonesia's economy. The next section analyses how the gap in installed power capacity has a tendency to increase across the regions.

CONVERGENCE ANALYSIS

There has been a lack of detailed information regarding installed capacity at the provincial level, especially for the island of Java, as the power system in Java was networked. This shows that the power generated in one province can be sold to other provinces. As a result, it is better if one compares the capacity of power supply for selected islands, such as Java–Bali, Sumatra, Kalimantan, Sulawesi, Papua, West Nusa Tenggara, East Nusa Tenggara, and Maluku. The rated capacity was selected instead of installed capacity because rated capacity indicates the real capacity that can be generated. The convergence on power capacity across the regions is measured using the standard deviation of electrification ratio, which is normalized using the mean values.

A trend towards electrification convergence would be observed if the measured coefficient of variation decreased over time. This is simply calculated based on the standard deviation (σ) of power capacity (x_{it}) across the regions, divided by the mean $\bar{x}_t$ in any given year. The formula (σ) is given as (Wei et al. 2007):

$$\sigma_t = \left[\sqrt{\frac{1}{N} \sum (x_{it} - \bar{x}_t)^2} \right] / \bar{x}_t \qquad (2.1)$$

As can be seen in Table 3.6, one does not obtain convergence in rated capacity between 2009 and 2013, that is, the rated capacity became divergent across the regions. This indicates that the growth rate of rated capacity tends to be unequal across the regions. This implies that the electricity consumption gap will also increase across the provinces. Furthermore, it can be observed that there are increasing divergence rates due to the increase in Java–Bali's share from 77 per cent in 2009 to about 84 per cent in 2013; other regions showed stagnancy and even a decline in terms of share. Sadly, the decline in absolute rated capacity occurred in several regions such as Sumatra and Kalimantan as they are regions that are rich in energy sources (coal).

As seen in Figure 3.12, there is a convergence in the electrification ratio among the Indonesian provinces. This means that the gap in the electrification ratio across the provinces is expected to decline. Thus, household access on electricity is improving. On the other hand, the convergence showed an increasing trend for kWh sold

Figure 3.12
Convergence in Electrification Ratio and kWh Sold per Capita

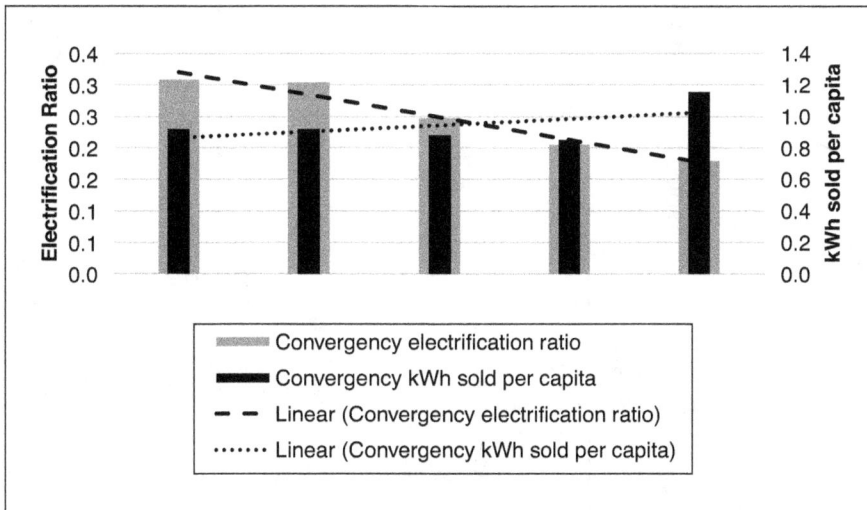

Source: Author's calculation.

Table 3.6
Rated Capacity (MW) and Convergence Rated Capacity

No.	Region	2009	2010	2011	2012	2013
1	Sumatra	3,327.59 (15.1)	3,761.68	3,157.38	3,020.89	2,885.76 (9.9)
2	Java-Bali	16,991.45 (77.1)	17,535.23	20,611.98	23,379.62	24,267.10 (83.7)
3	Kalimantan	766.04 (3.5)	1,063.27	674.23	664.29	695.76 (2.4)
4	Sulawesi	605.73 (2.7)	762.45	639.72	632.72	721.49 (2.5)
5	Papua	93.49 (0.4)	192.13	100.81	93.91	103.07 (0.4)
6	Maluku	92.05 (0.4)	96.96	91.19	94.61	99.82 (0.3)
7	West Nusa Tenggara	97.88 (0.4)	99.91	82.13	96.87	129.47 (0.4)
8	East Nusa Tenggara	73.40 (0.3)	29.22	93.48	103.31	107.30 (0.4)
	Convergence rated capacity	1.987	1.915	2.093	2.155	2.165

Note: Figures in bracket showed share.
Source: PLN (2009, 2010, 2011, 2012, and 2013).

per capita. Electricity is sold to several economic sectors such as residential, industrial, business, social, and the government. The growing gap on electricity sold per capita indicates that the growth in sales are different across the sectors for each province. As the rate of electricity sold depends on the provincial power supply capacity, one may expect that the gap in power capacity across the provinces would also increase (the data in Table 3.5 has corroborated this).

Notes

1. Captive power is electricity generation for private use, such as for industrial plants and commercial operations. The owners of captive power plants are prohibited from selling electricity to the public but would need to sell excess electricity to PLN. Kristov (1995) indicated that many of the captive power plants belonged to state-owned enterprises and did not have an economic rationale in terms of their sale agreements. For example, in 1993/94, the PLN bought electricity from captive power plants at an average price of Rp 37.5 per kWh; however, the average retail price for that period was Rp 152 per kWh (Kristov 1995).
2. The following model was applied in order to measure the growth: $Y = Ke^{\lambda t}$, where Y = electricity consumption/production, K and λ are parameters, and t = years.
3. Solicited projects are constructed based on the Public Plans for National Electric Power (*Rencana Umum Ketenagalistrikan Nasional*/RUKN), whereas unsolicited projects come about when the private sector developed the power plants based on its own proposal for government consideration.
4. This is in accordance with the 2012 Government Regulation No. 14, which concerns the Electricity Supply Business Activities [*Kegiatan Usaha Penyediaan Tenaga Listrik*].
5. Founded in 1993, PT Cikarang Listrindo generated and distributed power to industries and residential estates located in the Jababeka industrial zone, Cikarang, Bekasi, West Java. PT Cikarang Listrindo has an installed capacity of about 518 MW. The electricity is generated by a gas turbine that consume gas and oil. According to Kristov (1995), Cikarang Listrindo had a monopoly on the concessions due to their political connections and were able to sell their electricity to PLN. The company is owned by Mr Sudwikatmono (the step-brother of former President Soeharto).

6. PPP aims to ensure the availability of investment funds, the improvement of quantity-quality-efficiency of services, the betterment of the quality of management and maintenance, and the promotion of use and pay services or, for some circumstances, the need to consider the affordability of users. There are two types of PPP: (i) cooperation agreement; and (ii) permit to manage.

7. In 2013, according to the Head of the Directorate General for Electricity, the total national installed capacity was about 49 GW. Of this total capacity, the PLN, IPP, Private Power Utility (PPU), and Operation Permit (OP) Holder held 72 per cent, 21 per cent, 4 per cent, and 3 per cent of the total installed capacity respectively. The PPU and OP's proportion of the total national installed capacity is expected to reach 12 per cent by 2018. "Pemerintah Terbitkan Peraturan Baru Untuk Tambah Kapasitas Listrik", 9 May 2014, <http://www.djlpe.esdm.go.id/modules. php?_act=detail&sub=news_media&news_id=3732> (accessed 12 May 2014).

8. Author's calculation based on the *Handbook for Statistik Ekonomi Energi 2006* and *2007*.

9. "PLN Rugi Rp 14.2 miliar akibat pencurian listrik" [PLN Lost Rp 14.2 billion due to electricity theft], 13 February 2004, <http://www.bumn.go.id/20999/ publikasi/berita/pln-rugi-rp142-miliar-akibat-pencurian-listrik/> (accessed 29 April 2014).

10. The industrial sector experienced a 2 per cent negative growth in the years 1979/80–1980/81 and 1 per cent for the 2002–3 period.

References

Badan Pusat Statistik (BPS). *Statistik Captive Power 2011* [Captive Power Statistics 2011]. Jakarta: BPS, 2011.

———. *Indikator industri besar dan sedang* [Indonesia Large and Medium Manufacturing Indicator]. Jakarta: BPS, various years.

Departemen Pertambangan dan Energi (DPE). *55 Years of Mining and Energy Development*. Jakarta: DPE, 2000.

Energi dan Sumber daya Mineral (ESDM). *Handbook Ekonomi dan Energi*. Jakarta: ESDM, 2006.

———. *Handbook Ekonomi dan Energi*. Jakarta: ESDM, 2012.

Kristov, Lorenzo. "The Price of Electricity in Indonesia". *Bulletin of Indonesian Economic Studies* 31 (1995): 73–101.

PT. PLN (Persero). *50 Years of PLN Dedication*. Jakarta: PT PLN (Persero), 1995.

————. *Rencana Usaha Penyediaan Tenaga Listrik PT PLN (Persero) 2009–2018* [PT PLN Business Plan for Electricity Utility 2009–2018]. Jakarta: PT PLN (Persero), 2009.

————. *Rencana Usaha Penyediaan Tenaga Listrik PT PLN (Persero) 2013–2023* [PT PLN Business Plan for Electricity Utility 2013–2023]. Jakarta: PT PLN (Persero), 2013.

————. *Rencana Usaha Penyediaan Tenaga Listrik PT PLN (Persero) 2015–2024* [PT PLN Business Plan for Electricity Utility 2015–2024]. Jakarta: PT PLN (Persero), 2014a.

————. *Statistik PLN* [Statistics PLN]. Jakarta: PT PLN, various years (2002, 2009, 2010, 2011, 2012, 2014b).

Sambodo, Maxensius Tri. "Kebijakan Sektor Kelistrikan" [Policy in Electricity Sector]. In *Pengaruh Kebijakan Bahan Bakar Minyak (BBM) dan Tarif Dasar Listrik (TDL) terhadap Kegiatan Ekonomi dan Kesejahteraan Masyarakat: Studi Kasus Sektor Industri* [The Impact of Gasoline and Electricity Policy on Economic Activities and People Welfare: Industrial Sector Case Study], edited by Maxensius Tri Sambodo. Jakarta: LIPI Press, 2009.

Sen, Kunal and Liesbet Steer. "Survey of Recent Development". *Bulletin of Indonesian Economic Studies* 3 (2005): 279–304.

Thee Kian Wie. *Indonesia's Economy since Independence*. Singapore: Institute of Southeast Asian Studies, 2012.

Wei, Kailei, Shujie Yao, and Liu Aying. "Foreign Direct Investment and Regional Inequality in China". University of Nottingham — *Research Paper Series*, 2007/32.

4

ECONOMIC CRISIS AND ITS IMPACT ON THE POWER SECTOR

Chapter 3 indicated that between 1969 and before the economic crisis in 1997/98, the electricity sector in Indonesia grew healthily in terms of production, consumption, and efficiency (declining in transmission and distribution losses). This period can be considered as the period with the best performance of the electricy sector after independence. However, the rapid development of the power sector was not based on strong foundations of good governance and good corporate governance. As a result, after the economic crisis in 1997/98, the power sector was under critical conditions with poor performance and a lack of investment. This chapter highlights that PLN still needs to resolve the financial problem due to pricing and exchange rate policy. Mishandling of the situation and inappropriate strategies to overcome the challenges will lead to more problems in the power sector in the future.

Indonesia experienced two major economic crises in the mid-1960s and late 1990s. The two crises led to deep economic contractions. Economic growth was –3.0 per cent in 1963 and –13.1 per cent in 1998; the two crises increased the number of poor people in absolute terms (Thee 2012). The origins of the two crises were different. The economic crisis in the mid-1960s was due to a mismanagement of the domestic economy while that in the late 1990s was due to the creditor and investor panic that began in Thailand in mid-1997 and spread to other Asian countries such as Malaysia, the Philippines, and Indonesia (Thee 2012). The two crises led to a serious political predicament which resulted in the downfall of the first and second Indonesian presidents. Thee (2012) also noted the major differences between the two crises: the mid-1960s crisis was preceded by a steady economic decline during the previous five or six years, while the crisis in the late 1990s was preceded by three decades of rapid and sustained economic growth.

As seen in the previous chapter, the 1997/98 economic crisis caused a substantial decline in the growth of sold electricity and most of the decreases were from the industrial sector. This indicates that the industrial sector was hit more severely than the other sectors. Even though the electricity consumption from the industrial sector rapidly increased after the crisis, the consumption from the household sector increased much faster than that of the industrial sector. As a result, in 2006, the electricity consumption from the household sector exceeded that of the industrial sector. Furthermore, it seems likely that the commercial sector would be able to surpass the industrial sector in the next three decades.[1]

Further, power production efficiency which can be measured by investigating the added value and input-output ratio showed declining trends after the 1997/98 crisis (see Figure 4.1). The added values for power production increased significantly between 1980 and 1996 by 17 per cent per year. However, after the economic crisis in 1997/98, the values did not reach pre-crisis levels. Even between 2006 and 2011, the values were negative. This indicates that the input costs were higher than the output rates. The input-output ratio indicates how much input is needed to produce one unit of output. The figure indicates that when the added value increases, the input-output ratio has a tendency to decrease, and vice versa. Basically, when the added value increases, the output grows much higher than the input cost; thus, the input-output ratio would also have the tendency to decrease. After the economic crisis in 1997/98, the input-output ratio had a tendency to increase, indicating that in order to produce one unit of output, more input was needed.

Figure 4.1
Added Value and Input-Output Ratio, 1980–2011

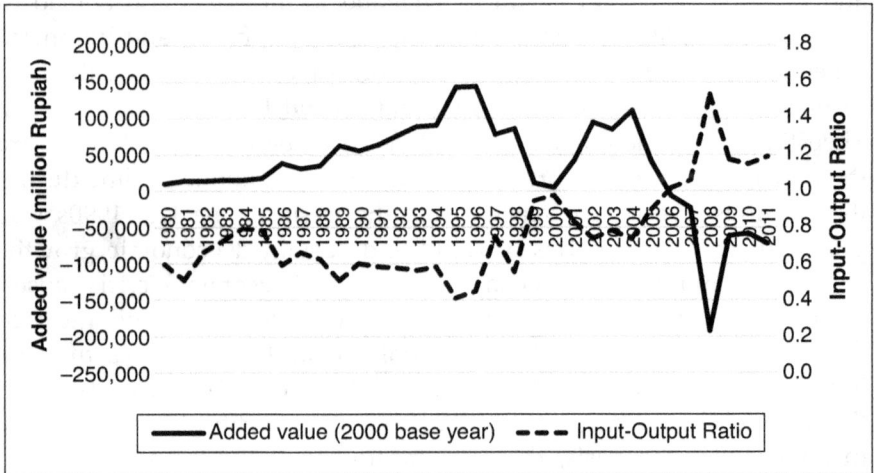

Note: The input cost consists of expenditures for fuel and lubricants, stationaries, spare parts, maintenance cost of machineries, rental costs, and the cost of other services; the output cost covers the rate of electricity sold and distributed to customers with the addition of income from other services; the added value rate is the output minus input.
Source: BPS (various years).

Although this result indicated that production became less efficient, we need to be careful in interpreting such results for two reasons. Firstly, the movement of output price was less flexible than the input price as the central government regulated the prices of sold electricity. Secondly, the expenditure rates for fuel and lubricants increased significantly from about 45 per cent in 2006 to about 71 per cent in 2011. Increases in fuel costs could not be fully passed on to customers through increases in electricity tariffs. As a result, the central government provided more electricity subsidies (see Figure 4.2). For example, in 2000, the electricity subsidy was at about US$0.5 billion and in 2015, it reached approximately US$5.8 billion. Then the share of electricity subsidy to the total central government expenditure reached a peak of 12 per cent in 2008, before it declined to about 5.5 per cent in 2015.

Figure 4.2
Electricity Subsidy in Indonesia

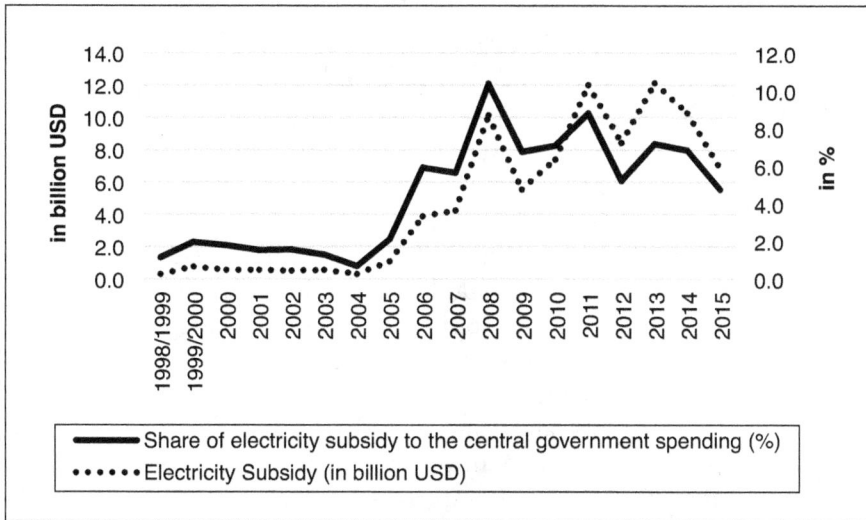

Source: Ministry of Finance (various issues).

UNDERSTANDING THE FINANCIAL PROBLEM OF PLN

By mid-July 1998, the State Minister for the Empowerment of State-owned Enterprises, Tanri Abeng, suddenly replaced the Director of PLN, Djiteng Marsudi. Even though Djiteng was still eager to lead PLN, Tanri Abeng had planned to give him a higher position as the head of the team for the restructuring of PLN,[2] particularly as PLN went into financial trouble due to the depreciation of the Rupiah against the US dollar. PLN suffered an operating loss which amounted to Rp 2.7 trillion in 1998, and this occurred after it achieved a profit of Rp 1.6 trillion the year before. The operating loss was continued for six consecutive years after the economic crisis. PLN (2013) claimed that there was a lack of investment funds due to the 1997/98 economic crisis and by 2008, their capital had been depleted by Rp 15 trillion.

Ultimately, PLN's financial loss was driven by a mismatch between their revenue streams (which were calculated mostly in Rupiah) and their operating expenses (which were paid in US dollars). As the economic crisis in the late 1990s was driven by external factors and affected the currency as well as the banking and economic sectors, it is important to investigate the financial dimensions of PLN's loans and power purchase agreements as these two elements can increase its financial risks.

PLN'S LOAN

Between 1957 and 1968, the role of donor countries such as France, the United States, Czechoslovakia, Germany, Hungary, Yugoslavia, and Russia were important in developing the power facilities in Indonesia. The total assistance or soft loans from friendly nations reached nearly US$173.45 million. During 1974–94, the role of foreign aid became more important and it was managed by the government after having obtained approval from the Minister of Finance. There are two forms of foreign aid — technical aid and project aid. Project aid can take the form of multilateral sources, bilateral sources, and export credits. In the case of multilateral sources, due to the rise of economic welfare, the World Bank and ADB upgraded the loan status from a soft loan (the terms included a 3–4 per cent interest rate and thirty years repayment) into a semi-commercial loan (the terms included 6–8 per cent interest rate, twenty years repayment, and a five-year grace period). The government of Indonesia passed the loan to PLN through a sub-loan agreement. PLN bore the currency risk and paid a higher interest rate (0.5 per cent) above the original rate from the Bank of Indonesia. However, since 1990, the World Bank had not offered loans for state-owned power generation (Wells 2007).

PLN also obtained foreign aid from bilateral sources such as Japan International Cooperation Agency (JICA) and the Overseas Economic Cooperation Fund (OECF). Under institutions such as Inter-Governmental Group on Indonesia (IGGI) or Consultative Group on Indonesia (CGI), countries like Netherlands, Germany, France, United Kingdom, Austria, Norway, Denmark, Finland, and Australia also provided soft loans for the development of the power sector in Indonesia. The soft loans usually had a 3–4 per cent interest rate with a loan period of thirty years (inclusive of a grace period)

(PLN 1995). Besides soft loans, foreign aid also came in the form of export credits. The Overseas Economic Cooperation and Development (OECD) could provide US dollars for the disbursement of export credits at an interest rate of about 6.7 per cent with a thirteen-year maximum loan period (inclusive of a grace period). However, the Indonesian government or PLN needed to give a 15 per cent down payment for the disbursement of export credits.

Prior to 1994, the Indonesian government undertook a Jumbo Loan (commercial loan) from Bank Indonesia for the down payment. However, after August 1994, when PLN became a limited company (it could now pursue profits), it needed to prepare its own down payment. Indonesia could also use the Purchase and Installment Sales Agreement (PISA) for companies which were affiliated with Japanese banks, as they would be considered part of their export credit (PLN 1995).

The lack of domestic financing and flexibility to borrow money from international institutions caused PLN's debt portfolio to change. Figure 4.3 indicates that between 1974/75 and 1993/94, foreign

Figure 4.3
Financial Realization of Electric Power Development
(as % of account)

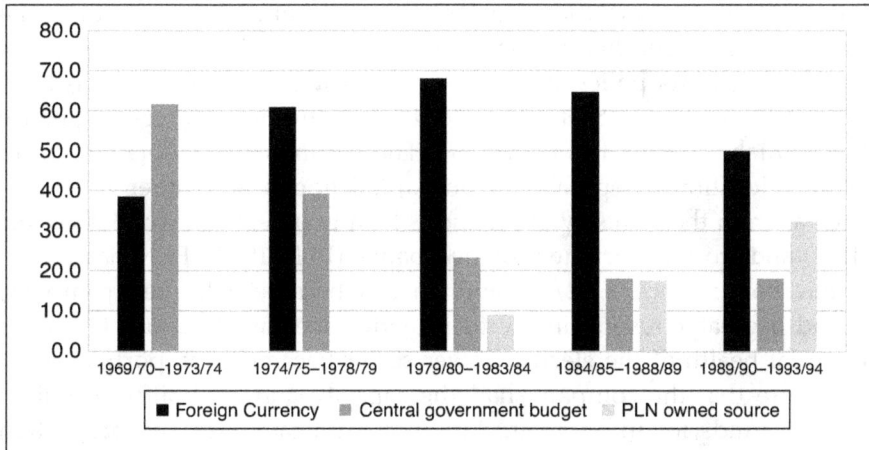

Source: PLN (1995), Table 16.

currency was the dominant financial currency for the development of the power sector. However, most of the funds were gathered under the multilateral, bilateral and export credit schemes. The funds came mostly in the form of financial aid packages: soft loans and semi-commercial loans.

The state budget also contributed and supported investments for the power sector. The two oil booms (in 1973/74 and 1979/80) over the 1974–81 period positively impacted infrastructure development in Indonesia. The nominal price of Indonesian crude oil increased from US$1.6 per barrel in 1970 to US$35 in 1980 (Odell 1981, as cited in Thee 2012). The oil boom had eased foreign exchange constraints, increased the government's capacity to provide subsidies for basic commodities, and improved the government's capacity for capital expenditure. As seen in Figure 4.3, between 1974/75 and 1978/79, the central government's budget for power supply reached nearly 40 per cent, and after the oil boom this proportion decreased. When the oil price declined, the central government's support for the power sector had a tendency to decrease (PLN 1995). As a result, there was a shortage of Rupiah as a counterpart to foreign currency funds. In order to obtain more Rupiah, the government used the Rupiah from Foreign Loan (RPLN) strategy. This meant that the government would seek foreign loans from international institutions such as the International Bank for Reconstruction and Development (IBRD) and the Asian Development Bank (ADB), convert the loans into Rupiah, and then distribute the Rupiah to projects that require foreign aid (PLN 1995).

As part of its policy to promote domestic financing, PLN has been obligated since 1982/83 to provide its own funding sources to finance the Rupiah counter fund (APLN). These funds were obtained from profit allocations, depreciation on capital goods and other revenues, such as from the Ministry of Finance's loan to investment fund accounts (RDI) and from government-owned banks (PLN 1995). PLN has issued public bonds since 1992/93, and once it became a limited company, it had a greater responsibility to provide investment funds. Thus, the financial health of the electric power sector became an important factor to ensure that the company had the capacity and credibility to obtain enough funds for investment.[3] Figure 4.3 indicates that the proportion of PLN's own investment funds increased from 9 per cent to about 32 per cent between 1979 and 1994. The proportion of PLN's investment funds was much higher than the allocation of the central government's budget to PLN. This indicates that PLN became less dependent on government support; as a corporate entity, PLN became more reliant on public and overseas funds for investment.

PLN has also issued long-term financing options such as bonds, *syariah ijarah* and *sukuk*, which amounted to Rp 21.3 trillion (until 2013),[4] whereas the outstanding international bonds totalled US$5,550 million or Rp 64.2 trillion between 2006 and 2012.[5] According to PLN (2013), the total investment funds for the period 2013–22 amounted to approximately US$71,079 million or Rp 822 trillion; these funds consisted of approximately US$40,901 worth of foreign currency and approximately US$30,196 local currency.[6] Thus, even though the proportion of PLN funds on power sector development became significant, most of the funds consisted of long-term financing, soft loans and semi-commercial loans. This can be seen in both a positive and negative light. It is positive in the sense that PLN would have more capacity to obtain funds for investment. However, this may create other problems such as currency risks (explained in the next section) and interest rate risks.

POWER PURCHASE AGREEMENT

Before the 1997/98 economic crisis, PLN signed twenty-six agreements with private investors to develop power generation. There was a plan to add approximately 10,925 MW to the total power generation capacity; it was estimated that the total required investment was about US$13,706 million (Wells 2007). When the 1997 Asian currency crisis hit Indonesia, approximately 9,000 MW worth of the planned total capacity were either still under construction or in the advanced planning stages (Gray and Schuster 1998, as cited in Wells 2007). PLN had a commitment to purchase electricity when the planned electricity generation would be able to support PLN's network system. The agreement for power buying was developed under the power purchase agreement (PPA). However, the energy pricing policy made the Indonesian government or rather, its state-owned enterprises, vulnerable to many risks, such as short-falls in demand and any Rupiah devaluations (Wells 2007). For example, due to currency depreciation post the economic crisis in 1997/98, the contract price for Paiton I jumped to about 8.56 cents per kWh, which was much higher than the average tariff at the time or even before the crisis (which was at approximately 7 cents per kWh) (Wells 2007).

In 1997, the average Rupiah exchange rate was Rp 2,880/USD and in 1998, it rose to Rp 10,194/USD; between 1997 and 1998, Rupiah depreciated more than 347 per cent against the US dollar.[7] As a result, if one considers the average electricity tariff in dollar terms, it decreased from about 7 cents per kWh to about 1.7 cents per kWh (Tripathi and McBeth 1998, as cited in Wells 2007). This condition affected PLN's financial position as it needed to purchase electricity from private power producers at a rate of 5.7–8.5 cents per kWh, which was several times above the selling price (Wells 2007). PLN's commitments to buy electricity was also supported by a "letter of comfort" from the Ministry of Finance. Basically the letter ensured that the Indonesian government "would support the PLN in honoring its obligations" (Wells 2007). Wells (2007) also indicates that the letter for Paiton I in 1995 was issued following considerable pressure from the US and Japanese governments[8] as the contract was also subjected to international arbitration should the PLN fail to honour the agreements.

The 1997/98 economic crisis worsened, and the Indonesian government "postponed" — or rather, set for "review" — several power projects in response to IMF pressure (Wells 2007). The central Indonesian government prepared a team of negotiators who would review the prices and production schedules for these power projects. The government focused its attention on the Paiton I project as it was a costly investment and would soon come into operation (in May 1999) (Wells 2007). In June 2003, the negotiation was concluded after much effort.[9] PLN claimed that renegotiating the contract would save Indonesia US$5.5 billion (Wulandari 2003, as cited in Wells 2007). However, there would also be some costs to bear, such as the US$217.5 million needed to reimburse the Overseas Private Investment Corporation (OPIC); the US$15 million paid to the World Bank's Multilateral Investment Guarantee Agency (MIGA); and Karaha Bodas' claims of approximately US$300 million (this would be paid to Caithness Energy and Florida Power & Light, the project's foreign investment partner for Karaha Bodas Company/KBC) (Wells 2007).[10]

In response to falling value of the Rupiah and the decline in the demand for power, Mr Djiteng, head of PLN, said that he would need to terminate the power purchase agreements with PT Cikarang Listrindo by mid-July 1998. He also claimed that the power contract agreements with private producers were not conducted under proper conditions. He said the following:[11]

> Ketika itu saya tidak berada dalam keadaan yang wajar untuk berunding. Ini karena semua proyek listrik swasta punya backing politik. Dengan adanya perubahan kurs, kondisi menjadi berbeda. Saya kan tidak mengeluarkan izin swasta dan yang mengeluarkan Dirjen. Lalu mereka datang ke saya untuk merundingkan masalah harga. [At that time I was not in a reasonable condition to conduct negotiations. This was because all of the private electricity projects had political support. With the changes in currency exchange (the depreciation of the Rupiah), the conditions have changed. I was not in the position to issue permits for the private sector as those permits were issued by the Directorate General. They would then come to me to negotiate the price.]

Further, Djiteng also said that:[12]

> Dalam setiap penandatanganan jual beli listrik swasta, biasanya direksi tinggal tanda tangan. Karena proses perundingannya 'di atas', kami tinggal dipanggil untuk hadir menandatangani perjanjian itu. Proyek listrik swasta ini sepertinya bagi-bagi kalpling saja. [For every power purchase agreement with the private sector, usually the PLN Director would only be required to authorize the agreement with his/her signature. As the negotiation procedure was already conducted at a "higher level", we would only be called in to attend the signing of the agreement. These private sector projects seem to serve as a way to distribute interests.]

Wells (2007) also reported that political interests were being served in these private sector contracts (summarized in Table 4.1). Even though the 1998 fall of Soeharto resulted in a significant decline in his children's influence, several of the Indonesian partners remained influential and likely weakened the government's position during contract disputes (Wells 2007). For example, CalEnergy (Mid American) (which owned two unfinished geothermal projects,

Table 4.1
Indonesian Partners in Foreign-owned Power Plants

Project	Influential Participant(s)
Paiton I	Hashim Djojohadikusumo (Siti Hediati Hariyadi's brother-in-law), Siti Hediati Hariyadi ('Titiek', President Soeharto's second daughter), and Agus Kartasasmita (brother of Ginandjar, the Minister for Mines and Energy).
Tanjung Jati B	Siti Hardiyanti Rukmana ('Tutut', Soeharto's first daughter)
Paiton II	Bambang Trihatmodjo (Soeharto's second son)
Sengkang	Siti Hardiyanti Rukmana ('Tutut', Soeharto's first daughter)
Palembang Timur	Bob Hasan (Chinese businessman, Soeharto's closest crony)
Salak	Bob Hasan
Sarulla	Hutomo mandala Putra ('Tommy Soeharto', Soeharto's third son) and Bob Hasan
Wayang Windu	Bambang Trihatmodjo (Soeharto's second son); another report says 'Tommy Soeharto'
Cilacap	Bambang Trihatmodjo (second son of Soeharto)
Tanjung Jati A	Siti Hediati Hariyadi ('Titiek', President Soeharto's second daughter) and Bakrie, a *pribumi* (indigenous Indonesian) business group close to Soeharto
Tanjung Jati C	Siti Hardiyanti Rukmana ('Tutut', Soeharto's first daughter)
Dieng	Himpurna (retired military officers)
Patuha	Muhammad Lutfi (son-in-law of Hartarto, the Coordinating Minister for Development Supervision and State Administrative Reform)
Bedugul	Sigit Hardjojudanto (Soeharto's first son)
Karaha Bodas	Tantyo Sudharmono (son of the vice president) and possible friends of Soeharto's wife
Pasuruan	Bambang Trihatmodjo (Soeharto's second son) and known crony Chinese businessmen

Source: Wells (2007), Table 3.

namely Patuha and Dieng) proceeded to have an arbitration lawsuit against PLN and the Indonesian government; CalEnergy won the arbitration and was awarded a large sum. Although the Indonesian government did not pay the sum, the company filed and collected its political risk insurance from OPIC (Wells 2007, p. 348). Wells (2007) pointed out that Hartarto's son-in-law (Hartarto was the Coordinating Minister for Development Supervision and State Administrative Reform) was a partner in a Patuha geothermal project (see Table 4.1). Hartarto had also taken charge of the renegotiation process on the geothermal project. Wells (2007, p. 357) interviewed several Indonesians as well as the counsel for Indonesians; the interview results indicated that "Hartarto prohibited the use of what may have been Indonesia's strongest defence." Wells (2007, p. 357) also said that "the decisions protected Hartarto's son-in-law, but perhaps at a cost of hundreds of millions of dollars to the Indonesian people."

A lack in good governance and good corporate governance has depressed the situation of the power sector in Indonesia. About a decade after the 1997/98 Financial Crisis, the financial condition of PLN was difficult and this resulted in difficulties for new investment in the power sector. PLN needs to adopt more transparent procurement procedures, both the independent power producer (IPP) procurement process and the power purchase agreements (PPA). Currently, there are three types of IPP procurement processes (see Table 4.2): (i) direct appointment; (ii) direct selection; and (iii) open tender. There is a clear guideline on IPP procurement process and the selection is based on the location of primary energy sources, the level of energy shortage in the region, and the source of primary energy (renewable and non-renewable energy). The Minister of Energy and Mineral Resources (MEMR) Regulation No. 3/2015 had stated the maximum tariff for power purchasing and this is based on two main elements: (i) levellized-based cost on generating power; and (ii) the price at commercial operating date. Further, the maximum tariff can be adjusted according to the power purchase agreement.

PLN gave the example of PPA, and Article 10 on pricing policy stated that the basic price of electricity is determined in US dollar per kWh.[13] Then 25 per cent of basic price can be calculated based on the

Table 4.2
Criteria on Independent Power Producer Procurement

No.	Criteria	Direct appointment	Direct selection	Open tender
1.	Conditions	Mine mouth CFSPP (coal-fired steam power plant), marginal gas-fired power plant, hydroelectric power plant, emergency of crisis of electric power supply, expansion project of power plant in the same location of the same system.	Energy diversification to non-fuel oil, expansion project of power plant in different location on the same system, more than one (1) direct appointment proposal.	IPP project(s) that is not eligible for direct appointment or direct selection, or PLN requires open tender.
2.	Project type	Mine mouth CFSPP, non-mine mouth CFSPP, (engine/turbine/combined cycle) gas-fired power plant, hydroelectric power plant	Mine mouth CFSPP, non-mine mouth CFSPP, (engine/turbine/combined cycle) gas-fired power plant, hydroelectric power plant	All kinds of power plants
3.	Tariff	Based on Minister of Energy and Mineral Resources (MEMR) Regulation No. 3/2015 and/or negotiation and/or applicable regulation issued by MEMR.	Based on Minister of Energy and Mineral Resources (MEMR) Regulation No. 3/2015 and/or lowest price proposal submitted by the participants.	Lowest price proposal submitted by the bidders.

Source: <http://www.pln.co.id/wp-content/uploads/2011/03/Buku-IPP.pdf>.

average value of US consumer price index at the last quarter using the following formula:

$$P_m = P_b \times (0.75 + 0.25 \times (USCPI/USCPI_b))$$ (3.1)

where,

P_m = Electricity price at current time

P_b = Electricity price at commercial operating date

$USCPI$ = the average value of US consumer price index at the last quarter

$USCPI_b$ = the average value of US consumer price index at the last quarter before the commercial operating date

Buyer (PLN) makes a payment in Rupiah at the spot exchange rate on the date of payment (at 11 a.m., based on the Central Bank's exchange rate). Thus, following the current example of PPA, PLN needs to consider the exchange rate risks. The example of PPA also mentioned that in case of dispute, all parties agreed that the final stage needs to be settled at the Indonesian Arbitrage National Agency (*Badan Arbitrase Nasional Indonesia*/BANI).

IN RETROSPECT

Contract pricing negotiations were crucial as the central Indonesian government approved automatic tariff adjustment (ATA) mechanism in November 1994. With the new mechanism, electricity tariffs would be adjusted every three months in light of fluctuations in the fuel price levels, the prices of purchased power from the IPP, and the depreciation of Rupiah against other currencies (Kristov 1995). Even though it was believed that the new policy would depoliticize electricity pricing, the President still had the veto power to suspend pricing adjustments under undesirable political, social and economic conditions. The ATA mechanism also provided some room for PLN to negotiate prices with the IPP so that they would be able to obtain the lowest possible wholesale tariff prices (Kristov 1995).

Kristov (1995) said that for the period 1980/81 to 1993/94, if the government had considered exchange rate fluctuations, the domestic interest rate, a 12 per cent rate of return on equity, and that 25 per cent of earnings would be retained in order to fund system expansions, the cost of supplying electric power would be about 45.5 per cent higher than PLN's average sales revenue. The central government kept electricity tariffs low in order to support economic development and this became a hidden subsidy in the PLN's budget. Kristov's calculation also had an important implication; in order for PLN to become commercially viable, the government would need to allocate a subsidy budget for targeted groups and set electricity tariffs that would be able to cover all the costs of supplying electricity; this would include bulk power purchases from private producers (Kristov 1995).

Although the price of electricity failed to cover the full cost of power production, PLN still managed to obtain a profit of Rp 1.67 trillion in 1997.[14] However, as seen in Figure 4.4, PLN's operating revenues went

Figure 4.4
PLN's Operating Profit/Loss and Subsidy

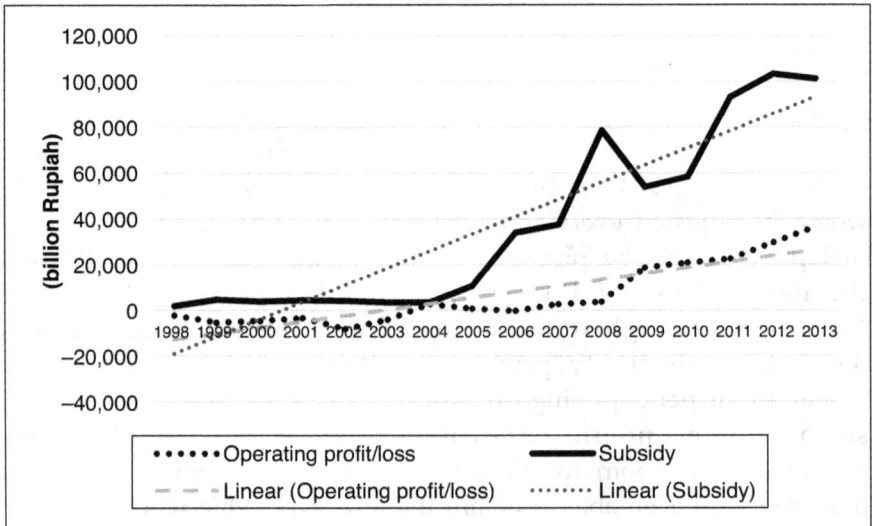

Sources: 1998–2007 data (PLN's Financial Report, various issues); 2008–13 data (PLN 2013).

into the negative by Rp 2.77 trillion; this loss continued until 2003. In 1998, the Indonesian government provided Rp 1.9 trillion worth of direct subsidies to PLN. While PLN obtained a net profit of Rp 2.56 trillion in 2004, the amount of electricity subsidies had a tendency to increase even as PLN's profit increased. PLN (2013) claimed that it had obtained PSO (Public Service Obligation) margins by 5 per cent since 2009, which increased to 8 per cent (in 2010 and 2011), and 7 per cent (in 2012).

Currently, PLN still bore risks based on currency exchange rate fluctuations. Due to the depreciation of the Rupiah in 2013, PLN needed to re-evaluate bond payments that were denominated in US dollars. PLN (2013) stated that exchange rate losses amounted to approximately Rp 48.1 trillion, which was an increase of 809.9 per cent from the 2012 losses of Rp 5.94 trillion. Furthermore, the real account payables in US dollar denominations also increased by 22.5 per cent (from Rp 24.61 trillion in 2012 to about Rp 30.15 trillion in 2013). As a result, PLN's operating expenses in 2013 increased by 165.6 per cent to a total of Rp 75.72 trillion.

The depreciation of the Rupiah against the US dollar increased PLN's liabilities which were denominated in US dollars. However, most of PLN's projects were financed by long-term loans and soft loans, as illustrated in Table 4.3. In 1998, the proportion of short-term to long-term liabilities increased rapidly, so much so that the proportion of short-terms liabilities became much higher than long-term ones. In 1998, PLN made a substantial loss on the foreign exchange which amounted to approximately 22.2 per cent of the electricity sold (more than Rp 3 trillion). The currency losses occurred as PLN needed to purchase energy inputs such as fuel, machinery, spare parts and equipment in US dollar denominations. According to Table 4.3, the total expenditure for fuel and lubricants in relation to the total share of electricity increased to about 68 per cent in 1998 and decreased slightly to about 62 per cent in 1999. Total fuel spending was about Rp 9.4 trillion in 1998 and it increased to about Rp 9.7 trillion in 1999, whereas in 1997, it was about Rp 4.3 trillion.

PLN obtained fuel through a tendering process whereby the fuel was purchased at market prices. It was not necessary for PLN to purchase fuel from Pertamina (the state-owned oil and gas company). When Pertamina and PT Trans Pacific Petrochemical Indotama (TPPI)

Table 4.3
Basic Indicators

Year	Proportion of short-term to long-term liabilities	Proportion of fuel and lubricant expenses to the total amount of electricity sold	Proportion of net losses on foreign exchange to the total amount of electricity sold	Proportion of purchasing power to the total amount of electricity sold
1996	0.202	0.357	0.001	0.019
1997	0.215	0.399	0.000	0.030
1998	0.567	0.683	−0.222	0.137
1999	1.072	0.618	0.220	0.324
2000	0.639	0.469	−0.248	0.424
2001	0.660	0.495	0.017	0.308
2002	0.312	0.460	0.070	0.286
2003	0.371	0.431	0.020	0.218
2004	0.365	0.421	−0.029	0.206
2005	0.525	0.591	0.011	0.215
2006	0.374	0.896	0.025	0.210
2007	0.448	0.859	0.011	0.222
2008	0.330	1.279	−0.110	0.246
2009	0.244	0.845	0.084	0.282
2010	0.263	0.818	0.022	0.245
2011	0.246	1.162	−0.012	0.263
2012	0.236	1.077	−0.047	0.078*
2013	0.236	0.962	−0.313	0.068*

Note: The original data was represented in monetary units prior to the conversion into percentages; * denotes a change in accounting terminology (see the following paragraph for more detailed explanations).
Source: Author's calculation from PLN's Financial Report (various issues).

(a private sector company) competed by submitting bids during the PLN tendering process, TPPI won the contract to supply 1.25 million kilolitres of diesel fuel per year to PLN. As a result, Pertamina was not happy with the result and sent a petition letter to PLN.[15]

Table 4.3 indicates that the proportion of short-term to long-term liabilities decreased gradually. In 2013, the proportion of short-term to long-term financing was slightly higher than the 1997/98 pre-crisis level. However, the share of fuel and lubricant expenses tended to increase, and they were much higher than the total sale of electricity for several years. Such figures indicate that there were no automatic adjustments for retail prices due to increases in fuel costs. As a result, the central government needed to provide electricity subsidies and the amount tended to increase when the demand on electricity increased and the world fuel prices rose.

The cost of fuel was one of the important components of PLN's operating expenses; in 2013, most of PLN revenues from sold electricity went into paying for fuel expenditures. Another component that was also important was the losses that occurred based on foreign exchange fluctuations. Table 4.3 indicated that there were times when PLN was able to gain from currency exchange rates, but the cumulative losses due to foreign exchange rates between 1996 and 2013 reached an amount of Rp 46 trillion, with the highest loss reported at approximately Rp 48.1 trillion in 2013.[16] PLN (2013) indicated that 46 per cent of the company's total loans were in US dollars. PLN's estimate also indicated that for any depreciation of Rp 100/USD, it would increase the potential for loan burdens by Rp 2.25 trillion (PLN 2013). It would be vital and necessary for PLN to implement a currency hedge to deal with currency risks. Currently, only two (Bank Negara Indonesia and Garuda Indonesia) of the 138 state owned companies have implemented this policy.

The proportion of purchased electricity increased substantially from about 2 per cent in 1996 to about 42 per cent in 2000. Increases in the share of electricity purchases were due to two factors, namely quantity and price. In 1996, PLN bought about 1,344 GWh and over the years it increased to about 9,135 GWh (ESDM 2006). The proportion of geothermal and steam-coal power plant electricity production to the total increases in private production capacity amounted to about 28.5 per cent and 67.1 per cent respectively. The private steam-coal plants increased their production capacity by 1,200 MW in 1998, while geothermal power plants increased theirs by 180 MW in 2000. In 1999, the privately installed power generating capacity increased by 1,200 MW. Thus, privately owned steam-coal plants contributed 2.4 GW worth of the total installed capacity until 2003. Most of the increases in the private steam-coal power plants was supported by Paiton I, which had a design capacity of about 1,230 MW (2 × 615 MW) in 1998 and Paiton II which had a capacity of about 1,220 MW (2 × 610 MW).[17]

PLN increased its spending on power purchases and as a result, there were increases in electricity production from the IPP. However, as discussed in the previous section, the power purchase agreement conditions were disadvantageous to the Indonesian populace (Sudja 2003). Sudja (2003) pointed out that the payback rates upon investment indicated that the price of electricity from Paiton should be within the range of US$3.21–3.64 per kWh instead of US$4.93 per kWh that came about from the negotiating process. Sudja (2003) argued that the US$2.5 billion project development cost was an overestimate if one compares it to the Lavalin Consultants' estimate of approximately US$1.29–1.61 billion. According to Sudja (2003), even the cost of the Suryalaya coal fired power plant (3 × @600 MW) project amounted to approximately US$1.1 billion. Table 4.3 indicates that the proportion of electricity purchases from the private sector had a tendency to increase after 2004 and was at 26.3 per cent in 2011.

However, in 2012 and 2013, the share of electricity purchases from the private sector decreased to less than 10 per cent. This is mainly due to changes in accounting practices. In 2013, through the adoption of new Indonesia Financial Accounting Standards (PSAK) and a new Interpretation of Financial Accounting Standards (ISAK), the PLN reclassified their electricity purchases into three elements: finance leases, operating leases, and normal purchase transactions. As a result, the power purchase agreements were sorted into three classifications (PLN 2013). The finance lease category consisted of thirty-four power plant management companies, the operating lease category consisted of five power purchase agreements, and the normal purchase transaction category consisted of thirty-two electric companies which supplied power to the network. From the three categories, we can conclude that the majority of the previous power purchase agreements fell under the finance and operating lease agreements. This implies that the risks and rewards need to be clearly divided in terms of power purchases. Under the financial leases, there is a substantial transfer of risks and rewards to the owner of an asset (such as PLN); under this scheme, PLN would still own the equipment and would be responsible for the operating costs, which include servicing. On the other hand, under the operating leases, PLN would not have any rights to the equipment after it has been used; PLN would need to return the equipment to the lessor. On the basis of accounting practices, the financial leases would be a part of the assets (as a balance sheet item) of PLN, while operating leases would be part of its expenditures and would be taken off the balance sheet of items. With this classification, it would become clear which risks would belong to PLN and which to third parties.

Notes

1. It has been assumed that the consumption from commercial and industrial sectors increased by 7 per cent and 4.5 per cent respectively.
2. "Djiteng tersandung listrik swasta" [Djiteng Stumbles Over Private Electricity Purchases], 20 December 1999, <http://www.angelfire.com/oh/mEmeX/kontrareformasi.txt> (accessed 9 May 2014).
3. In October 2013, the Export-Import Bank of Korea (K-EXIM) supported Korean manufacturing companies which bid for power generation tenders. The K-EXIM provided this facility to Korean companies without demanding a guarantee from the Indonesian government.
4. Calculated from various issues of the PLN Annual Report
5. Calculated from various issues of the PLN Annual Report. An exchange rate of Rp 11,577.5/USD was used.
6. This investment budget did not consider investment from independent power producer (IPP). According to PLN (2013), this investment included only the base cost while financing cost was excluded. An exchange rate of approximately Rp 11,575/USD (8 May 2014) was assumed.
7. Data is obtained from <http://aric.adb.org/macroindicators?category=6&sel_country=4&frequency=5> (accessed 8 May 2014).

8. Paiton I was one of twenty-six electric power projects. The project was located in East Java with a total capacity of approximately 1,230 MW and a total investment of about US$2,500 million (Wells 2007). The plant generates coal-based power. This project was guaranteed by the Japanese and American Export-Import Bank and the US Overseas Private Investment Corporation (OPIC).

9. "Kalo Saya Diganti Apakah PLN Akan Untung?" [If I Am Replaced, Would PLN Still Remain Profitable?], interview between Djiteng and Alu Nur Yasin, *Tempo Interactive*, 23 July 1998, <http://tempo.co.id/ang/min/03/21/ekbis2.htm> (accessed 9 May 2014).

10. "Djiteng tersandung listrik swasta" [Djiteng Stumbles Over Private Electricity Purchases], 20 December 1999, <http://www.angelfire.com/oh/mEmeX/kontrareformasi.txt> (accessed 9 May 2014).

11. The results of the power project review in June 2003 were as follows: out of a total of 26 projects, 7 projects were terminated, to be revived only with the possibility of new investment offers in the future; 14 projects were renegotiated; the PLN acquired 2 projects; Pertamina acquired 1 project; the government acquired 2 projects from OPIC.

12. Karaha Bodas was one of twenty-six geothermal power projects. It has a power generation capacity of 220 MW and is located in West Java.

13. See <http://www.pln.co.id/dataweb/ESC/draft_esc_pln.pdf> (accessed 15 June 2015).

14. Data was obtained from Table 2, "Analisis Peran Subsidi Bagi Industri dan Masyarakat Pengguna Listrik" [An Analysis of the Role Subsidies Play for Industries and the Electricity Consumers], *Jurnal Keuangan dan Moneter*, vol. 6, no. 2 (2003): 44–62.

15. See "Menteri BUMN: Saya pilih PLN beli BBM dari Pertamina" [Minister for BUMN: I prefer that PLN purchase fuel from Pertamina], 7 October 2010, <http://finance.detik.com/read/2010/10/07/130320/1457985/4/2/menteri-bumn-saya-pilih-pln-beli-bbm-dari-pertamina> (accessed 19 May 2014).

16. According to PLN (2013), the Rupiah depreciated against the US dollar by 20.8 per cent (it depreciated against the Yen and Euro by 3.4 per cent and 23.8 per cent respectively). In 2013, the accumulated losses due to currency depreciation amounted to Rp 48.1 trillion, but if one considers interest debts and other items, the total loss from these other items amounted to approximately Rp 75.72 trillion. Thus in 2013, the total loss of PLN was about 29.57 trillion.

17. Paiton I operated under the BOT (build, operate, transfer) model; the contract period for the project lasts for forty years and the termination

year is 2039. Banks involved with the funding of the project were mainly foreign commercial banks, such as the Japan Bank of International Cooperation (JBIC), the OPIC, and the US EXIM. There were three companies which sponsored the project, namely International Power (United Kingdom), Mitsui (Japan), and Tokyo Electric Power Co. (Japan) which held ownership shares of 31 per cent, 50 per cent, and 14 per cent respectively. In 1995, the investment commitments in physical assets amounted to approximately US$2,470 million. For more details, refer to <http://ppi.worldbank.org/explore/PPIReport.aspx?ProjectID=10>. The Paiton project has been further expanded and in 2012, the PLN purchased 18.34 per cent (8,514 GWh) of its total purchased electricity from PT Paiton Energy Company (PLN 2012).

References

Badan Pusat Statistik (BPS). *Statistik Indonesia* [Indonesia Statistics]. Jakarta: BPS, various years.

Energi dan Sumber daya Mineral (ESDM). *Handbook Ekonomi dan Energi*. Jakarta: ESDM, 2006.

Kristov, Lorenzo. "The Price of Electricity in Indonesia". *Bulletin of Indonesian Economic Studies* 31 (1995): 73–101.

Ministry of Finance. *National Budget*. Jakarta: Ministry of Finance, various years.

PT PLN (Persero). *50 Years of PLN Dedication*. Jakarta: PT PLN (Persero), 1995.

———. *Laporan Tahunan* [Annual Report]. Jakarta: PT PLN, 2012.

———. *Laporan Tahunan* [Annual Report]. Jakarta: PT PLN, 2013.

Sudja, Nengah. "Questioning the Electricity Price of Paiton I". <http://iacconference.org/documents/11th_iacc_workshop_QUESTIONING_THE_ELECTRICITY_PRICE_OF_PAITON_I.pdf> (accessed 19 May 2014).

Thee Kian Wie. *Indonesia's Economy since Independence*. Singapore: Institute of Southeast Asian Studies, 2012.

Wells, Louis T. "Private Power in Indonesia". *Bulletin of Indonesian Economic Studies* 43 (2007): 341–63.

5

ELECTRICITY AND ECONOMIC GROWTH

The analysis from the previous chapters indicated that economic growth and electricity consumption and production has a strong correlation. This chapter investigates empirically whether availability (in terms of power consumption) has a causality link to economic growth in Indonesia through the application of econometrics; more specifically, through a time series analysis. This assessment is important in understanding the long-term perspective on economic growth *vis-a-vis* electricity consumption between 1960 and 2012 (this is the longest time series analysis in the case of Indonesia). Interestingly, the data from the time series analysis approach has supported the conservative hypothesis; this is where electricity consumption conservation may be implemented with little or no adverse effect on economic growth. One can expand on these empirical results of the time series analysis for policy refinement. This analysis adds on to the data available on the issue as a larger data series has been used in comparison to previous studies on Indonesia, such as Squalli (2007) and Sambodo (2011). Furthermore, a diagnostic test has been carefully conducted in order to ensure that the model is econometrically robust.

There are two main reasons why it is important to investigate the relationship between electricity consumption and economic growth. Firstly, Indonesia has a chronic power shortage problem. This has led to unexpected blackouts and forced the government to implement a fast track programme and demand side management, such as by replacing conventional lamps with energy saving lamps. The second reason is because the electricity sector has a direct impact on global warming. In 2008, calculations made at the global level indicated that the proportion of electricity and heat generation to total carbon dioxide emissions amounted to 41 per cent, which made up the highest category when compared to other contributors (IEA 2010). There are three main ways to control carbon dioxide emissions from the electricity sector (IEA 2009): (i) improving energy efficiency for electricity end users; (ii) providing policy incentives (such as through a tax on carbon dioxide emissions or providing subsidies that promote low carbon technology); (iii) enhancing research and development in low carbon generation technologies.

LITERATURE REVIEW

The relationship between electricity consumption and economic growth can be explained using four hypotheses. As seen in Table 5.1, the direction of causality determines the type of policy action. By conducting literature reviews from several countries, Payne (2010) showed that 31 per cent of the studies supported the neutrality hypothesis; 28 per cent supported the conservation hypothesis; 23 per cent supported the growth hypothesis; and 18 per cent the feedback hypothesis. According to Apergis (2011), the lack of consensus in the empirical results may be attributed to differences in variable selection, model specifications, the time horizon that was selected for study, and the econometric approaches which were undertaken.

Table 5.1
Hypothesis Test between Electricity Consumption and Economic Growth

No.	Relationship Type	Policy Type
1.	Uni-directional causality, from electricity consumption to economic growth (*Growth hypothesis*)	Do not restrict the electricity usage because it may adversely affect economic growth.
2.	Uni-directional causality, from economic growth to electricity consumption (*Conservative hypothesis*)	Conserving electricity consumption may be implemented with little or no adverse effect on economic growth.
3.	Bi-directional causal relationship (*Feedback hypothesis*)	Electricity consumption and economic growth are jointly determined and affected at the same time.
4.	No causal relationship (*Neutral hypothesis*)	Neither conservative nor expansive policies in relation to electricity consumption have any effect on economic growth.

Source: Chen, Kuo and Chen (2007, p. 2611).

Several studies have been conducted in order to investigate the relationship between electricity consumption and economic growth in Indonesia. However, the studies have been inconclusive (see Table 5.2). Majority of the previous studies on causality emphasized on the bivariate framework; that is, they focused on economic growth and electricity consumption with a maximum data span of thirty years. For econometric estimations, it is better to apply a trivariate analysis as Odhiambo (2009) argued that the causality studies based on the bivariate framework were very unreliable as the introduction of new variables can change the inference and the estimation magnitude. Alternatively, Narayan and Singh (2007) have mentioned capital, energy price, and labour input as some of the variables which have been used by many scholars. This indicates that there are several options to select the candidate of the third variable. In this analysis, energy price as the third variable for investigating Indonesia's case was selected.

Table 5.2
Summary of the Granger Causality Study in Indonesia

No.	Authors	Methodology	Main Variable	Time Period	Causality Relationships
1.	Murry and Nan (1996)	Standard Granger causality, VAR	Electricity consumption, real GDP	1970–90	Income → Electricity
2.	Yoo (2006)	Johansen-Juselius; No cointegration; VAR	Electricity consumption per capita, real GDP per capita	1971–2002	Income → Electricity
3.	Yoo, S.H., and Kim, Y. (2006)	Standard Granger causality and Hsiao's version of Granger causality method	Electricity production; electricity consumption; real GDP	1971–2002	Income → Electricity
4.	Lean and Smyth (2010)	Johansen-Fisher panel cointegration; cointegration; VEC	Electricity consumption per capita, real GDP per capita Other variables: carbon dioxide emissions per capita	1980–2006	Electricity → Income
5.	Chen, et al. (2007)	Johansen-Juselius; Pedroni panel cointegration; cointegration; VEC	Electricity consumption; real GDP	1971–2001	Electricity → Income
6.	Squalli, J. (2007)	ARDL bound test; cointegration; Toda-Yamamoto causality	Electricity consumption per capita; real GDP per capita	1980–2003	ARDL: Income → electricity TY: Electricity → ⇸Income
7.	Sambodo (2011)	Variance decomposition analysis, Bayesian Model Averaging, bivariate and trivariate causality	GDP, electricity consumption, gross capital formation	1971–2007	Neutral hypothesis, but shock on GDP has larger impact on electricity consumption

Source: Apergis and Payne (2011).

METHODOLOGY

This analysis covers a longer data period in comparison to previous studies (this study spans fifty-three years, focusing on the period between 1960 and 2012). The longer data period improves the quality of estimation. The data for GDP per capita came from World Development Indicators and the International Financial Statistics, whereas the data for electricity consumption per capita came from the World Development Indicators, Statistical Year Book of Indonesia, and from PLN's own statistics reports.

In order to determine causality, the Granger causality test was conducted. The test was based on the error correction models (ECM) which have the following specifications:

$$\Delta \ln Y_t = a + \sum_{i=1}^{p} v_i \Delta \ln Y_{t-i} + \sum_{i=1}^{p} \kappa_i \Delta \ln EC_{t-i} + \pi_1 ECT_{t-i} + \varepsilon_{1t} \qquad (5.1)$$

$$\Delta \ln EC_t = b + \sum_{i=1}^{p} \kappa_i \Delta \ln EC_{t-i} + \sum_{i=1}^{p} v_i \Delta \ln Y_{t-i} + \pi_2 ECT_{t-i} + \varepsilon_{2t} \qquad (5.2)$$

Y is defined as real GDP per capita (this measurement uses the 2005 USD rate as constant), and EC is defined as electricity consumption per capita. ECT is the error correction term at lagged intervals and p is the optimal lag length. By letting $M_1 = (v_1, ..., v_p)$, and $M_2 = (\kappa_1, ..., \kappa_p)$, the causality test was conducted by generating χ^2 statistics. This would establish whether the null hypotheses can be accepted or rejected. In the case of bivariates, the null hypothesis has been set as follows:

1. Equation 1: H_0: $M_2 = 0$, this indicates that there is no causality relationship between the electricity consumption per capita and GDP per capita growth.
2. Equation 2: H_0: $M_1 = 0$, this indicates that there is no causality relationship bwtween GDP per capita growth and electricity consumption per capita.

ECT is the error correction term at lagged intervals and p is the optimal lag length. It should be noted that ECT is used if we find that there is a long run relationship between electricity consumption and economic growth. Alternatively, if we do not find such a relationship, we delete the *ECT* terms from Equations 5.1 and 5.2 so that we will have the vector autoregressive model (VAR).

ECONOMIC GROWTH AND ELECTRICITY CONSUMPTION REVISITED

Both GDP per capita and electricity consumption per capita showed a tendency to increase, as illustrated in Figure 5.1. The figure also indicated that Indonesia experienced negative growth for GDP per capita for several years (such as in 1962, 1963, 1965, 1967, 1982, 1998, and 1999). However the largest decline occurred in 1998, when GDP per capita declined significantly by 14.4 per cent. Similarly, electricity consumption per capita also showed negative growth for some years, such as in 1966–68, 1973, 1976, and 1998. However, even though the GDP decreased significantly in 1998, electricity consumption per capita only declined by 0.1 per cent. The highest record for the declining

Figure 5.1
GDP and Electricity Consumption

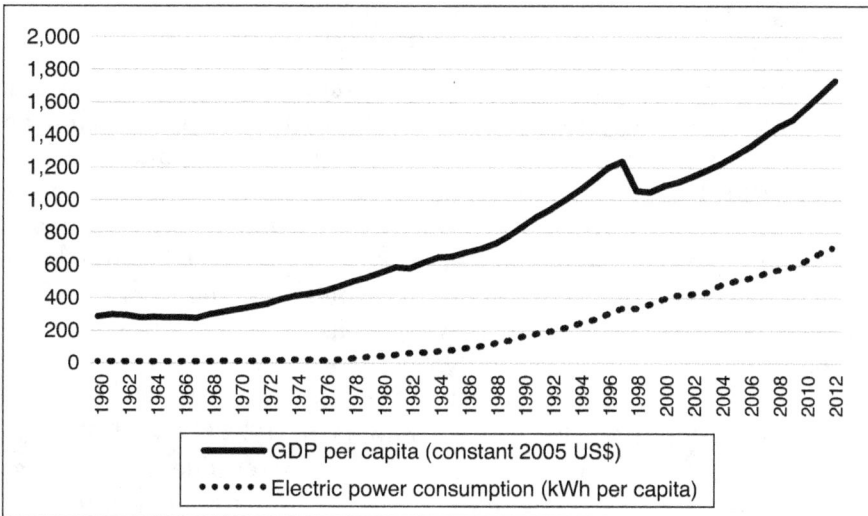

Sources: World Development Indicators for 1971–2012 data and BPS for 1960–70 data.

electricity consumption per capita occurred in 1976 (−14.5 per cent). This indicates that the 1997/98 economic crisis had a marginal effect on electricity consumption per capita; that is, one may also argue that a sharp contraction in economic growth did not significantly affect electricity consumption per capita. This is because electricity is a basic necessity. Thus a decline in economic growth would not have much effect on consumption.

We argued that electricity consumption cannot be separated from the dynamics of economic growth. Economic growth in Indonesia is driven by economic policy and external factors. Thee (2002) identified three major phases of the Soeharto era based on economic challenges, policies, and performance.

1. 1966–73: stabilization, rehabilitation, partial liberalization and economic recovery;
2. 1974–82: oil booms, rapid economic growth and increasing government intervention;
3. 1983–96: post-oil boom, deregulation, renewed liberalization and rapid export-led growth.

In 1966 (the first phase), Indonesia's economic performance was very poor and the inflation rate reached 636 per cent (Thee 2002). However, the Soeharto's New Order era made economic recovery a top priority and was able to drastically reduce inflation rates to about 112 per cent in 1967, 85 per cent in 1968, 10 per cent in 1969 and 9 per cent in 1970 (Thee 2002). The two-year stabilization plan consisted of four objectives: halting hyperinflation; decontrol; rescheduling foreign debts and obtaining new credits; and a new, open-door policy towards foreign direct investment (Arndt 1984, as cited in Thee 2002). After 1966, the economic performance improved gradually. Even the World Bank indicated that the Indonesian growth rate in the 1970s was better than that of the other "populated petroleum economies", such as Nigeria, Mexico, and Venezuela (World Bank 1983, pp. 150–51, as cited in Booth 1998).

The period from 1973 to 1981 was considered to be the oil boom years for Indonesia. The two oil booms in 1973/74 and 1978/79 increased not only export earnings but also tax revenues from foreign oil companies operating in Indonesia. The Indonesian government was able to undertake substantial public investments as well as expand and improve the efficiency of the public administration sector due to higher oil revenues, including new investments in the electricity sector. As we have seen in Chapter 3, during the oil boom period, the growth in installed capacity increased rapidly. The higher oil revenues, in turn, contributed to economic growth (Thee 2002) and Booth (1998) pointed out that there was an accelerating growth in manufacturing and public utilities compared to the other sectors. In the second phase, average economic growth was maintained at 7 per cent, while electricity consumption grew by 17.8 per cent. However, in 1982, economic growth was at approximately 1.1 per cent. There were a number of internal and external factors which led to this situation, such as recessions in several major industrial countries, the terms of trade which deteriorated due to falling oil prices, currency realignments that led to a rapid increase in debt, and Pertamina's bankruptcy (Thee 2002).

In the third phase, the average economic growth was higher than in the second phase which reached 7.2 per cent, but the growth of electricity consumption was lower than the previous period's rate of 14.3 per cent. The fast economic growth at that time was not only caused by a rapid increase in investment, which was reflected through the increased imports of capital goods, but was also the result of the modernization process and the technological products which were embodied in the imported capital goods (Sundrum 1986, as cited in Thee 2002). Indonesia's ability to sustain such high economic growth as well as the ability to shift from a dependency on primary exports to manufactured exports led the World Bank to classify Indonesia as one of the "Newly Industrializing Economies" (Thee 2002).

In 1997, economic growth was about 4.7 per cent, lower than that of the previous year's, which was at about 7.6 per cent. The Thai baht depreciation in July 1997 had a contagion effect on other Asian countries such as the Philippines, Malaysia and Indonesia. This brought negative sentiment towards investment in the region. Further, the Rupiah depreciation against the US dollar caused a huge debt burden to many Indonesian firms and also led to a banking crisis. The economic crisis in Indonesia was more persistent than in other Asian countries as it led to political instability and a loss of confidence in the market. The 1997/98 economic crisis reduced the economic growth to

–13 per cent in 1998. Although the economic growth rebounded in 1999, economic growth did not recover from the pre-crisis levels.

During the 1997/98 economic crisis, electricity consumption still had a 1.2 per cent positive growth. However, it decreased sharply from the previous period's rate of 13.7 per cent (see Table 5.3). Furthermore, after the economic crisis, electricity consumption grew by about 4.3 per cent on average, which was lower than the economic growth. As can be seen in Table 5.3, the highest growth in electricity consumption was during the oil boom period. This indicates that substantial investment in the electricity sector was started in the early 1970s and the investments grew steadily prior to the economic crisis in 1997/98.

Although the post-oil boom period had economic growth rates which were higher than those during the boom, the growth of electricity consumption during the oil boom period was higher than that after the boom. This indicates that economic growth acceleration was faster than electricity consumption. This was not surprising because during the post-oil boom period, the government issued a series of deregulations for the banking, trade, and investment sectors. Furthermore, stability in the global economic condition also benefitted Indonesia. However, the growth of electricity consumption after the economic crisis was lower than in the previous period. One might argue that this is mainly due to a lack of investment in

Table 5.3
Annual Economic Growth and Electricity Consumption (%)

Time Period	Description	Economic Growth	Electricity Consumption Growth
1971–73	Stabilization	8.83	6.18
1974–82	Oil boom	7.04	17.79
1983–96	Post oil boom	7.27	14.27
1997	Early crisis	4.70	13.73
1998	Economic crisis	–13.13	1.16
1999–2012	Post crisis	5.3*	4.3

Note: * GDP (constant 2005 USD).
Source: Calculated from World Development Indicators.

the power sector and also due to an uncertainty in government regulations. A more detailed analysis on this matter has been discussed in Chapters 2, 3 and 4.

From the previous chapter, we have indicated that the total electricity consumption from the residential sector surpassed that of the industrial sector. However, we have to be careful in interpreting these conditions because many large firms constructed their own power plants. There are many reasons for this, such as predicting that energy costs will rise in the future; PT PLN's unreliable power supply; and the fact that Indonesia is rich in primary energy supply sources such as coal and gas. Furthermore, the electricity law provided an opportunity for the private sector to generate its own power both for internal consumption and for selling its excess generation to PLN.

EMPIRICAL RESULTS (BIVARIATE AND TRIVARIATE MODELS)

Standard tests, such as the Augmented Dickey-Fuller test and the Phillips-Peron test, for the unit root was applied. It was found that the log level of real GDP per capita (Y) and the log electricity consumption per capita (EC) were not stationary at all common significance levels for both tests. However, after taking the first difference into consideration, both GDP per capita and electricity consumption per capita were found to be stationary under the Phillips-Peron test, but not for the Dickey-Fuller test. But, after taking the second difference into consideration, both GDP per capita and electricity consumption per capita became stationary for both tests. From this, it can be inferred that the Phillips-Peron test is more robust than the Dickey-Fuller test; the former has a more robust estimate by taking into account heteroskedasticity and autocorrelations consistent with covariance matrix estimators (StataCorp 2007). Thus, the author relied on the Phillips-Peron result and concluded that both GDP per capita and electricity consumption per capita were stationary for the first difference.

Next, in order to investigate the lag order (which indicates the best period to start the Granger casuality test), pre-estimation and post-estimation tests were conducted. The pre-estimation test indicated that with the likelihood-ratio test, AIC, FPE, HQIC, and SBIC were optimal for the model with one lag. The post-estimation test also indicated the same result as that of the pre-estimation test. Thus it was concluded that lag 1 was the optimal lag for the model. Then, one needed to consider the possibility of a long-term relationship between GDP per capita and electricity consumption per capita. In order to do this, the Johansen cointegration test was conducted; the result indicated that there was no long run relationship between real GDP and electricity consumption. Thus, the Granger causality test was estimated by applying the VAR model.

According to the results (which have been summarized in Table 5.4), while there was a unidirectional causality relationship from GDP per capita growth to electricity consumption per capita, there was no significant relationship in the other direction. Thus the VAR model supports the conservative hypothesis. This implies that conservative policies for electricity consumption may be implemented with little or no adverse effect on economic growth.

Tests for residual autocorrelation (LM test), normality distributed disturbances and stability conditions were also conducted. The LM test supported the hypothesis that there was no autocorrelation in the residuals. Both the single-equation Jarque-Bera statistics and the joint Jarque-Bera statistics did not reject the null hypothesis. This implies that the disturbance for the VAR equation has a normal distribution. Furthermore, the test also implied that the model is specified correctly. Finally, as each eigenvalue was less than 1, the estimate satisfied the eigenvalue stability conditions. Thus, the diagnostic test indicates that the VAR model is well accepted.

Table 5.4
VAR Bivariate Model Estimation Results

Variables	ΔY	ΔEC
ΔY_{t-1}	(–)	0.5136 (0.283)*
ΔEC_{t-1}	−0.0069 (0.0678)	(–)

Note: Standard error in ( ); (–) we do not report irrelevant parameters; at 10% significance level.

Table 5.5
VAR Trivariate Model Estimation Results

Variables	ΔY	ΔEC	$\Delta Price_{t-1}$
ΔY_{t-1}	(–)	0.529 (0.285)*	10.837 (45.689)
ΔEC_{t-1}	–0.0071 (0.0678)	(–)	11.718 (21.948)
$\Delta Price_{t-1}$	0.00005 (0.0004)	–0.00033 (0.00086)	(–)

Note: Standard error in ( ); (–) we do not report irrelevant parameters; at 10% significance level.

In the case of the trivariate model, energy prices from the World Development Indicators were selected (2000 = 100, at constant 2000 dollars). Similar procedures to the bivariate case were conducted (as seen in the previous section). Energy price was stationary at first difference. No long-run relationship was found and the VAR model was applied. The result from the trivariate model showed the same results as the bivariate case (see Table 5.5). There was a positive causality from GDP per capita growth to electricity consumption per capita. Thus, introducing the third variable did not change the directionality; that is, the bivariate model did not suffer from variable bias omissions. The energy price variable did not have any significant impact on GDP per capita growth and electricity consumption as the government provided energy subsidies. Thus fluctuations in world energy prices were not fully absorbed by the economy.

ANALYSIS AND IMPLICATIONS

The estimation concluded that the electricity consumption per capita could be induced by increases in GDP per capita. The causality test showed that economic growth per capita causes an increase in the growth of electricity consumption per capita. This implies that as GDP per capita increases, the demand on electricity per capita will also increase. As seen in the previous chapters, the calculations on electricity demand and consumption were underestimated as Indonesia was still short on electricity supplies.

From the energy input perspective, the direction from electricity consumption to economic growth was assumed. However, there has been no strong evidence in support of the growth hypothesis in Indonesia. I argue that there are three reasons as to why the growth hypothesis does not exist. Firstly, there has been a strong growth in the electricity consumption from the household sector; the rise in household consumption was more significant than productive consumption. Secondly, after the economic crisis, electricity consumption from the industrial sector decreased. As such, many companies developed their own power plants due to a lack of power supplies and poor quality of power supplied by PLN. By doing this, companies could obtain two benefits. They could ensure the quality and quantity of the power supply. They could also sell excess power to PLN or other users.

Thirdly, after the 1997/98 economic crisis, the growth of electricity consumption decreased substantially, from double digit growth to single digit. On the other hand, although the economic growth after the 1997/98 crisis had not reached pre-crisis levels, the situation was relatively better than the growth in electricity consumption. This was due to the fact that when electricity consumption decreased rapidly, it only caused a modest impact on economic growth; it seemed that economic growth was less sensitive to the decline in electricity consumption. This also confirmed the results by previous studies, such as that of van der Eng (2002) who argued that the mobilization of productive resources (mineral resources, labour, domestic and foreign savings) had played an important role on the economic growth between the 1960s and 1990s. Furthermore, van der Eng (2009) indicated that between 1971 and 2007, capital stock growth contributed to 70 per cent of Indonesia's economic growth.

This analysis supports the conservative hypothesis instead of the growth hypothesis. While recent studies such as Sambodo (2011) have supported the neutral hypothesis, the analysis on variance decomposition suggested that GDP had more influence on electricity consumption than the other way round. Thus, when planning for electricity expansion, one would need to consider future economic growth prospects.

Surprisingly, although electricity consumption per capita in Indonesia is still below that in Vietnam, China, Malaysia, and

Thailand, and slightly higher than India, Indonesia still has some room to conserve its electricity consumption. This indicates that the conservative hypothesis also prevailed for countries that had relatively low electricity consumption per capita. This result may challenge the ideology of the growth hypothesis because the Indonesian case showed that electricity conservation had a neutral effect both on consumption and production. Thus, it did not matter if the econometric model suggested for a growth hypothesis or a conservation hypothesis — even for Indonesia which has a relatively lower electricity consumption compared to other countries — there is evidence to support the conservation policy. Thus, electricity conservation should be considered a way of life.

Energy conservation, energy saving and energy efficiency are interchangeable terminologies that can support sustainable development. The 2009 Indonesian Government Regulation No. 70 stated that energy conservation was a systematic, planned, and integrated effort to ensure the sustainability of energy supplies at the national level and to improve the efficiency of energy usage. The potential rewards of energy conservation do not only benefit consumers, but also humanity and the environment. One of the indicators in measuring energy sustainability is energy intensity. The formula will need to be modified where

Table 5.6
Electricity Consumption and Production

Country	Electric Power Consumption (kWh per capita)			Electricity Production (million kWh)		
	1971	2011	Increase (times)	1971	2011	Increase (times)
Indonesia	14	680	47	1,756	182,384	104
Philippines	236	647	3	9,145	69,176	8
Vietnam	41	1,073	26	2,300	99,179	43
India	98	684	7	66,384	1,052,330	16
China	151	3,298	22	138,400	4,715,716	34
Malaysia	310	4,246	14	3,795	130,090	34
Myanmar	20	110	6	691	7,327	11
Thailand	120	2,316	19	5,083	155,986	31

Source: World Development Indicators.

instead of measuring the ratio of total primary energy supply (TPES) to GDP, the ratio for electricity consumption to GDP will need to be calculated. An efficient economy is able to use less energy to produce the same unit of output. Thus, more developed nations will have lower energy intensity. As seen in Figure 5.2, Indonesia had the lowest electricity intensity when compared to the BRIC (Brazil, Russia, India and China) countries. The BRIC countries had shown a tendency to decline in terms of electricity intensity. However, electricity intensity is also dependent upon the structure of the economy, as economies with many energy-intensive industries will have relatively high ratio of electricity intensity.

The Indonesian government has taken steps to implement energy conservation policies due to increases in the price of fossil fuel, depletion of fossil fuel, increasing energy import, power shortages and increases in energy subsidies. For example, the 2005 Presidential Decree No. 10 on Energy Saving was issued in response to the increase in oil prices that led to the increase in energy subsidy. In 2009, the Government Regulation No. 70 on Energy Conservation was issued. Similarly in

Figure 5.2
Electricity Intensity

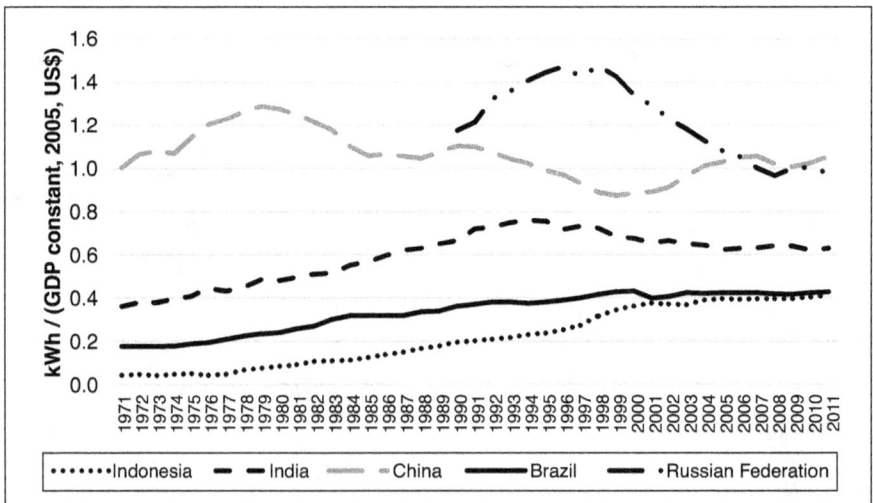

Source: Calculated from the World Development Indicators.

2011, Presidential Decree No. 13 on Energy and Water Saving was issued. In the electricity sector, the government determined that there were 20 per cent electricity savings to be had from the average daily electricity usage rates for the last six months.

However, the Indonesian government needed to make more effort to improve the effectiveness of electricity conservation policy. There are four main obstacles that need to be overcome and they are a lack of information, inappropriate organizational arrangements, finance, and environmental and political factors (Hill et al. 1995; United Nations 2004). Energy education at both the consumer and producer levels can improve people's awareness with regards to energy conservation. Fiscal and non-fiscal incentives can also be provided to reduce the severity of the problems that may arise due to organizational arrangements and financial problems. However, political factor is a major challenge to overcome in order to rationalize energy pricing.

While the government needs to pursue energy conservation policy, promoting investment in the power sector needs to be considered a priority. As seen in Figure 5.3, the average yearly additional capacity by

Figure 5.3
Additional Capacity by PLN (average at yearly level)

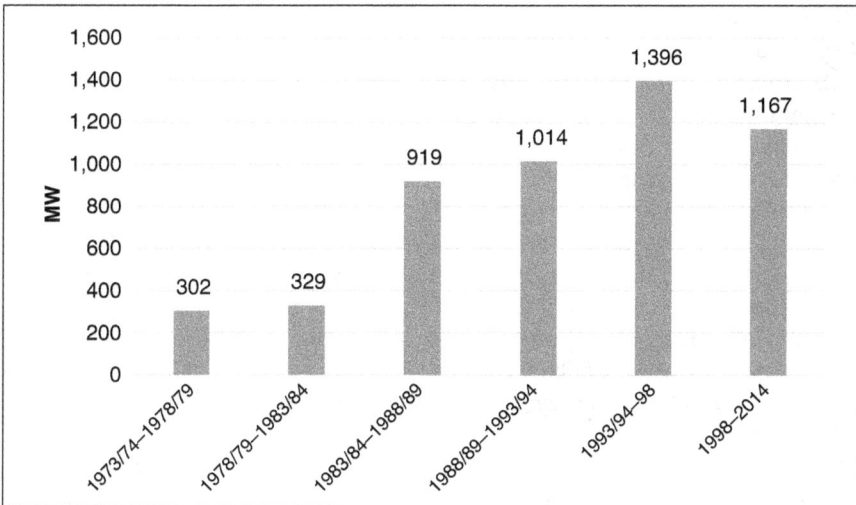

Source: Calculated from Table 3.1 on p. 48 of this book.

PLN increased from about 302 MW in 1973/74 to about 1,396 MW in 1998, after which it decreased to about 1,167 MW in 2014. Technically, new capacity needs to grow with increasing rate because it replaces the old capacity and adds to the power demand that increases every year. A lack of investment in the power sector causes many regions to suffer a power crisis.

References

Apergis, Nicholas and James E. Payne. "A Dynamic Panel Study of Economic Development and the Electricity Consumption-Growth Nexus". *Energy Economic* 33, no. 5 (2011): 770–81.

Booth, Anne. *The Indonesian Economy in the Nineteenth and Twentieth Centuries: A History of Missed Opportunity*. New York: Palgrave, 1998.

Chen, Sheng-Tung, Hsiao-I Kuo, and Chi-Chung Chen. "The Relationship between GDP and Electricity Consumption in 10 Asian Countries". *Energy Policy* 35 (2007): 2611–21.

Hill, Robert, Phil O'Keefe, and Colin Snape. *The Future of Energy Use*. London: Earthscan Publications, 1995.

International Energy Agency (IEA). *Sectoral Approaches in Electricity: Building Bridges to a Safe Climate*. Paris: IEA, 2009.

————. *CO_2 Emissions from Fuel Combustion Highlights*. Paris: IEA, 2010.

Narayan, Paresh Kumar and Baljeet Singh. "The Electricity Consumption and GDP Nexus for Fiji the Islands". *Energy Economics* 29 (2007): 1141–50.

Odhiambo, N.M. "Electricity Consumption and Economic Growth in South Africa: A Trivariate Causality Test". *Energy Economics* 31 (2009): 635–40.

Payne, James E. "A Survey of the Electricity Consumption-Growth Literature". *Applied Energy* 87 (2010): 723–31.

Sambodo, Maxensius Tri. "Investigating Relationship between Electricity Consumption and Economic Growth in Indonesia: A Comparative Perspective from China, Japan, and the US". Report on Waseda University Organization for Japan–US Studies (WOJUSS) International Symposium on Japan and the United States in Changing Asia, 2011.

Squalli, Jay. "Electricity Consumption and Economic Growth: Bounds and Causality Analyses of OPEC Members". *Energy Economics* 29 (2007): 1192–1205.

StataCorp. *Stata Statistical Software: Release 10. College Station*. Texas: StataCorp LP, 2007.

Thee Kian Wie. "The Soeharto Era and After: Stability, Development and Crisis, 1966–2000". In *The Emergence of National Economy: An Economic History of Indonesia, 1800–2000*, edited by Howard Dick, Vincent J.H. Houben,

J. Thomas Lindblad, and Thee Kian Wie. Crow's Nest, NSW: Allen & Unwin, 2002.

United Nations (UN). "End-use Energy Efficiency and Promotion of a Sustainable Energy Future." *Energy Resource Development Series* 39. New York: UN, 2004.

van der Eng, Pierre. "Indonesia's Growth Performance in the Twentieth Century". In *The Asian Economies in the Twentieth Century,* edited by Angus Maddison, D.S. Prasada Rao and William F. Shephered. Massachusetts: Edward Elgar Publishing, 2002.

———. "Total Factor Productivity and Economic Growth in Indonesia". <https://crawford.anu.edu.au/acde/publications/publish/papers/wp2009/wp_econ_2009_01.pdf> (accessed 29 May 2014).

6

ELECTRICITY AND THE ENVIRONMENT

TRAPPED CARBON IN THE POWER SECTOR

The electricity sector is not only important for economic development but it also has a strong impact on the environment. One of the major contributors of carbon dioxide emissions comes from the energy sector, particularly from electricity generation. According to IEA (2011), direct carbon dioxide emissions from fossil-fired power generation amounted to 27 per cent of the global greenhouse gas emissions in 2005. Furthermore, about 73 per cent of the total greenhouse gas emissions from power generation in 2007 originated from coal-fired power generation. Almost half of the 2020 energy-related carbon dioxide emissions are expected to be emitted by the major emerging economies, where the power sector and industries play an even larger role (IEA 2009).[1]

As can be seen in Table 6.1, in 2010, the carbon dioxide emissions in Indonesia amounted to 434 million tons (about 5 per cent and 22 per cent of the total carbon dioxide emissions from China and India respectively). Although Indonesia was higher than India in terms of carbon dioxide emissions per capita, Indonesia had a lower ratio intensity for carbon dioxide emissions with respect to GDP and energy use compared to China and India. This indicates that Indonesia's economy is less carbon intensive compared to China and India. For a single unit of energy use, Indonesia also emitted less carbon dioxide than the other two countries. However, it does not imply that Indonesia has the "right" to emit more carbon dioxide from energy production. In fact, the Indonesian energy sector needs to emit less carbon dioxide in the future.

In 2011, the total carbon dioxide emissions in Indonesia amounted to approximately 447.18 $MtCO_2$ and excluding LUCF (Forestry and Land Use Changes), the energy sector contributed 435 $MtCO_2$ of that amount.[2] Most of the carbon dioxide emissions in the energy sector consisted of emissions from the electricity generation, manufacturing and transportation sectors (see Figure 6.1). In Indonesia, electricity and heat made up the highest contributions to carbon dioxide emissions from the energy sector; their proportions of the total will increase in the future if the planned energy systems continue to be dependent on carbon intensive sources such as steam coal.

There are three main policies that will determine the structure of Indonesia's power system in the future. The first of these policies came

Table 6.1
Comparative Indicators, 2010

Indicators	Indonesia	China	India
CO_2 emissions (kt)	433,989	8,286,892	2,008,823
CO_2 emissions (metric tons per capita)	1.80	6.19	1.67
CO_2 emissions (kg per 2005 US$ of GDP)	1.15	2.16	1.62
CO_2 emissions (kt) per Energy use (kt of oil equivalent)	2.05	3.29	2.78

Note: Carbon dioxide emissions stem from the burning of fossil fuels and cement manufacture. They include carbon dioxide produced during consumption of solid, liquid, and gas fuels and gas flaring. Energy use refers to the use of primary energy before its transformation to other end-use fuels, which is equal to indigenous production plus imports and stock changes, minus exports and fuels supplied to ships and aircraft engaged in international transport.
Source: International Energy Agency (IEA Statistics © OECD/IEA, <http://www.iea.org/stats/index.asp>) and Carbon Dioxide Information Analysis Center, Environmental Sciences Division, Oak Ridge National Laboratory, Tennessee, United States.

Figure 6.1
Carbon Dioxide Emissions from the Energy Sector

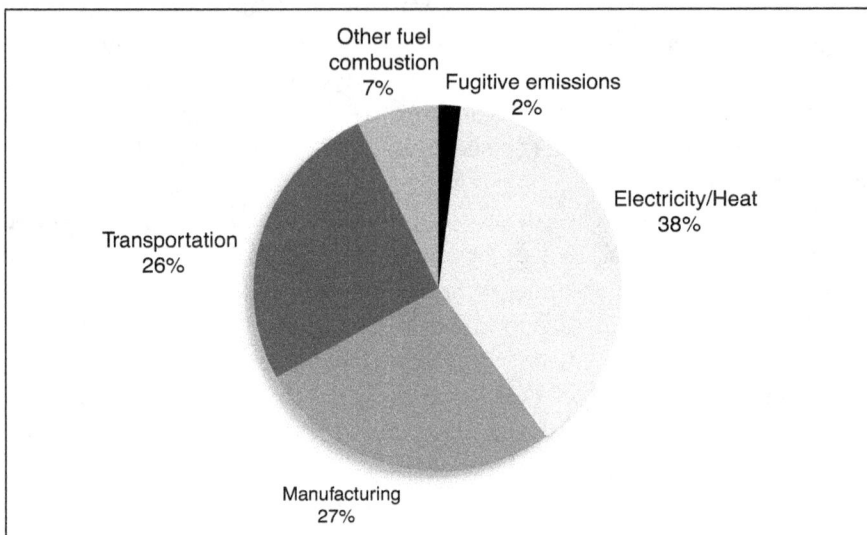

Other fuel
combustion
7%   Fugitive emissions
2%

Electricity/Heat
38%

Transportation
26%

Manufacturing
27%

Source: International Energy Agency (IEA Statistics © OECD/IEA, <http://www.iea.org/stats/index.
asp>) and Carbon Dioxide Information Analysis Center, Environmental Sciences Division, Oak
Ridge National Laboratory, Tennessee, United States.

in July 2006 when the government launched a fast track programme
(which for the sake of simplicity was) called the 10,000 MW Fast Track
Program. Between 2006 and 2009, it added a national electricity capacity
which ranged between 7,900 MW and 11,422 MW. This first fast track
programme focused on steam coal power plant mechanism. As Java
was the main target of the first fast track electricity programme, about
83 per cent of that additional capacity was located in Java. The second
programme came in January 2010 when the government launched the
second fast track programme that would add about 10,000 MW more
capacity. However, as it stands, the additional capacity is not only
based on coal sources but also on renewable energy and gas sources.
Finally, between 2015 and 2019, government plans to develop 35 GW
of new power capacity and 25.8 GW, or about 73.7 per cent of it
will be based on steam coal. This policy will bring new challenges in
managing carbon dioxide emissions from the power sector.

Figure 6.2
Carbon Dioxide Emissions from the Electricity Sector

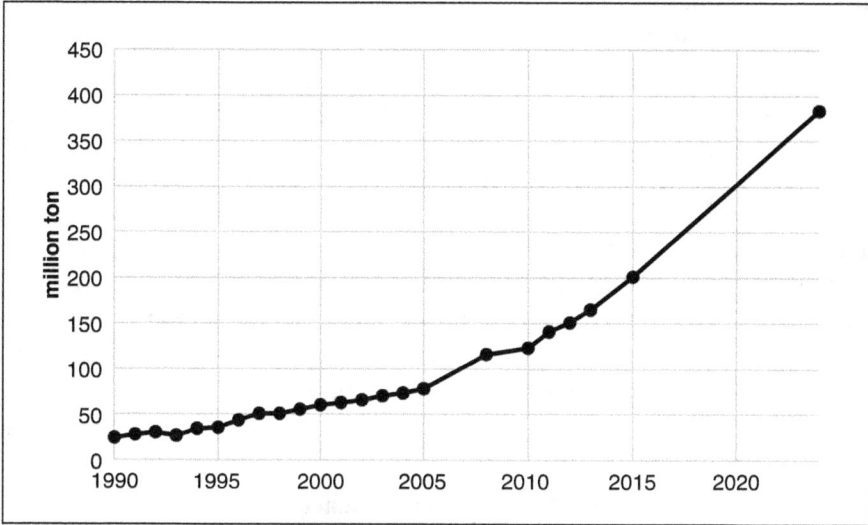

Sources: *Handbook Statistik Ekonomi Energi 2006* (Ministry of Energy and Mineral Resources) for 1990–2005 data; PT PLN Business Plan for Electricity Utility (various years) for 2008–24 data.

The proportion of steam power plants (coal based) to the total installed capacity would rise from about 48.8 per cent in 2006 to about 63 per cent in 2014 based on the work plan of the power sector's fast track programme (Sambodo and Oyama 2010). According to PLN (2014), between 2015 and 2024, the new capacity of steam coal power plants is about 42 GW or about 60 per cent of the total new capacity. It is expected that more than 60 per cent of electricity supply in Indonesia will be generated by steam coal power plants. This also indicates that coal would become the backbone of the primary energy supply for the national electricity system in the intermediate term. Furthermore, according to PT PLN's business plan for 2015–24, carbon dioxide emissions from the power generating system would increase from about 201 million tons in 2015 to about 383 million tons in 2024 (see Figure 6.2) and 87 per cent of the total emissions will be contributed by coal burning (PT PLN 2014).

As can be seen in Figure 6.3, the proportion of coal-based electricity production increased from about 2.4 per cent in the mid-1980s to about 44.4 per cent in 2011, while the actual production increased from 339 GWh to about 81,000 GWh for the same period. Coal-based electricity generation is projected to increase in the future. This indicates that the power system for Indonesia will likely be trapped into a "carbon-locked" situation should there be no well-designed green power system in the future. A green power system is defined as a power system which uses sustainable energy and has less carbon dioxide emission. Sustainable energy rests on two pillars (John and Rubbelke 2011): (i) energy from renewable sources, and (ii) energy efficiency. Furthermore, Lee (2010) said that there needs to be incentives for using renewable energy such as cost reduction (in comparison to the unsustainable path) and less greenhouse

Figure 6.3
Electricity Production from Coal

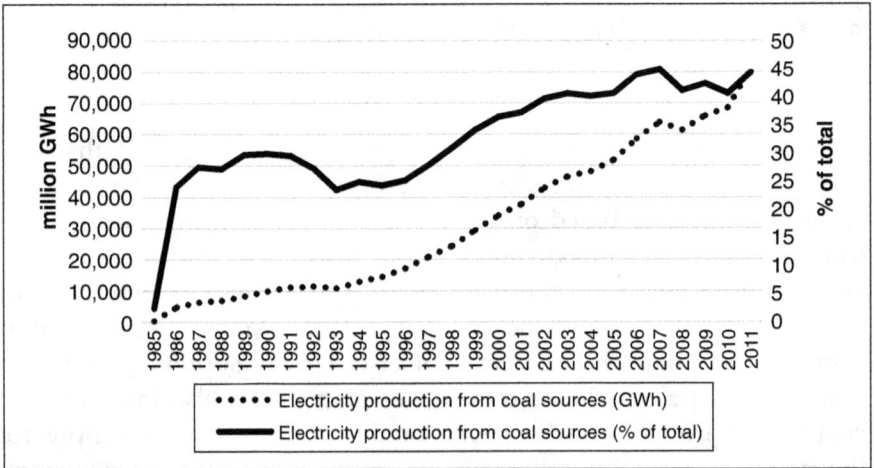

Note: The sources of electricity refer to the inputs used to generate electricity. Coal refers to all coal and brown coal, both primary (including hard coal and lignite-brown coal) and derived fuels (including patent fuel, coke oven coke, gas coke, coke oven gas, and blast furnace gas). Peat is also included in this category.
Source: International Energy Agency (IEA Statistics © OECD/IEA, <http://www.iea.org/stats/index.asp>), Energy Statistics and Balances of Non-OECD Countries, Energy Statistics of OECD Countries, and Energy Balances of OECD Countries.

gas emissions. The biggest challenge is how the Indonesian power sector needs to be designed to avoid carbon "lock-ins" in the future. It can be argued that participation via the sectoral approach (SA) could help Indonesia to obtain more effective carbon dioxide emission reduction. The sectoral approach here refers to an approach that reduces carbon dioxide emissions from the electricity sector.

UNDERSTANDING THE SECTORAL APPROACH

Indonesia has shown strong commitment to mitigate climate change. In order to achieve the nation's target of reducing carbon dioxide emissions by at least 26 per cent (without international assistance) and 41 per cent (with international assistance) by 2020, the government released the Presidential Regulation No. 61 on 20 September 2011 — the National Action Plan (NAP) for the greenhouse gas emissions reduction. The NAP covers six major areas and they are agriculture, forestry and peat land, energy and transportation, industry, waste management, and other supporting activities.

Power expansion and carbon dioxide emissions reduction will need to be pursued simultaneously. This was stated in Huenteler et al. (2012), who emphasized the importance of having balanced priorities between energy security, environmental policy, and climate policy, as well as economic and industrial policies. Indonesia's electricity system can play an important role in its transition to a low-carbon economy. However, Indonesia needs a broader approach or multiple approaches to ease the transition. Several approaches can be conducted such as demand side management (DSM), technology switching, fuel switching, and price incentives which reflect the cost of service. Thus, decision-makers would need to balance between supply- and demand-side investment policies.

A new framework or architecture for addressing global climate change has been proposed by institutions such as the Harvard Project on International Climate Agreements.[3] The 13th Conference of the Parties to the United Nations Framework Convention on Climate Change (COP 13) in December 2007 reached an agreement on the Bali Action Plan, which had five major elements (Aldy and Stavins 2009): a long-term global climate policy goal, emissions mitigation, adaptation, technology transfer, and financing. As part of the recommended mitigation actions, sectoral approaches have been developed for the electricity sector.[4]

Similarly, Sawa (2008) stated that the "cooperative sectoral approach" (which was coined in the Bali Action Plan), was one where, for example, "the Japanese government … led the world in making specific proposals for employing a sectoral approach as a basis for negotiations on the next framework to follow the Kyoto Protocol". Sectoral approval was designed for developing countries to meet voluntary "no-lose" greenhouse gas emissions targets for a particular sector. The no-lose target means that there is no penalty for not meeting the target, but there are positive incentives for exceeding it (Schmidt et al. 2008). Schmidt et al. (2008) proposed electricity and five major industrial sectors to implement the sectoral approach: iron and steel; chemical and petrochemical; aluminium; cement and limestone; and paper, pulp and printing.

With respect to the power generating sector, Sawa (2008) argued that there was a need to shift the power mix to low carbon resources when considering particular national circumstances. He also argued that improvement in the efficiency of the power sector, especially improvement in thermal power plants that combust fossil fuels, would have significant implications for countering global warming. He also suggested that the most appropriate measure would be to increase the average efficiency level of coal-fired power plants. He proposed three channels: (i) transferring technology and know-how from private companies in developed countries; (ii) extending information on best practices and providing on-site diagnosis and guidance; and (iii) financial support for such activities by private companies should be a major feature in government policies and measures.

The two instruments for sectoral mitigation consist of sectoral crediting and sectoral trading (IEA 2009).[5] Under both options, the baseline would be set below the business-as-usual rate so that the host country could contribute to the global mitigation process. There are two ways to estimate crediting baseline (IEA 2009). The first is to use a sectoral crediting baseline approach that is inspired by clean development mechanism (CDM). The second is the dynamic baseline method. According to the CDM model, the baseline emissions factor (the combined margin) is calculated from a weighted average of the emissions factors from all existing power plant units and the emissions factor. The emissions factor is calculated for a cohort of the most recently-built power units. The

CDM model assumes a baseline which is fixed once and for all, over the agreed crediting period. The dynamic model is defined as (IEA 2009):

$$CB_t = A \times CO_2/MWh_{t_{existing}} + (1 - A) \times CO_2/MWh_{t_{newplants}} \qquad (6.1)$$

where CB = crediting baseline, A = weight for the existing capacity

The critical assumption is that this crediting baseline would apply only to new plants, with the aim of triggering as much transformation as possible in new investments and to reduce the carbon "lock-ins" related to new power demand growth. In general, this baseline equation would function as follows (IEA 2009):

1. The higher "A" is, the less stringent the baseline. The negotiation over the baseline, once there has been an agreed measure of the carbon dioxide intensity of existing plants, would focus on the value for parameter A.[6]
2. As the performance of new plants improves and more new plants come on board over the years, the baseline moves further away from the initial performance of the sector, which provides an incentive to invest early in new, cleaner power generation.

Schmidt et al. (2008) included Indonesia as one of ten candidate countries that could participate in a sector-based approach to electricity. According to Schmidt et al. (2008), there was a two-step process in establishing "no-lose" targets:

1. Experts would assess and define energy intensity benchmarks for each sector to use as a starting point for discussions.
2. Non-Annex I countries would pledge a carbon intensity level that they could achieve without assistance.

Annex I countries would negotiate with developing countries on specific financial and other support through a Technology Finance and Assistance Package to encourage non-Annex I countries to ultimately commit to stricter "no-lose" emissions intensity levels. Schmidt et al. (2008) argued that a Technology Finance and Assistance Package was needed because this could provide greater support for developing advanced technologies than a simple awarding of carbon credits. It is possible that the revenues from the emissions reduction credit would be insufficient to fund the initial levels of investment and technology transfer.

Sambodo (2012) argued that as the additional steam capacity sources are coal based and fossil fuel based power plants which dominate the power generation sector, it is difficult to obtain carbon credits from the power system unless Indonesia can promote the latest technology on steam coal power plants, such as the ultra-supercritical generator. Sambodo (2012) also said that Indonesia would fully benefit from carbon credits as the government would need to choose the less stringent option among the various baselines (A = 0.6 for example). The less stringent option would have the highest cumulative emissions reduction. It has also been pointed out that a DSM policy would also need to be developed. One observation that can be seen is that DSM policy is likely to reduce the total emissions credit. Thus, aside from negotiating on the "A" parameter, it is also important to investigate the state of DSM policy as the policy could significantly affect the amount of carbon credits that can be attained. If Indonesia shows firm commitment in implementing DSM, then Indonesia could also demand for carbon credits to implement similar policies during the next policy cycle.

The Indonesian government has been participating in CDM. Table 6.2 lists the CDM projects that are directly related to the energy sector for the implementation period between 2007 and 2020. There are thirty-one projects on the list with a total carbon dioxide reductions of about 35.2 million tons. As can be seen in the table, the geothermal projects category shows the highest reduction in emissions, followed by the cement industry. Furthermore, even though emissions reductions from the biogas and biomass sectors can be considered quite low in terms of per project units, the aggregate reduction from the total number of projects is high. PT PLN has signed five emissions reduction purchase agreements (ERPA) since 2002 and started three projects under the voluntary carbon mechanism (VCM). According to Schmidt et al. (2009), sector-based programmes improve the CDM project by providing a focused package of technology investments (see Table 6.2 for details).

Furthermore, according to the National Action Plan (NAP) for Greenhouse Gas Emissions Reductions, there were several actions taken in the electricity sector which are as follows: according to the

Table 6.2
Clean Development Mechanism (CDM) Projects

	Project Name	Emission Reduced (tons)
1.	CDM Solar Cooker Project Aceh 1	21,000
2.	MSS Biomass 9.7 Mwe Condensing Steam Turbine Project	537,778
3.	MNA Biomass 9.7 Mwe Condensing Steam Turbine Project	447,780
4.	Indocement Alternative Fuel Project	936,784
5.	Indocement Blended Cement Project	4,468,569
6.	Lampung Bekri Biogas Project	188,260
7.	Derajat Unit III Geothermal Project	4,961,954
8.	PT Navigate Organic Energy Indonesia Integrated Solid Waste Management (GALFAD) Project in Bali	863,961
9.	PT BUDI ACID JAYA Tapioca Starch Production Facilities Effluent Methane Extraction and On-Site Power Generation Project in Lampung	2,171,488
10.	Nagamas Biomass Cogeneration Project	542,297
11.	Amurang Biomass Cogeneration Project	211,841
12.	Tambun LPG Associated Gas Recovery and Utilisation Project	3,655,816
13.	MEN Tanggerang 13.6 MW Natural Gas Co-generation Project	340,976
14.	4 MW Biomass Power Plants Using Waste Wood Chips and Sawdust in Central Java Province	102,214
15.	Pontianak GHG Emissions Reduction Through Improved MSW Management LFG Capture, Flaring and Electricity Generation	343,689
16.	Gas Turbine Co-Generation Project in Indonesia	227,960
17.	Emissions Reduction Through Partial Substitution of Fossil Fuel with Alternative Fuels in the Two Cement Plants of PT Holcim Indonesia Tbk	5,167,066
18.	Listrindo Kencana Biomass Power Plant	346,704
19.	Energy Efficiency Improvement Project	214,655
20.	Kabil II 11.4 MW Gas Fired Project	89,586
21.	Biogas Project, BAJ Unit 6	246,949
22.	Biogas Project, BAJ Way Jepara	350,420
23.	BAJ Gunung Agung Factory Tapioca Starch Wastewater Biogas Extraction and Utilisation Project, Lampung Province	441,798
24.	AANE Belitung Biogas Recovery from Palm Oil Mill Effluent (POME) Ponds and Biogas Flaring/Utilisation	197,180
25.	Biogas Project, BAJ Terbagi	365,302
26.	Lahendong II-20 MW Geothermal Project	466,990
27.	BAJ Pakuan Agung Factory Tapioca Starch Wastewater Biogas Extraction and Utilisation Project, Lampung Province	441,798
28.	Wayang Windu Phase 2 Geothermal Power Project	6,358,656
29.	Ranteballa Small-Scale Hydroelectric Power Project	68,159
30.	Belitung Energy Biomass Power Plant	313,184
31.	Jembo II 24 MW Gas Fired Project	136,773
	Total Emissions Reduction	35,227,587

Source: Calculated from <www.unfccc.int/cdm>.

NAP, between 2010 and 2014, about 352 MW of power supply was constructed from renewable energy sources, such as micro and mini hydro, solar panels, wind, and biomass sources. Between 2015 and 2020, the new capacity from renewable energy sources is expected to increase by about 873 MW. The total emissions reductions from the supply side would amount to about 4.4 million tons. From the demand side, carbon reductions would be achieved by implementing power saving at the household level. Total carbon dioxide emissions from the enhancement of the efficiency of household appliances was 5.58 million tons in 2014 and expected to be about 4.17 million tons in 2020. Thus, the projected total emissions reductions from both the supply and demand sides would amount to about 14 million tons.

The sectoral approaches give three major findings. First, by adopting more advanced technologies for steam power plants such as that of the ultra-supercritical generator, Indonesia would be able to substantially reduce carbon dioxide emissions. Second, as coal would form the backbone of primary energy sources in the power sector, Indonesia would need to be more flexible in the early stages of the sectoral approach negotiations. Finally, thirty-one projects with a total carbon dioxide reduction of about 35.2 million tons were obtained from information on listed CDM projects are directly related to the energy sector between 2007 and 2020. The geothermal and biogas projects have shown the highest reduction rates in terms of emission targets, followed by the cement industry. If one compares the cumulative emissions reductions among the CDM, NAP, and SAs, the SAs have larger emissions reduction than CDM and NAP in the electricity sector. Therefore, Indonesia still has the opportunity to have huge carbon savings if the new steam coal investments with ultra-supercritical technology are locked-in.

MANAGING CARBON DIOXIDE EMISSIONS FROM THE ELECTRICITY SECTOR

Technology Choices for Coal Based Power Plants

Sambodo (2012) pointed out that the total carbon dioxide emissions depend on three major factors: the type of steam-coal technology, policy on energy efficiency, and proportion of renewable energy in the system.

According to PT PLN's business plan, the company dominated the electricity production for most types of power plants, except for the geothermal sector. Table 6.3 shows the policies on the power plant expansion process. There were also indications that the private sector produced more electricity from geothermal energy sources than those provided by PT PLN. PT PLN has policies regarding different types of power plants (PT PLN 2010), such as:

1. PT PLN would plan for a coal based steam power plant project.
2. PT PLN would include hydropower and pumped storage energy generation projects.
3. While there will be an open tender for the geothermal power plant projects in general, for geothermal sites which are owned by Pertamina (State Oil Company), PT PLN can pursue two approaches regarding its generation, such as through energy service contracts and power purchase agreements.
4. PT PLN would include turbine power plants.
5. PT PLN would include combined cycle (gas) generation if there is funding support. The combined cycle project would be part of a development project from the open gas cycle that is owned by PT PLN.

Furthermore, as can be seen in Table 6.3, the new steam power plants would be based on coal. They would also use technology from the subcritical to supercritical types. However, Sambodo (2012) argued that if one has adopted supercritical and ultra-supercritical technologies for the new steam coal power plants, carbon dioxide emissions can be reduced by 10 per cent and 12 per cent per year, respectively. Furthermore, Sambodo (2012) said that as the new steam technology would have a lower generating cost when the fuel costs increase, the new technology could help to minimize electricity subsidies when there are unexpected increases in fuel cost. Thus, government support would be needed in order to boost new investments for more advanced steam coal technology.

It seems that Indonesia can learn from China in controlling carbon dioxide emissions from coal-fired power plants. Sambodo (2012) indicated that to produce one MWh of power, Indonesia needs to burn 0.886 tons of coal. In the case of China, for coal-fired power plants to generate a unit MWh, coal consumption decreased from 0.370 tons in 2005 to

Table 6.3
Policies on Power Plant Expansion, 2010–19

Region	Type	Specification	Technology
Java–Bali	Steam	1,000 MW 600 MW 400 MW	boiler supercritical (coal) coal subcritical
	Combined cycle	750 MW 750 MW	gas LNG
	Gas turbine	200 MW	oil
	Geothermal	55 MW, 110 MW	
	Hydro-pump storage	250 MW	in 2013
	Nuclear	1,000 MW	

Region	Location	Policy
Outside Java–Bali	Small islands	Small scale diesel power plant and gradually introduce LNG (Liquefied Natural Gas), biomass, and coal.
	Sumatra	Power plant is contracted near coal mining.

Source: PLN (2010, 2014).

about 0.339 tons in 2009 (Kahrl et al. 2011). Similarly, the Chinese central government agencies have led an effort to shut down small (≤ 50 MW) and old (>20 years, ≤200 MW) units, retiring 60.6 GW of these units between 2006 and 2009 (Kahrl et al. 2011). Further, the average thermal efficiency of coal-fired power plants in China has been able to sustain a linearly increasing trend since the 1960s, and now reportedly surpasses the average efficiency of US coal plants by a significant margin (Kahrl et al. 2011).

Indonesia would require international support in order to mitigate carbon dioxide emissions. In 2017, the first ultra-supercritical technology is expected to operate (with a capacity of 2 × 1,000 MW) in central Java. Ultra-supercritical technology has the lowest carbon dioxide emissions intensity compared to subcritical and supercritical technologies (Sambodo 2012). This would be the first public-private partnership (PPP) with a project value of about US$3.2 billion and the winning consortium includes Japan-based Electric Power Development (J-Power), local coal mining company Adaro Energy, and the Japan-based Itochu Corporation.[7] The government has provided support in facilitating and supporting the investment process; these include expediting measures for items such as the power purchase agreements, the guarantee agreements, and the recourse agreements. Unfortunately, land acquisition and the potential impact on the environment has caused delay in project implementation.

Efficiency in Electricity Used

According to IEA (2009), such energy efficiency policies had several benefits, such as a reduced exposure to rising international energy prices; energy cost savings for end-users; lower needs for expensive energy infrastructure; lower local pollution; and lower carbon dioxide emissions. A DSM policy can be implemented to reduce the demand for electricity due to energy efficiency and energy conservation. A clear distinction between energy efficiency and energy conservation is that the former refers to the adoption of a specific technology that would reduce the overall energy consumption without changing the behaviour of the consumers, while the latter merely implies a change in consumers' behaviour (Oikonumou et al. 2009). Shrestha and Marpaung (2006) used methods such as the replacement of inefficient appliances in the residential areas (for example, incandescent lamps with fluorescent lamps (CFL) and standard motors with energy efficient motors). Similarly, Hu et al. (2011) also said that "worldwide experiences have proved that DSM is useful [for] energy efficiency on the consumer side and could be the first priority in [the] face of climate challenge". Further, Sambodo and Oyama (2011) found that in Indonesia there was a negligible relationship between electricity consumption and economic growth; that is to say, electricity conservation policy would have no impact on economic growth. Chapter 4 highlighted that Indonesia still has room for improvement in electricity conservation with neutral impact on economic growth.

Sambodo (2012) said that if technology improvements are difficult to promote, DSM could be pursued to offset the lack of technology improvements. DSM policy can also help in reducing the generating cost because it can ease utilization of old power plants that have much higher generating cost compared to that of the latest technology. As generating costs can be decreased by implementing the DSM policy, electricity subsidies can be reduced. The Indonesian government will need to promote power-saving policies as one of the most important parts of its exit strategy from electricity subsidies.

Renewable Energy

In Chapter 2, we know that in the early 1950s, about 55.8 per cent of the total installed capacity was contributed by hydropower. However, in 2013, the share of hydropower to the total installed capacity was about 10 per cent. In 1978, the first power supply from geothermal power plant was produced with a capacity of about 0.25 MW in Kamojang, West Java. In 2013, the share of geothermal power plant to the total installed capacity was about 2.6 per cent. Thus, in 2013, the total share of large scale renewable power (hydropower and geothermal) to the total installed capacity was about 12.6 per cent. Because the share of renewable installed capacity tended to decline, the share of electricity production from renewable energy sources also decreased from about 24 per cent in 1986 to about 12 per cent in 2013 (see Figure 6.4).

The proportion of renewable energy has a tendency to increase if there is a huge investment in geothermal and hydropower plants. Following PLN's business plan, most of the additional capacity from geothermal sources would be constructed by independent power producers (IPP), while most of the hydropower plants would be developed by PT PLN. The share of renewable energy declines not because Indonesia lacks renewable resources, but due to a lack of efforts to optimize the potential resources. As seen in Table 6.4, only about 9 per cent of hydropower has been used. Similarly, with geothermal and biomass, only about 4 per cent and 3 per cent respectively have been used. Further, a limited amount of energy can be generated from solar, wind, and ocean power.

It is also important to note that climate factor becomes a challenge for the sustainability of power supply, especially for hydropower. Hydropower plants have a relatively low availability factor (AF). If one

Figure 6.4
Renewable Energy and Electricity Sector

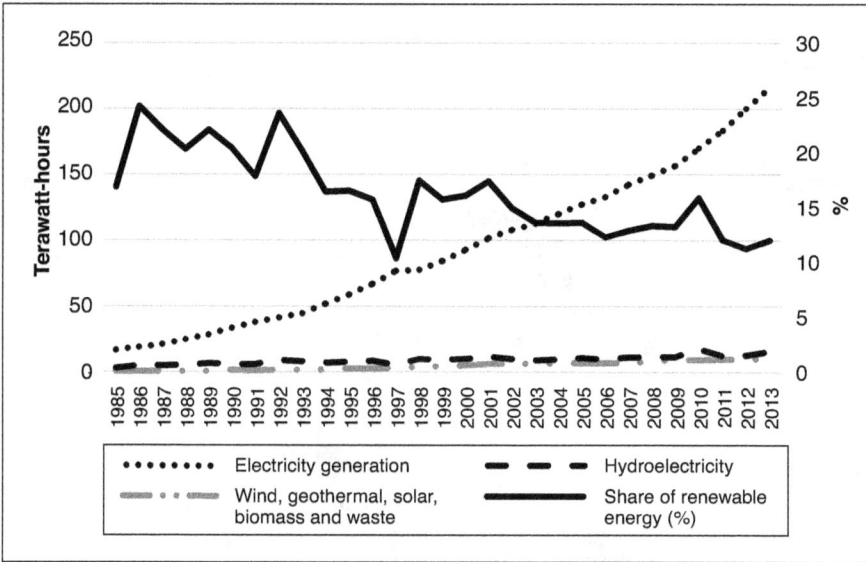

Source: Calculated from *BP Statistical Review of World Energy*, June 2014.

looked back to 1996, the year when AF had the highest value, one can argue that it was heavy rainfall that increased water availability in the dams (due to the *La Nina* phenomena), which in turn improved hydropower output. On the other hand, in 1997, Indonesia experienced a long dry season (due to *El Nino*), and thus hydropower plants had the lowest AF. In contrast, geothermal power plants have the highest AF value. This indicates that on average, geothermal sources operate about 86 per cent of the total calendar period. It can be argued that geothermal sources would be a more consistent primary renewable energy supply. With this type of energy source, geothermal energy can be used most of the time. Besides the climate factor, overlapping of land ownership has become one of the major obstacles in dealing with the declining operational age of dams in Indonesia. For example, due to land changes, the area around the Saguling Dam has showed rapid sedimentation. This reduces the lifespan of the dam from fifty to thirty years.[8]

Table 6.4
Reserve, Capacity and Rate of Utilzation of Renewable Energy in Indonesia

Renewable Sources	Reserve (1)	Capacity/Production (2)	Rate of Utilization (2) : (1)
Geothermal	30 GW	1.3 GW	4%
Hydro	75GW	6.8 GW	9%
Biomass	49.8 GW	1.6 GW	3%
Solar	4.8 kWh/m²/day	22.45 MW	—
Wind	3-6 m/s	1.87 MW	—
Ocean	49 GW	0.01 MW	—

Source: Ministry of Energy and Mineral Resources (2013).

Box 6.1
Availability Factor

According to the Glossary of Nuclear terms (Koelzer 2012), availability factor is a measure of the ability of power plants, a unit or a plant section to perform its operational function. The distinction made between equipment availability and energy availability are as follows:

1. Equipment availability is said to be the ratio of available time (operating and standby time) to the calendar period. Equipment availability would characterize the reliability of a power plant.
2. Energy availability is said to be the ratio of available energy to the theoretically possible energy for the period under report. It would characterize the reliability of a power plant in general, once one has considered all complete and partial outages.

One can define the availability factor as

$$AF = \frac{\text{available time}}{\text{calendar period}} = \frac{\text{operating time} + \text{stand by}}{\text{calendar period}}$$

Land acquisition has become the main problem in constructing most power plants in Indonesia, including geothermal and hydropower plants. For example, location permit for Hydropower Asahan Unit III in North Sumatra was submitted in 2004, but legal permit on the land's status has still not been obtained. Asahan Unit III is located in protected forest area and is under the authority of the Ministry of Forestry. Although in 2014 the Supreme Court annulled the land from the Ministry of Forestry, construction cannot be started before the Ministry of Forestry revised the land's status.[9]

The Indonesian government has issued regulations to solve land acquisition problems, such as: (i) Law No. 2/2012 on Land Acquisition, and (ii) Presidential Regulation No. 71/2012 on the Land Acquisition for Public Interest. Then the Presidential Regulation No. 71/2012 was revised three times: (i) Presidential Regulation No. 40/2012; (ii) Presidential Regulation No. 99/2014; and (iii) Presidential Regulation No. 30/2015. The revisions aim to simplify and quicken the process of obtaining permits and to provide certainty on land compensation. However, it seems that Indonesia needs to first solve the overlapping land ownership that has spread across the various levels of governments.

Similarly for the case of geothermal energy, the Indonesia Geothermal Association also pointed out seven challenges that need to be resolved by the government (Azimudin 2014). First, the government needs to simplify the process of obtaining licences on the environment, location, permit to borrow and use forest areas, permit for obtaining and utilization of water, permit to construct buildings, and local regulations. Second, the government needs to solve the disputes on geothermal projects that are located within the protected forests areas. Third, the government needs to provide certainty on feed-in tariff (FIT). Based on the Ministry of Energy and Mineral Resources Regulation No. 17/2014, PLN must buy electricity from geothermal sources based on the government's ceiling price which is guaranteed for thirty years. The ceiling price is different following the commercial operation dates and regions. The government has indicated the price for the years between 2015 and 2025. Fourth, the government needs to provide more incentives such as fiscal incentives for import purposes. This regulation is important to facilitate import of machineries and components for geothermal power plants. Fifth, according to Electricity Law No. 30/2009, there is no open access network, but it is possible to rent transmissions network. Because most of the geothermal power plants are located in remote areas, access on transmissions is important to supply electricity to the national grid. Sixth, PLN is still the single buyer of electricity, and this may affect competition among potential buyers. Finally, the tender process on geothermal working areas needs to be settled both at the local and central government levels. Due to the complexity of the situation and since the geothermal law has been introduced in 2003, out of eleven geothermal working areas, none has come to the stage of commercial operation date (COD).

TOWARDS GREEN PATH POWER SYSTEM

Sambodo (2012) argued by considering the long-term power expansion model. Indonesia has the opportunities to reduce carbon dioxide emissions not only by utilizing natural gas and upgrading steam coal technology to ultra-supercritical, but also by combining this policy with renewable energy. However, it seems that the capacity for renewable energy grows slowly. It is hoped that the share of renewable energy would increase rapidly by providing incentives for using renewable energy. Similarly, Resosudarmo et al. (2011) also recommended providing more incentives for investments in electric power generation from clean resources.

The government has issued regulations that aim to support industries, including renewable energy. For example, Law No. 17/2006 on Custom allows for the abolishment and exemption of import duties, although this permission needs to be approved by the Ministry of Finance. Government Regulation No. 31/2007 on the abolishment of value-added tax for strategic commodities covers capital goods such as machineries. Government Regulation No. 94/2010 also provides tax abolishment and exemption on corporate income tax for companies that are involved in pioneer industries. Pioneer industries are defined as industries with large forward and backward linkages, having large added value and positive externalities, introducing new technologies, and having strategic values for national interest. The regulation is supported by the Ministry of Finance Regulation No. 130/2011 that stated the renewable energy industry as part of pioneer industries. Finally, Government Regulation No. 52/2011 also mentioned that renewable energy such as geothermal, hydro, solar power, wind, and ocean are parts of specific businesses and these industries can enjoy income tax facilities such as: (i) income tax deduction in the sum of 30 per cent capital investment over six years; (ii) accelerated amortization and depreciation; (iii) 10 per cent tax on dividend or lower, according to tax treaty; and (iv) extended tax loss carry forward up to ten years.

Further, the government has implemented FIT. According to the Ministry of Energy and Mineral Resources Regulation (MEMR) No. 4/2012, PT PLN has to buy electricity and excess capacity from renewable energy sources. The incentives on FIT not only depends on the type of renewable energy, but also the type of connection and the region. In the case of outside Java, such as in Maluku and Papua, the government provides more incentives. According to MEMR Regulation No. 2/2011, the geothermal FIT was 9.70 cents per kWh, but according to MEMR Regulation No. 17/2014, for geothermal power plants with commercial operation date in 2025, the FIT is US\$29.6 per kWh.[10] Thus, there have been a substantial increase in the price of electricity from geothermal sources.

However, it seems that providing more monetary incentives for renewable energy will not be effective unless the government can provide permanent solutions on land acquisition and other permits. Further, there are also risks by providing monetary incentives without considering the deliverability of the projects. As seen in Tables 6.5, 6.6, and 6.7, most of the renewable energy producers are dominated by a few big players. If the government does not have a strategic plan, monetary support for renewable energy will create more barriers for other firms to participate in the market. Alternatively, subsidizing only renewable energy will make the production of renewable energy fall below potential level.

Sambodo (2013) argued that improving the contribution of renewable energy to the total installed capacity needs to be pursued in three ways: (1) improving the diversification ratio; (2) increasing the share of renewable energy; and (3) reducing emissions intensity. For a better emission target, the government needs to determine: (1) renewable energy target; (2) intensity target (kg CO_2/kWh); and (3) renewable energy consumption per capita (kWh/capita).

Oil is still considered the primary energy source. For example, based on PT PLN's business plan for 2010–19, oil consumption was expected to amount to about 3.53 million kilolitres (KL) in 2010, but the actual oil consumption was about 4.64 million KL, about 31 per cent above the planned level. Similarly, according to PT PLN's business plan for 2013–22, the consumption for high speed diesel

Table 6.5
Top Five Producers of Biodiesel in Indonesia

No.	Company	Capacity (Mt/Year)	Share to the Total National Capacity (%)
1.	PT Wilmar Bioenergy Indonesia	1,050,000	27.0
2.	PT Musim Mas	850,000	21.9
3.	PT Wilmar Nabati Indonesia	690,000	17.7
4.	PT Cemerlang Energy Perkasa	400,000	10.3
5.	PT Ciliandra Perkasa	250,000	6.4

Table 6.6
Top Five Producers of Solar Panel Module in Indonesia

No.	Company	Capacity (MW per year)
1.	PT LEN Industri	10
2.	PT Adyawinsan Electrical and Power	10
3.	PT Surya Utama Putra	15
4.	PT Swadaya Prima Utama	15
5.	PT Azet Surya Lestari	10
6.	PT Wijaya Karya Intrade Energi	10
Total National Capacity		60–80

Table 6.7
Top Three Producers of Geothermal Energy in Indonesia

No.	Company	Share to the Total National Production (%)
1.	Chevron Geothermal	50.8
2.	Pertamina	22.7
3.	PT Indonesia Power	19.3

(HSD) in 2014 was 5.4 per cent above the planned level. Further, there is also a tendency that the share of electricity production from rental genzet (oil based) increased from 2.8 per cent to about 8 per cent between 2009 and 2014. As the share of rental genzet increased,

PLN consumes more oil fuel. This implies that genzet is still the first solution in solving a power crisis, especially outside Java, rather than promoting renewable energy. It has been noted that Government Regulation No. 23/2014 also provides opportunities to use more diesel power because PLN can directly purchase electricity from the private sector if the customer location is classified as suffering from a power shortage.

Notes

1. According to World Energy Outlook (WEO) 2008 scenarios, the other major economies included Brazil, China, India, Indonesia, Russia, and Saudi Arabia.
2. <http://cait2.wri.org/wri#Country GHG Emissions?indicator[]=Electricity/Heat (CO_2)&indicator[]=Manufacturing/Construction (CO_2)&indicator[]=Transportation (CO_2)&indicator[]=Other Fuel Combustion (CO_2)&indicator[]=Fugitive Emissions (CO_2)&year[]=2011&act[]=Indonesia &sortIdx=&focus=&chartType=geo> (accessed 6 June 2014).
3. The Harvard Project proposed three criteria that are important for implementing the new international climate regime: the regime has to be scientifically sound, economically rational, and politically pragmatic.
4. Mitigation refers to the reduction of greenhouse gas emissions.
5. IEA (2008, pp. 50–51) provides this summary:

    Sectoral crediting. A crediting mechanism based on ambitious, negotiated mitigation goals at the sectoral level. The goals may be of a non-binding or "no-lose" nature: A country could commit one of its sectors to a target generate emissions reduction credit if it outperformed the target, and not be penalised otherwise. The baseline can be expressed in absolute terms as a total amount of emissions, or in intensity terms as tCO_2-eq per unit of output. *Sectoral trading.* A country could adopt a sector-wide emissions commitment. This would enable it to trade emissions allowances internationally, even if the country were not covered by a country-wide emission goal.

6. In the simulation, the International Energy Agency used three values of A: 0.2, 0.4, and 0.6 for China; and 0.1, 0.2, and 0.3 for India.
7. However, the project has not shown substantial progress. Since it was approved in 2011, land accusation and environmental problems have become major obstacles. Although the government claimed that land accusation has been resolved, the fishermen whose fishing areas are near the plants are worried about the environmental impacts of the project. The Greenpeace Indonesia also provides strong support to the fishermen.

8. See "Tanah diserobot, usia PLTA Saguling menyusut 20 tahun" [Due to Land Grabbing, the Age of Saguling Hydropower Decrease by 20 Years], 8 June 2015, <http://bisniskeuangan.kompas.com/read/2015/06/08/0945008/Tanah.Diserobot.Usia.PLTA.Saguling.Menyusut.20.Tahun> (accessed 9 June 2015).

9. See "Pembangunan PLTA Asahan III Tunggu SK Pengganti Register 44" [Development of Asahan Hydropower is Still Waiting for Replacement Letter No. 44), 4 September 2014, <http://medanbisnisdaily.com/news/read/2014/09/04/115423/pembangunan_plta_asahan_iii_tunggu_sk_pengganti_register_44/#.VXgIZiyjX7w> (accessed 9 June 2015).

10. This price is directed to the construction of geothermal plants in isolated regions or in regions that are highly dependent on diesel power.

References

Azimudin, Tafif. "Tantangan Pengembangan Industri Panas Bumi di Indonesia" [Challenge on Developing Geothermal Industry in Indonesia]. Paper presented at the Pertamina Energy Outlook 2015, Jakarta, 3–4 December 2014.

Aldy, Joseph E. and Robert N. Stavins. *Post-Kyoto International Climate Policy: Summary for Policymakers*. New York: Cambridge University Press, 2009.

Huenteler, Joern, Tobias S. Schmidt, and Norichika Kanie. "Japan's post-Fukushima Challenge-Implications from German Experience on Renewable Energy Policy". *Energy Policy* 45 (2012): 6–11.

Hu, Zhao Guang, Jiahai Yuan, and Zheng Hu. "Study on China's Low Carbon Development in an Economy-Energy-Electricity-Environment Framework". *Energy Policy* 39 (2011): 2596–2605.

International Energy Agency (IEA). *Sectoral Approaches in Electricity: Building Bridges to a Safe Climate*. Paris: IEA, 2009.

———. *CO$_2$ Emissions from Fuel Combustion: Highlights*. Paris: IEA, 2011.

John, Klaus D. and Dirk T.G. Rubbelke. "Sustainable Energy: An Introduction to the Topic". In *Sustainable Energy*, edited by Klaus John and Dirk Rubbelke. London: Routledge, 2011.

Kahrl, Fredrich, Jim Williams, Ding Jianhua, and Hu Jenfeng. "Challenges to China's Transition to a Low Carbon Electricity System". *Energy Policy* 39 (2011): 4032–41.

Koelzer, Winfried. "Glos°sary of Nuclear Terms". <http://www.euronuclear.org/info/encyclopedia/pdf/Nuclear%20Glossary_2012-03-30.pdf> (accessed 7 April 2012).

Lee, Jisoon *Green Growth: Korean Initiatives for Green Civilization*. Seoul: Random House Korea Inc., 2010.

Ministry of Energy and Mineral Resources. *Handbook Statistik Ekonomi Energy 2013*. <http://prokum.esdm.go.id/Publikasi/Handbook%20of%20Energy%20&%20 Economic%20Statistics%20of%20Indonesia%20/HANDBOOK%20ESDM%20 2013.pdf> (accessed 11 May 2014).

Oikonomou, V., F. Becchis, L. Steg, and D. Russolillo. "Energy Saving and Energy Efficiency Concepts for Policy Making". *Energy Policy* 37 (2009): 4787–96.

PT PLN (Persero). *Rencana Usaha Penyediaan Tenaga Listrik PT PLN (Persero) 2010–2019* [PT PLN Business Plan for Electricity Utility 2010–2019]. Jakarta: PT PLN (Persero), 2010.

———. *Rencana Usaha Penyediaan Tenaga Listrik PT PLN (Persero) 2015–2024* [PT PLN Business Plan for Electricity Utility 2015–2024]. Jakarta: PT PLN (Persero), 2014.

Resosudarmo, Budy P., Frank Jotzo, Arief A. Yusuf, and Ditya A. Nurdianto. "Challenges in Mitigating Indonesia's CO_2 emission: The Importance of Managing Fossil Fuel Combustion". <http://ccep.anu.edu.au/data/2011/ pdf/wpapers/CCEP1108Resosudarmo.pdf> (accessed 12 January 2012).

Sambodo, Maxensius Tri. "Mathematical Modeling Analyses for Investigating the Future Expansion of Electric Power System in Indonesia". PhD dissertation, National Graduate Institute for Policy Studies, 2012.

———. "Facilitating the Penetration of Renewable Energy into the Power System". In *Energy Market Integration in East Asia: Renewable Energy and Its Deployment into the Power System*, edited by Fukunari Kimura, Han Phoumin, and Brett Jacobs. Jakarta: Economic Research Institute for ASEAN and East Asia (ERIA), 2013.

Sambodo, Maxensius Tri and Tatsuo Oyama. "The Electricity Sector Before and After the Fast-Track Program". *Economics and Finance in Indonesia* 58 (2010): 285–308.

———. "Investigating Electricity Consumption and Economic Growth in Indonesia: A Time Series Analysis". Paper presented at the Waseda University Organization for Japan–US Studies (WOJUSS) International Symposium, Waseda University, Okuma Memorial Tower, 9–10 June 2011.

Sawa, Akihiro. "A Sectoral Approach as an Option for a Post-Kyoto Framework". Discussion Paper 2008–23, Harvard Project on International Climate Agreements, December 2008.

Schmidt, Jake, Ned Helme, Jin Lee, and Mark Houdashelt. "Sectoral-based Approach to the post-2012 Climate Change Policy Architecture". <http:// www.ccap.org/docs/resources/539/CPOL8-5_05_Schmidt%20(2).pdf> (accessed 12 January 2012).

Shrestha, Ram M. and Charles O.P. Marpaung. "Integrated Resource Planning in the Power Sector and Economy-wide Changes in Environmental Emissions". *Energy Policy* 34 (2006): 3801–11.

7

THE RURAL ELECTRICITY PROGRAMME IN INDONESIA

This chapter analyses the trend of the rural electrification programme in Indonesia. It presents analysis on the affordability dimension that is also linked to energy equity. The first part analyses the current position of electricity access from both regional and provincial perspectives. The second part investigates the affordability dimension of electricity and evaluates it both in nominal and real terms. The third part discusses the characteristics of households without electricity access using several indicators, such as housing and infrastructure conditions and social protection benefits from the government. The fourth section discusses the rural electrification programme in Indonesia, underlining the changing institutional actors and the outcome dimensions. Section five analyses the existing conditions of the rural electricity programme. Finally, the lessons learned from the rural electrification programme in Nusa Tenggara Province are discussed. To conclude, although Indonesia has contributed to reducing the number of people in the world without access to electricity and alleviating the huge disparity in electricity access and consumption among the provinces, the rural electrification programme has not yet devised a robust method or comprehensive strategies throughout the last six decades. The decision-makers seemed to lack an understanding of present and historical contexts in designing the programme. This affects the sustainability of electricity access. Resolving the problem of electricity access in Indonesia will require many more years.

CURRENT CONDITION OF ELECTRICITY ACCESS

The report of the Commission on Sustainable Development/CSD (2001) said that energy is central to achieving the goal of sustainable development. Access to affordable energy services is a prerequisite to reduce the number of people living on less than US$1 per day by 2015 (CSD 2001). The report also said that access to energy is crucial for economic and social development and the eradication of poverty. According to Birol (2007), there are three strategic challenges in global energy system, namely: (i) the growing risks of disruptions to energy supply; (ii) the threat of environmental damage caused by energy production and use; and (iii) persistent energy poverty, which is frequently overlooked in discussions. Birol (2007) has pointed out the vicious cycle of energy poverty and human under-development. Similarly, UNDP (2005) mentioned that access to electricity is a pre-condition to achieve the Millennium Development Goals (MDGs).

The World Summit on Sustainable Development in Johannesburg, South Africa, in 2002 highlighted energy for sustainable development. The summit mentioned that (UN 2002, p. 11):

> ... access to energy facilitates the eradication of poverty ... improve access to reliable, affordable, economically viable, socially acceptable, and environmentally sound energy services and resources ...

In September 2011, the UN General Assembly launched the "Sustainable Energy for All" initiative. UN Resolution No. 65/151 decided to declare the year 2012 as the International Year of Sustainable Energy for All (SE4A). Further, UN Resolution No. 66/288, under the outcome documents "the future we want" (27 July 2012) section on Energy, mentioned that:

> ... "Sustainable Energy for All" ... focuses on access on energy, energy efficiency, and renewable energies.

UN Resolution No. 67/215 at the 61st Plenary Meeting on 21 December 2012 decided to declare the years 2014–24 as the "UN Decade of Sustainable Energy for All". In the spirit of UN resolutions, developing countries, such as Indonesia, need to follow up and make plans to achieve the targets.

Indonesia has the second largest number of people without access to electricity in Asia, after India (see Table 1.1 of Introduction in this book). It contributed 9.7 per cent to the total population without electricity from developing Asia, or 43 per cent in Southeast Asia. Urban electrification rate in Indonesia is the lowest compared to other Southeast Asian countries, although the rural electrification rate in Indonesia is better than that in Cambodia, Myanmar, and the Philippines.

As seen in Table 7.1, electricity consumption per capita in Indonesia still falls below that in Vietnam, China, Malaysia, and Thailand, and it is slightly lower than India. However, between 1971 and 2011, electricity consumption per capita in Indonesia had increased by forty-seven times, the highest rate compared to other countries. Similarly, from the production side, Indonesia had the highest increase. However, the initial condition of electricity consumption and production in Indonesia lagged behind other countries, except Myanmar, and despite the substantial

Table 7.1
Electricity Consumption and Production

Country	Electricity Consumption (kWh per capita)			Electricity Production (million kWh)		
	1971	2011	Increase (times)	1971	2011	Increase (times)
Indonesia	14	680	47	1,756	182,384	104
Philippines	236	647	3	9,145	69,176	8
Vietnam	41	1,073	26	2,300	99,179	43
India	98	684	7	66,384	1,052,330	16
China	151	3,298	22	138,400	4,715,716	34
Malaysia	310	4,246	14	3,795	130,090	34
Myanmar	20	110	6	691	7,327	11
Thailand	120	2,316	19	5,083	155,986	31

Source: World Development Indicators.

increase in electricity production, it still falls behind other countries. In terms of promoting electric power consumption, Indonesia has been more successful than the Philippines. The Indonesian government has a target of increasing electricity consumption per capita to about 2,500 kWh in 2025 and 7,000 kWh in 2050 (Soerawidjaja 2011).

Both Indonesia and the Philippines share comparable figures on electricity access. Geographical factors seem to contribute to the low electrification ratios in both countries, especially in rural areas, possibly since archipelagic nature of the two countries influences access to electricity networks. The number of islands verified in Indonesia is 13,466 and more than 80 per cent of them are uninhabited.[1] Figure 7.1 shows that the average number of islands for each province is less than 300. Provinces with a higher number of islands seem to have a lower average energy sold per household. While this is not necessarily causality conclusion,[2] the geographical challenges imply that power system planning also needs to consider the geospatial factor.

Figure 7.1
Number of Islands and Average Energy Sold for Household in 2012

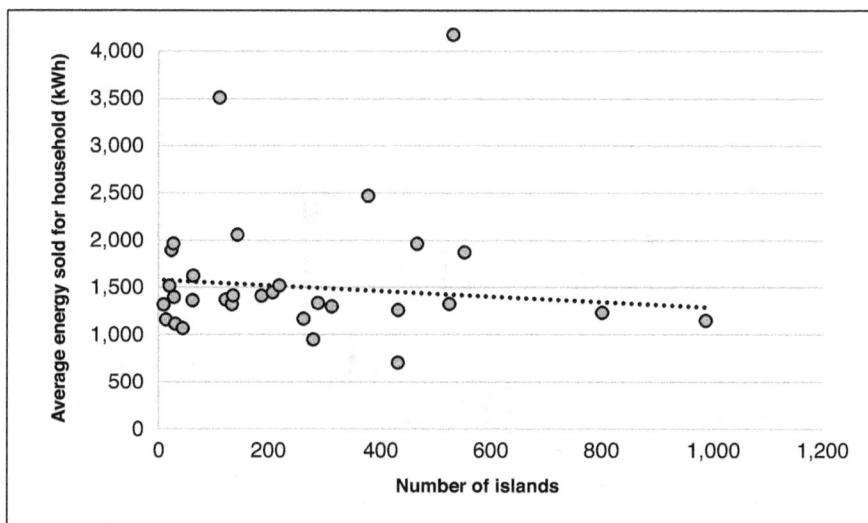

Source: PLN (2012) and KKP (2013).

According to the World Bank Policy Brief towards Universal Electricity Access in Indonesia, more than 50 per cent of the people without electricity access is located outside Java and Bali, far away from the main island grid (Sahai 2013). AusAID, ASTAE, and ESMAP have developed geospatial least-cost optimization to increase electrification ratio outside Java and Bali.[3] This is a promising approach as previous attempts to improve the rural electrification programme had focused on grid connections; this approach aims to broaden and diversify the options. It is not constrained by only the grid connection, but also gives the possibility of developing the communal solar mini grid and solar home system.

However, this geospatial approach in itself may not solve the complex problems of electricity poverty in Indonesia. It is only one technical aspect (hardware element); the institutional dimension (software element) also needs to be developed properly. Both elements are important to ensure the sustainability of energy poverty alleviation in Indonesia.

Despite the substantial increase in electric power consumption and production in Indonesia, electricity access is still relatively poor. Unequal electricity access across the islands and provinces contributes to this situation. Figure 7.2 shows the electrification ratio across

Figure 7.2
Electrification Ratio at Provincial Level, 2012 (%)

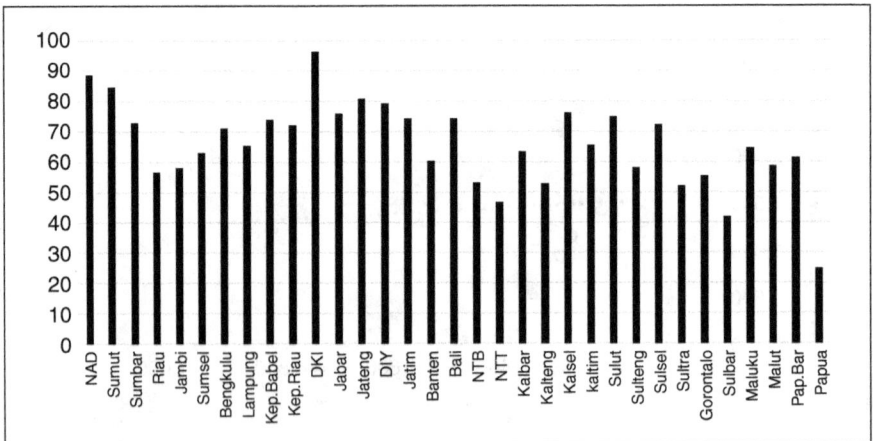

Source: PLN (2012).

thirty-three provinces in Indonesia in 2012. The electrification ratio of DKI Jakarta (Special Capital Region of Jakarta) was almost 100 per cent, but for Papua the ratio was only about 24.8 per cent. There were only four provinces with electrification ratio above 80 per cent. Low electrification ratio usually corresponds with low electricity sold per capita (see Figure 7.3, indicated by the dotted line). However, a province with high electricity sold per capita does not necessarily have relatively high electrification ratio. For example, Banten had the second highest amount of electricity sold per capita after DKI Jakarta, but in terms of electrification ratio, Banten was relatively low. This is because most electricity was consumed by the industrial sector instead of the household sector. In contrast, Aceh had a relatively high electrification ratio but low electricity sold per capita.

Figure 7.4 shows that there is positive correlation between the average energy sold for household and the electrification ratio. DKI Jakarta had both the highest electrification ratio and the average energy sold for household. In the case of Papua, although it had relatively

Figure 7.3
Electricity Sold and Electrification Ratio at Provincial Level, 2012

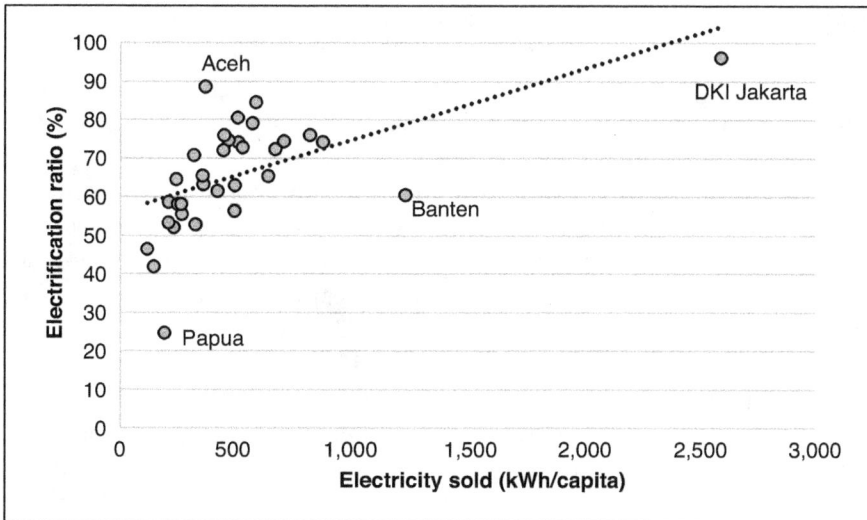

Source: PLN (2012).

Figure 7.4
Electricity Sold for Household and Electrification Ratio at Provincial Level, 2012

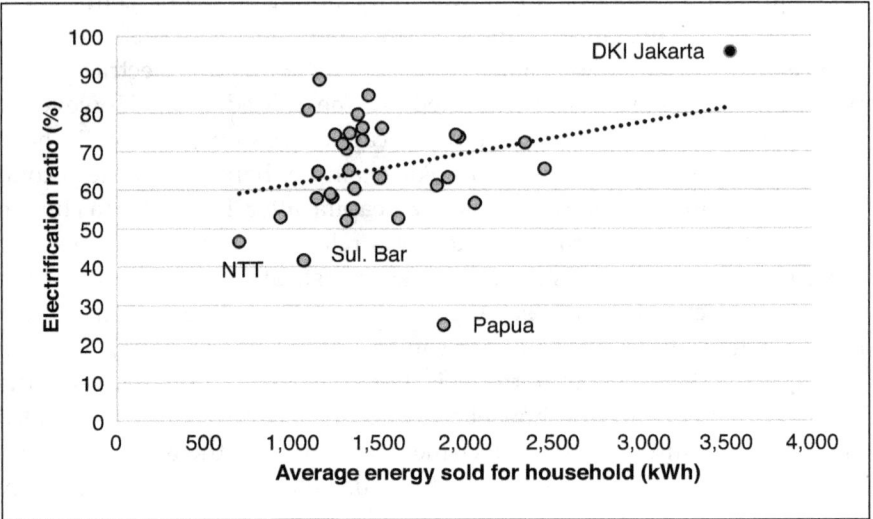

Source: PLN (2012).

high amount of energy sold compared to East Nusa Tenggara (*Nusa Tenggara Timur*/NTT) and West Sulawesi (*Sulawesi Barat*) Provinces, its electrification ratio was the lowest. Similarly, NTT had the lowest average energy sold for household, but had a higher electrification ratio than West Sulawesi and Papua, indicating that the electricity demand in NTT is relatively lower than West Sulawesi and Papua.

According to AGECC (2010), there is an increase of electricity consumption in fulfilling modern society needs in comparison to basic human needs (see Figure 7.5). In other words, the demand for electricity will increase as the income per capita increases, largely due to the increase dependency on electronic devices.

Electricity consumption can be divided into six areas, namely households, industries, social uses, government offices, public lighting and commercial sector. If we only consider electricity consumption at the household level and divide it by the number of people in the population (see Figure 7.6), we obtain two provinces consuming electricity below 100 kWh per person per year, specifically NTT and West Sulawesi,

Figure 7.5
Incremental Levels of Access to Energy Services

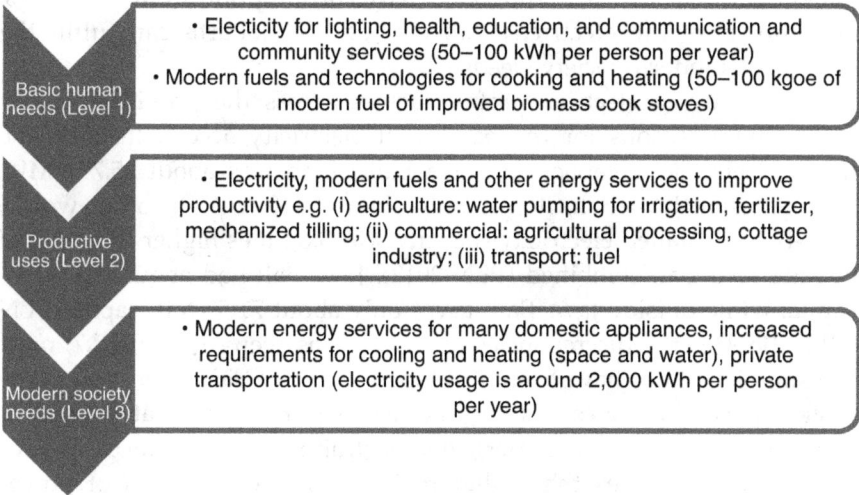

Basic human needs (Level 1)
• Electicity for lighting, health, education, and communication and community services (50–100 kWh per person per year)
• Modern fuels and technologies for cooking and heating (50–100 kgoe of modern fuel of improved biomass cook stoves)

Productive uses (Level 2)
• Electricity, modern fuels and other energy services to improve productivity e.g. (i) agriculture: water pumping for irrigation, fertilizer, mechanized tilling; (ii) commercial: agricultural processing, cottage industry; (iii) transport: fuel

Modern society needs (Level 3)
• Modern energy services for many domestic appliances, increased requirements for cooling and heating (space and water), private transportation (electricity usage is around 2,000 kWh per person per year)

Source: AGECC (2010).

Figure 7.6
Household and Total Electricity Consumption per Capita (kWh)

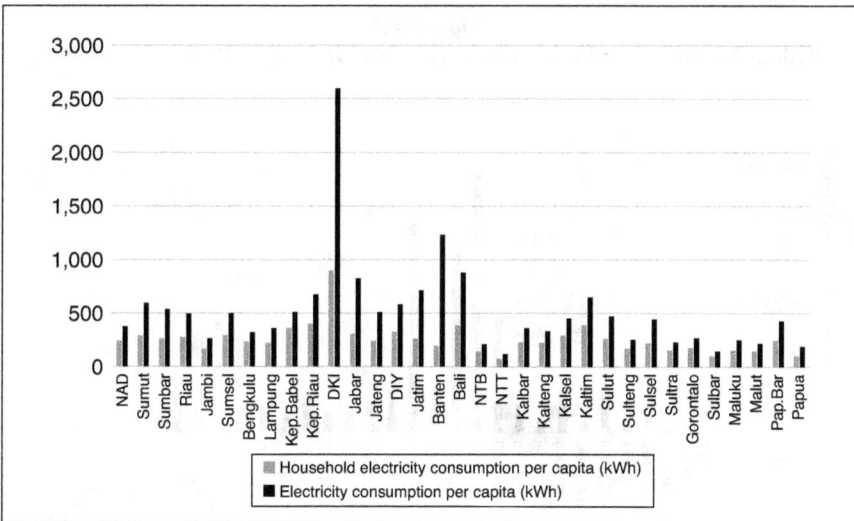

Household electricity consumption per capita (kWh)
Electricity consumption per capita (kWh)

Source: PLN (2012).

while the electricity consumption in Papua is slightly more at 105 kWh. Thus, if we assume the electricity consumption to be 2,000 kWh per person per year and including electricity consumption from all sectors, arguably only the electricity capacity of DKI Jakarta can fulfill the criteria of modern society needs.

Inequality in electricity infrastructure across the provinces is one of the main reasons for the paucity of electricity access. In 2012, the installed electricity capacity in Java–Bali island was about 25,791 MW, while outside Java–Bali, it was only about 7,110 MW. In other words, Java–Bali's installed electricity capacity was 3.6 times higher than that of outside Java–Bali combined (PLN 2012). Java–Bali had about 174 watt/capita, while outside Java–Bali it was only about 71.5 watt/capita (PLN 2012). Besides the discrepancies in capacity, as seen in Figure 7.7, most transmissions lines have been developed in Java. Grid connection in the eastern part of Indonesia is very limited. Figure 7.8 indicates installed capacity of travo (transformer), demonstrating that provinces in Java have more capacities than other regions. The construction of power infrastructures needs to be considered as a top priority for the eastern provinces in Indonesia. At the same time, the population size, land area, and geographical and topographical dimensions are key elements that must be taken into account in determining investment in the power sector.

Figure 7.7
Length of Transmission Lines (medium and low voltage) at Provincial Level, 2012

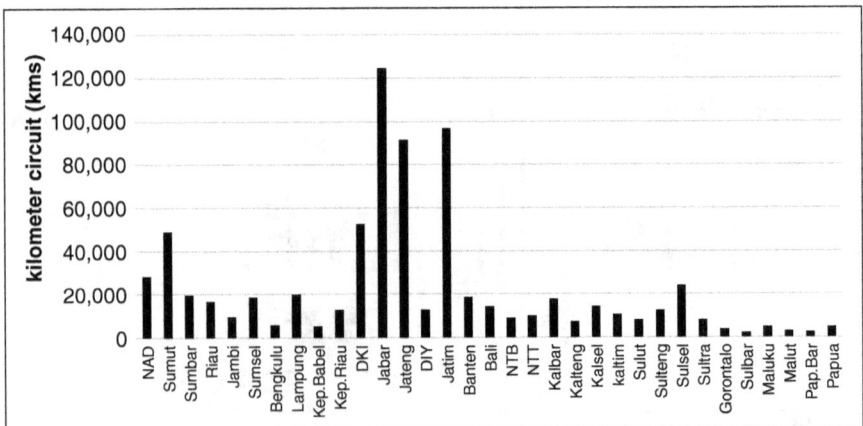

Source: PLN (2012).

Figure 7.8
Installed Capacity of Travo at Provincial Level, 2012

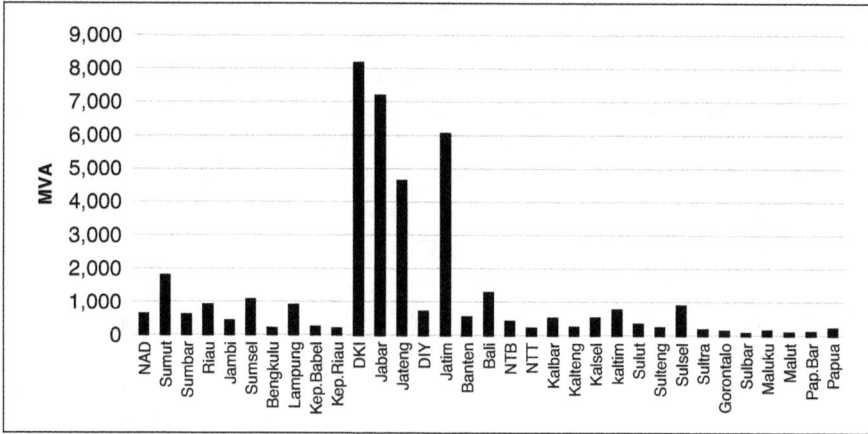

Source: PLN (2012).

This section raises three implications regarding the existing conditions of electricity access in Indonesia. Firstly, Indonesia has a significant number of people without electricity access. Thus national efforts, assistance, and support are needed not only to increase the supply of electricity but also to alleviate the inequality in power consumption across the provinces. Secondly, investments in power supply both on-grid and off-grid are needed to overcome the geographic challenges as an archipelagic nation. In dealing with the lack of electricity access, the government needs to take the lead by focusing on the rural areas and promoting rural electrification programmes. Lastly, since many islands do not have access to electricity, rural electrification programmes and small island electrification programmes will likely share many similar aspects and face common challenges.

MAKING ELECTRICITY AFFORDABLE

The government believed that by nationalizing electricity companies, electricity will be made more accessible to the poor. In compensation to the state electricity company, the government has provided both direct and indirect subsidies. According to Sudja (1993, as cited in Kristov

1995), the price of electricity from private developers was nearly 50 per cent higher than PLN's, because the private sector tends to reach excessive rates of return and also it depends on commercial loans with high interest rates. Further, McCawley in 1970, Munasinghe and Warford in 1982, and Amarullah in 1986 (as cited in Kristov 1995) indicated that electricity supply costs in Indonesia was higher than the average revenue which ranged between 40 per cent and 140 per cent. Similarly by comparing the electricity supply cost between 1980/81 and 1993/94, and considering the existence of hidden subsidies to PLN such as the exchange rate risks, interest rate subsidies, and opportunity costs of state equity in PLN, Kristov (1995) found that the supply cost was 45.5 per cent higher than PLN's average sales.

It seems that PLN's monopoly is necessary to avoid the high cost economy and to ensure that electricity is affordable for the poor. But this hinges onto the fairness issue of not only the allocation of subsidies, but also the opportunity cost for people that do not have access to electricity. As seen in Figure 4.2 on p. 75 of this book, after 2004, electricity subsidy increased rapidly. This is because between January 2003 and June 2010, the government did not increase electricity tariff. However, due to declining world energy prices between 2008 and 2009, electricity subsidy decreased by US$3.9 billion (see Table 7.2).

Electricity price consists of several components such as electricity purchase and diesel rented, fuel and lubricant oil, maintenance cost, personnel, depreciation of capital goods, and others. Most of the cost goes towards paying fuel and lubricant oil. Between 2008 and 2013, the share of fuel component reached 67 per cent of the total cost (PLN 2013). Because fuel cost has substantial impact on electricity cost, the distribution of electricity subsidy will be different across the regions. This is because the prime mover of generating electricity and technical efficiency of generators are diverse across the regions. In 2007, about 50.8 per cent of electricity subsidy was consumed by outside Java–Bali region, while in Java–Bali it was about 49.2 per cent (Sambodo 2009). In contrast, the rates of capacity in Java–Bali and outside Java–Bali were about 23 per cent and 77 per cent respectively (PLN 2009). This indicates that to generate the same amount of electricity, outside Java–Bali needs more subsidy than in Java–Bali. This is mainly because oil becomes the backbone of

Table 7.2
World Price of Crude Oil, Natural Gas, and Coal

	Spot Crude Price ($/bbl)	Natural Gas (US dollars per million Btu)	Coal (US dollars per tonne)
1998	13.0	1.9	29.5
1999	18.1	1.6	27.8
2000	28.4	2.7	31.8
2001	24.4	3.2	36.9
2002	25.0	2.4	30.4
2003	28.8	3.3	36.5
2004	37.9	4.5	72.4
2005	54.0	7.4	61.8
2006	64.9	7.9	56.5
2007	71.8	6.0	84.6
2008	98.3	10.8	148.1
2009	62.1	4.9	78.8
2010	79.5	6.6	105.4
2011	106.5	9.0	125.7
2012	107.3	9.5	105.5
2013	106.0	10.6	90.9

Note: Spot crude price (the average price of Dubai, Brent, Nigerian Forcados, and West Texas intermediate); natural gas (Heren NBP Index); coal (Asian Marker price).
Source: BP Statistical Review of World Energy, June 2014.

the outside Java–Bali system while in Java-Bali, the prime energy mover of generators is coal. Further, more than 65 per cent of PLN's customers are located in the Java–Bali region. In addition, in terms of electricity subsidy per capita, outside Java–Bali is higher than in Java–Bali (PLN 2009).

Further, Table 7.3 shows the distribution of electricity subsidies based on the type of customers (household, business and industry). Most of the subsidies was allocated for household customers at 450 VA and below. Between 2007 and 2013, the allocation of subsidy increased by Rp 10.9 trillion for customers who were connected at 450 VA and below. However, PLN's customers with 900 VA experienced the highest increase of electricity subsidy. This is because with 900 VA they can install more electronic devices and these consume more electricity. To be fair, consumers with the lowest voltage need to receive

Table 7.3
Electricity Subsidy Based on Type of Customer (in trillion Rp.)

Type of Customer	Voltage	2007	2013	Change (2013–2007)
Household	1. Up to 450 VA	10.23	21.15	10.92
	2. 900 VA	6.1	18.99	12.89
	3. 1,300 VA	2.27	5.64	3.37
	4. 2,200 VA	1.50	3.26	1.76
	5. > 2,200	1.01	1.51	0.5
Business	6. B.1, B.2, B.3	3.53	1.08	−2.45
Industry	7. I.2	0.742	1.75	1.01
	8. I.3–I.4	9.51	18.2	8.69

Note: B.1 (up to 2,200 VA); B.2 and B3 (> 2,200 VA); I.2 (up to 200 kVA); I.3 and I.4 (> 200 kVA).
Source: Sambodo (2009) and ISIS Malaysia (2014).

greater amount of electricity subsidies. Thus, electricity subsidy is regressive towards the lower income families.

Furthermore, in 2012, 60 million Indonesian people and 41 per cent of rural households did not have access to electricity. This implies that these people did not directly benefit from electricity subsidy. In fact, by increasing the amount of electricity subsidy, it may reduce their chance to obtain electricity as early as possible because more electricity subsidy means less funds for expanding electricity infrastructure.

In the business sector, electricity subsidy declined. This implies that the business sector pays electricity tariff at the market rate. However, the industrial sector still obtained electricity subsidy which mostly benefitted large companies (I.3–I.4). According to Sambodo (2009), in West Java Province, about 24 per cent of the electricity sold to industrial and commercial sectors was consumed by textile, garment, and leather industries; while the share to chemical, oil, coal, rubber, and plastic was about 16.5 per cent, with quarrying (excluding metal) at about 14.7 per cent. Thus, electricity subsidies benefitted mostly the labour intensive and resource-based industries.

However, electricity blackout is still frequent in West Java province, both with and without notice (Sambodo 2009). This affected the industrial performance due to lower product quality and delay in product delivery. The blackouts bring extra cost to the companies. Even textile companies, such as Panasia Indosyntec, developed its own steam coal power plants for two main purposes: (i) to ensure a reliable electricity supply for their own use, and (ii) to sell extra power supply to PLN. However, only a few companies can develop their own power supply and most of them need to rely on the supply from PLN. Thus providing electricity subsidy does not necessarily benefit companies. It would be more beneficial to obtain a high quality power supply at a reasonable price. Therefore, it is better to reallocate the electricity subsidy towards improving the infrastructure of the power supply.

The price of electricity at the household level in the early 1980s, 2003, and 2013 was investigated. These three time periods were selected due to data availability. As seen in Table 7.4, there are three major changes we can observe. First, in terms of the type of customers, the government has expanded it from three to six categories. Second, the government has also further expanded each category into several blocks. This means that calculating the price of electricity has become more complex and progressive pricing policy has been implemented. Finally, the government has removed the fixed cost component for customers with electricity consumption above 900 VA.

In order to make the prices comparable, we need to deflate the nominal price. Table 7.4 indicates the real price for each category of customers. However, we need to be careful when comparing the prices because in 2003 and 2013, the government implemented progressive tariff before the average price for each group was calculated. In 1980, the price gap between the lowest and the highest voltages was about Rp 1.32, but in 2003 and 2013, it increased to Rp 2.02 and Rp 3.08 respectively. This indicates that the government has become more progressive in implementing tariff policy. In real terms, the electricity price decreased between 2003 and 2013 (both for fixed and variable costs). Surprisingly, if we compare the variable cost for customers with less than 500 VA between 1980 and 2013, it decreased substantially from Rp 2.33 to about Rp 1.04, but the fixed

Table 7.4
Price of Electricity for Household Customer
(Nominal and real price in Rp.)

Type of Household Customer	May 1980 FC	May 1980 VC (kWh)	May 1980 (Real price, 2000 = 100) FC	VC (kWh)
R1 <=250, but less than 500 VA	@IDR 25	23	127.61	2.33
R2 >501 VA, but less than 2,200 VA	VA, IDR 70	31		3.14
R3 >2,201, but less than 6,600		36		3.65

	December 2003 FC	December 2003 VC (kWh)		December 2003 (Real price, 2000 = 100) FC	VC (kWh)	AP
R1 <=450 VA	11,000	Block I, 0–30	169	79.37	1.22	2.46
		Block II, 30–60	360		2.60	
		Block III, >60	495		3.57	
		AVG	341	2.46		
R1 900 VA	20,000	Block I, 0–20	275	144.31	1.98	2.92
		Block II, 20–60	445		3.21	
		Block III, >60	495		3.57	
		AVG	405	2.92		
R1 1300	30,000	Block I, 0–20	385	217.18	2.78	3.19
		Block II, 20–60	445	3.21		
		Block III, >60	495	3.57		
		AVG	442	3.19		
R1 2200	30,200	Block I, 0–20	390	217.90	2.81	3.20
		Block II, 20–60	445		3.21	
		Block III, >60	495		3.57	
		AVG	443	3.20		
R2 2200–6600	30,400	NA	560	219.35	4.04	
R3 > 6600	34,260	NA	621	247.20	4.48	

	October 2013 FC	October 2013 VC (kWh)		October 2013 (Real price, 2000 = 100) FC	VC (kWh)	
R1 <=450 VA	11,000	Block I, 0–30	169	33.55	0.52	1.04
		Block II, 30–60	360		1.10	
		Block III, >60	495		1.51	
		AVG	341	1.04		
R1 900 VA	20,000	Block I, 0–20	275	60.99	0.84	1.24
		Block II, 20–60	445		1.36	
		Block III, >60	495		1.51	
		AVG	405	1.23		
R1 1,300	NA	NA	975	NA	2.97	
R1 2,200	NA	NA	1,004	NA	3.06	
R2 3,500–5,500	NA	NA	1,145	NA	3.49	
R2 6,600	NA	NA	1,352	NA	4.12	

Note: FC = fixed cost for every month; VC = variable cost; AP = average price for the respective group; AVG = average cost for three blocks; we deflate the nominal price with GDP deflator which we obtained from World Bank national accounts data, and OECD National Accounts data files; blocks I–III indicate the level of electricity consumption in kWh.
Source: Author's calculation.

cost increased from Rp 127.6 to about Rp 341. Further, GDP per capita at real price between 1980 and 2013 increased more than 3.3 times. Thus, electricity has become more affordable. Later, we will see that although the real price has declined, low income families still experience difficulties receiving grid connection due to high installation cost.

WHO ARE THE ELECTRICITY-POOR PEOPLE?

Indonesia needs to increase the rural electrification ratio in order to reduce the number of people without access to electricity. However, Patunru (2013) argued that there are many other urgent non-income poverty problems that must also be given consideration. For example, low educational level of the people, insufficient sanitation facilities, lack of clean water, and unhygienic living conditions. Since all investment programmes have an opportunity cost, it is necessary to assess whether an investment in rural electrification programmes is worthwhile at present time or priority needs to be given to other purposes (McCawley 1978). Thus in improving policy design to reduce non-income poverty, the characteristics of electricity poor families must be studied and analysed in detail to better understand the larger problem as a whole.

To study the electricity-poor families in Indonesia, data from the National Socioeconomic Survey (SUSENAS) issued at the first quarter of 2013 was used.[4] The data covered 70,845 households from 33 provinces. About 92.3 per cent of the respondents had access to electricity, both from PLN and non-PLN,[5] while less than 8 per cent did not have access to electricity, or that they depended on oil lamp and other sources (see Figure 7.9).[6] The identified installed capacities for PLN's customers showed that they were mostly connected to 450 watt and 900 watt, or 41 per cent and 32.9 per cent respectively. Interestingly, about 14 per cent of PLN's customers did not have metering. Having no meter means that the customer pays a fixed amount monthly regardless of the amount of electricity consumed, and that PLN had the electricity constructed from off-grid connection, such as from hydropower, solar panel and other sources.

Generally speaking, customers who have metering obtain more benefits than those without metering. Customers with metering have at least a power capacity of about 450 watt (the minimum capacity level for household customers). Customers with non-metering power supply usually have power capacity much less than 450 watt. SUSENAS

Figure 7.9
Percentage of Households that use Electricity for Lighting by Sources

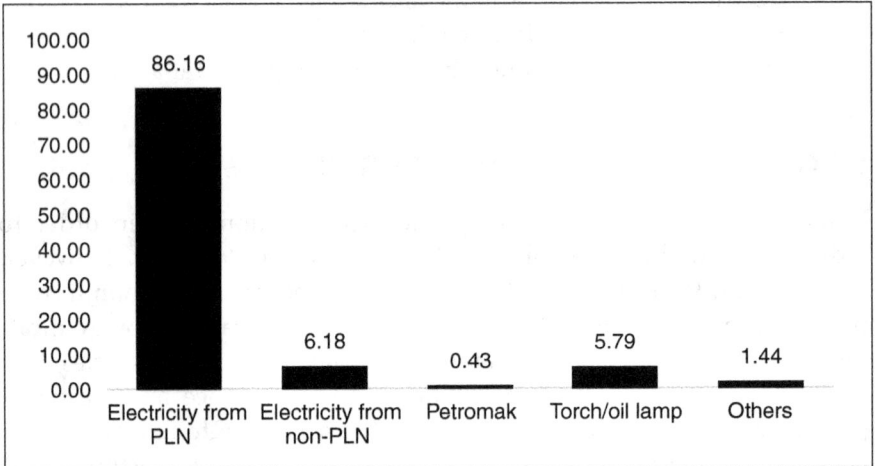

Source: Calculated from SUSENAS (first quarter 2013).

data also indicated that about 5,429 households do not have access to electricity (both from PLN and non-PLN sources) and 96.5 per cent of them live in rural areas. As a source of lighting, the shares of *petromak*, torch/oil lamp, and others were about 5.6 per cent, 75.5 per cent and 18.8 per cent respectively. This indicates that oil lamp is the main source for daily lighting.

To elaborate on the information about households without electricity access, three aspects were analysed: (i) housing conditions; (ii) social protection; and (iii) information and methods of communication. About 91 per cent of the respondents said that the houses they lived in belong to him/her. The roofs were made from zinc (53 per cent) and fiber or sago palm (*ijuk/rumbia*) (24 per cent). The walls were made from wood (66.7 per cent), bricks (13 per cent), and bamboo (11.9 per cent). The floors were covered by wood (41.5 per cent), land (23.4 per cent), and cement (22.4 per cent). The average floor area of the house was about 36.9 square metres (the minimum was 3 square metres and the maximum was 496 square metres). The source of drinking water came from unprotected spring water source (21.8 per cent), protected spring water source (19.3 per cent), river (16.8 per cent), unprotected well

(14.5 per cent), protected well (12.5 per cent), and rainfall (9.8 per cent).[7] This has implications on water consumption for cooking that also came from similar sources such as unprotected spring water source (20.9 per cent), protected spring water source (18.5 per cent), river (17.5 per cent), unprotected well (14.6 per cent), protected well (12.9 per cent), and rainfall (10.1 per cent).

Most households did not have toilet (54 per cent) and only about 27 per cent had their own toilet. The rest used joint toilets (10.7 per cent) and public toilets (7.7 per cent). Families that did not have a toilet depended on nearby beach/ground/farm (28.7 per cent), holes on the ground (27.8 per cent), river/lake/sea (24 per cent), indicating a high risk of exposure to community disease and poor sanitation. For cooking purposes, about 94 per cent of the respondents used firewood, 2.5 per cent used LPG (liquid petroleum gas), and less than 2 per cent used kerosene.

Social protection has become an important issue for the poor. The government has provided several programmes, such as: (i) rice for the poor (*Beras Miskin*, Raskin); (ii) family-based poverty alleviation programme (*Program Keluarga Harapan*/PKH); (iii) National Program for People Empowerment (*Program Nasional Pemberdayaan Masyarakat*/ PNPM); micro-credit loan (*Kredit Usaha Rakyat*/KUR); (iv) student assistance for the poor (*Bantuan Siswa Miskin*/BSM); and (v) social security and health. About 64 per cent of households obtained Raskin and 95.8 per cent did not participate in the PKH programme. About 1.8 per cent of households were included in the micro-finance programme. About 10 per cent of the respondents said that they obtained student assistance from the government and most of them were assistance for primary school education (4.7 per cent), junior high school education (1.9 per cent), and senior high school education (0.7 per cent). The relatively low beneficiaries of this programme may be due to few schools in the areas, especially for junior and high schools. In terms of health assistance, about 46.5 per cent of households said that they used *jamkesmas* (the community health protection scheme), *jamkesda* (the regional health insurance), *jampersal* (maternity insurance), and others.[7] Finally, only about 0.6 per cent of households have access to retirement benefits, indicating that most respondents worked in the informal sector.

Interestingly, mobile phone penetration in non-electrified households was relatively high. Only about 1.1 per cent of households had fixed telephone lines, but 37.6 per cent of households said that they owned mobile phones. Those without electricity access recharge their mobile phones at their neighbours' houses that have electricity. On average, people have more than one mobile phone, the maximum number being eight. In terms of possessions, 20 per cent of households said that they owned motorcycles; 6 per cent bicycles; and 9.6 per cent boats.

About 35.6 per cent of households said that their income was not enough to fulfill their daily needs. Several ways used to meet their daily needs include borrowing from family members (22.7 per cent); borrowing from friends and neighbours (18.4 per cent); selling goods that they have (8.2 per cent); and using their savings (5 per cent). Lack of income and unmanaged expenditure contribute to this condition. For example, although some households own motorcycles and mobile phones, but without the appropriate economic activities, these items result in extra expenditures instead. Lack of access to government programmes such as student assistance for education and Raskin may also result in having to spend more on education and food.

Lack of electricity access is only one element of non-income poverty. The majority of people who do not have access to electricity also lack access to safe water supplies and clean sanitation. They also depend on firewood for cooking. Some are partly excluded from social protection programmes due to exclusion error. Poor living conditions and inability to obtain social security force the community into unsustainable livelihood. Thus, lack in electricity access is only one among many complex problems that rural households face in improving the quality of their lives. Therefore, before any infrastructure project can be developed, the list of needs of the people have to be discussed and analysed in depth so that a proper sequence of developing infrastructure can be prepared (Nugroho 2012). It is also possible to provide a bundle of policy packages that aims to support sustainable livelihood.

MANAGING THE RURAL ELECTRIFICATION PROGRAMME

This section provides a brief historical background on the rural electrification programme in Indonesia. It investigates the dynamic organization and institution, actors and outcomes, before sketching out some lessons learned on why the rural electrification programme has not been successful for the past six decades.

The rural electrification programme in Indonesia was documented in the Planned Overall National Development (*Pembangunan Nasional Semesta Berencana*/PNSB) during the period 1961–68. PNSB was an economic development programme during President Sukarno's era. At that time, large power projects were given the highest priority, while medium projects were constructed to fill the gap between supply and demand. For small scale power supply, especially in the rural areas, microhydropower obtained the highest priority.[8] In the late 1950s, rural electrification was conducted in three distinct parts (McCawley 1978). The largest part was carried out with an assistance from an American aid for a total capacity of 23 MW that covered 40 separate sites. Then the Czech scheme with a total capacity of over 15 MW was installed at 54 sites. Finally, PLN also executed the programme 8 MW of diesel scheme, and it consists of German-made units. McCawley (1978) argued that these programmes run with increasing dissatisfaction in the outer islands that led to political problems and there were many difficulties encountered during the implementation process (McCawley 1978). They include: (i) logistic problems because many projects were located in remote areas; (ii) issues of maintenance and operation; (iii) lack in standardization and coordination; (iv) low utilization capacity; and (v) high running cost.

PLN has started the rural electrification programme on 9 July 1959 (PLN 1995). A special affair was established in the PLN Directorate of Construction, being the Rural Areas Electric Power Section, as stated in Decree No. 58/DDPLN/59 (PLN 1995). Up to 1976, most villages had their electricity supplied from the existing networks. Further, the Minister of Public Works and Electric Power Decree No. 16/PRT/1976 dated 20 October 1976 formed a Sub directorate of Rural Electrification within the PLN Directorate of Operation (PLN 1995). This Sub directorate conducted several activities such as research, construction, and development of rural electrification (PLN 1995). In the New Order era, according to the Minister of Public Works and Electric Power Regulation No. 16/PRT/1976 on 26 October 1976, the government asked PLN to manage the rural electrification programme.

According to Munasinghe (1988), rural electrification issues have become increasingly important since the mid-1970s. There are two objectives of the national rural electrification policy (Munasinghe 1988), namely achieving a high rate of economic growth, and realizing a more equitable distribution of income and social welfare. There is a higher interest in pursuing the first objective for two reasons (Munasinghe 1988). First, it can ensure a faster load growth and cost recovery, thus this will improve the capacities to supply electricity to remote areas. Second, providing output and employment through electricity-induced productivity gain can hopefully improve welfare of the people in the long run, rather than providing electricity subsidy under poorly targeted rural electrification scheme. Because the growth approach was important, the government set a higher priority to provide electricity to modern villages, instead of transitional and traditional villages.[9] However, Mohsin (2014) argued that during the New Order regime, the rural electrification programme, or better known as *Listrik Masuk Desa*, had two functions. First, it was a tool to improve the economic conditions of the villages. Second, it was a political instrument for the GOLKAR party to secure votes (vote-buying strategy) from rural people in the general elections.

The village unit cooperatives (*Koperasi Unit Desa*/KUD) had an important role in the early stages of the rural electrification programme. This can be seen from a joint decision between the Minister of Mining and Energy and the Minister of Trade and Cooperatives No. 755/ Kpts/M.Pertamb/1979 and No. 613/Kpb/XI/1979 on 9 October 1979 concerning the Implementation of the Development of Village Unit Cooperatives in Electric Power and Petroleum Fuel Distribution. Further, there was an agreement between PLN and the Directorate General of Cooperatives Development No. 001.NK/050/1990/M and No. 20/SKB/ BUK/I/1990 that stated that the PLN and the Directorate General of Cooperative Development agreed to support the increasing role of KUD in electric power business by making those KUDs which satisfied the criteria to participate in electric power work execution in the villages in PLN work areas all over Indonesia (ESDM 2000). Similarly, according to Munasinghe (1988), two ministries were involved in the rural electrification programme: (i) the Ministry of Mines and Energy (MME), its Directorate General for Energy and New Energy, and PLN; (ii) the Ministry of Cooperatives, its Directorate for the Promotion of Electricity Cooperatives, and the Project Development Office.

Cooperation between PLN and KUD was developed in several areas, such as education and training; survey, research, and development; information and guidance; design of pilot unit and general supervision of electric power; and other activities that may support KUD business in electric power (DPE 2000). KUD became PLN's partner in developing rural electrification. As seen in Table 7.5, there are four patterns of cooperation that can be promoted.

Four policies were implemented by the Department of Cooperative and Small Enterprises Development on the rural electrification programme. They were: (i) increasing the role of KUDs in executing the rural electrification programme by cooperating with PLN and the private sector; (ii) supporting independent KUDs (KUD Mandiri) through execution of rural electrification projects; (iii) assisting KUDs in executing rural electrification projects in areas which were unreachable by PLN distribution network; and (iv) planning of the programme outside Java. Since 1990/91, Management Service Arrangement (*Perjanjian Jasa Management*/MSA) was developed between PLN and KUD. Up till 1992/93, MSA Pattern had been developed with fifty-two KUDs in eleven provinces. In addition, Rural Electricity Cooperatives (KLP) had been operating since 1978[10] in Lampung (Sinar Siwo Megu), Luwu (Somabotuna), and Lombok (Sinar Rinjani). These three projects were supported by the US government (USAID) for US$9,168,953 and the Government of Indonesia through Investment Fund Account (*Rekening Dana Investasi*/RDI) for Rp 9,168.2 billion. Up till end 1991/92, the total installed power in the three KLPs were 10,294 kW with 1,660 kmc distribution network facility.

The government also provided rural electrification credit to prospective customers who were unable to pay the connection charges and home installation fees. Since 1982/83, the Directorate General of Budget and the Directorate General of Financial Institution has offered soft loan/credit to prospective customers under the Rural Electrification Credit scheme (*Kredit Listrik Perdesaan*/KLP). Between 1982/83 and 1994/95, KLP helped about 721,850 customers (PLN 1995). PLN also participated in the Armed Forces Rural Operation (*ABRI Masuk Desa*/ AMD) and up till 1994/95, this operation has covered 220 villages all over Indonesia (PLN 1995).

PLN (1995) argued that between 1977/78 and 1993, electricity consumption for the household sector in rural areas increased from 1.77 per cent to 10.3 per cent and the nature of rural consumption was mainly for consumptive purposes (85 per cent) and productive activities (15 per cent). Although the installed connection was about

Table 7.5
Pattern of Partnerships between PLN and KUD

Pattern	Description	Results in Repelita V (1989/90–1993/94)
I	KUD reads the kWh meter, collects the bills, maintains network and handles minor technical complaints.	Development programme for 4,000 independent KUDs by cooperation through patterns I and II.
II	KUD, in addition to the activities in Pattern I, also carries out installation of low voltage network and network maintenance.	In execution up to 1992/93 cooperation with PLN was achieved through patterns I and II for 2,297 KUDs which served 14,525 villages or 6.87 million households.
III	KUD buys bulk electric from PLN/private sector medium voltage network for distribution to KUD members as customers.	Development of Pattern III through utilization of PLN and private sector excess power, with a target of 549 villages. Through Pattern III, there was only one KUD, namely Wira Karya in Lhokseumawe (Aceh), which constructed the necessary facilities in 1987.
IV	KUD carries out commercial electricity power business, including power generation, transmission, distribution as well as connection and installation at the premises of KUD members as customers.	Using PLTM (microhydro power plant) with a target of 521 villages. KUD Wira Karya purchased 2 MW electric power from two fertilizer plants at Rp 25.00/kWh. Up to end 1991/92, this KUD had supplied electric power to 35 villages, serving 2,300 customers. Up to end 1992/93, the number of villages implementing Pattern IV reached 60 KUDs which utilized PLTD's (diesel power plant) as the generators of the electric power which was supplied to 476 villages with 63,636 customers.

Source: DPE (2000).

450 VA, the utilization was about 250 VA and it was used on average between 7–8 hours per day (PLN 1995). There is a target to obtain total rural electrification by the end of Repelita VII (five-year development planning) or by 2004/5 (PLN 1995).[11] In Repelita VI, or between 1994/95 and 1998/99, the total number of villages that plan to be served is about 18,619 with 6,578,210 customers and in Repelita VII, or between 1999/2000 and 2004/5, the target is about 13,033 villages with 7,041,825 customers. However, the target has not been achieved yet.

According to BPS in 2012, the number of villages was about 79,702 and between 2004 and 2012, the average number of new villages increased by 1,230 yearly.[12] The number of villages that had been electrified by PLN between 1977 and 1994 reached 34,790 with a total number of about 10.3 million customers (see Table 7.6). However, according to PLN (2012), by 1993/94, the total numbers of household customers and customers (include industries, commercial and others) were about 11.2 million

Table 7.6
Realization and Target of Rural Electrification Programme

Period	Year	Number of Villages	Number of Customers
	1977/78	76	3,800
	1978/79	2,244	280,085
	1983/84	7,636	1,377,233
	1984/85	9,194	1,814,437
	1985/86	10,660	2,334,608
	1986/87	13,101	2,933,589
	1987/88	16,773	3,954,372
	1988/89	18,794	4,708,626
	1989/90	20,559	5,440,670
	1990/91	23,142	6,310,950
	1991/92	24,889	6,844,036
	1992/93	27,090	7,562,512
	1993/94	31,689	8,916,716
End 1994		34,790	10,383,408
Target on Repelita VI (1994/95–1998/99)		18,619	6,578,210
Target Repelita VII (1999/2000–2004/5)		13,033	7,041,825
Total (1977–94)		205,847	52,481,634
Total (1977–2005)		237,499	66,101,669

Source: PLN (1995).

and 15.1 million respectively. Thus the share of household customers in rural areas to the total PLN's customers was about 80 per cent. It seems that by comparing 10.3 million customers in the rural area and 11.2 million PLN customers, the figure has overestimated the number of rural customers. This is probably due to the overlapping regions between the rural and urban areas.

It is difficult to determine the progress of rural electrification in Indonesia if agencies have their own definition of the rural territory. PLN (1995) said that,

> village or rural electrification is defined as the supply and operation of electricity in areas outside the capital city of the Republic, or outside of the capital cities of provinces, districts, municipalities, and administrative townships which are supplied by small scale electric power generators or medium voltage network.

However, McCawley (1971) argued that American aid for the rural electrification programme was targeted at semi-urban rather than the rural areas because it was planned at small towns and not in rural areas. Similarly, Table 7.7 states the definition of village or rural according to laws and also lists subsequent regions under rural areas. Before 1979, rural was administratively under the second or third level of regional government. However, the laws before 2014 did not clearly define the characteristics of rural areas beyond the administrative authority. Definition of rural is very complex and may vary among government institutions. Thus, decision-makers need to refer to BPS's definition.[13]

PLN (1995) mentioned two challenges regarding the rural electrification programme. Firstly, due to the generally low electricity consumption in rural areas, feasibility study must be conducted to assess the least costly option, for example through extending the grid connection and promoting small scale renewable energy sources, such as geothermal, mini-hydro and solar home system. Secondly, there should be a clear and sustainable financing structure for a long-term rural electrification programme. Because PLN has become a limited company on 16 June 1994, the problem of funding for long-term rural electrification development programme needs to be effectively resolved. Since Repelita II, the coalitions between PLN,

Table 7.7
Legal Definition of Rural Area

No.	Law Number and Name	Definition
1.	Law No. 19 of 1965 on Desa Praja (Rural Praja)	A unit of orderly community that has certain border, rights to manage its own community, select its own leader, and own property. In terms of organization structure Desa Praja is under First Level Region (Daerah Tingkat Satu/Province) and Second Level Region (Daerah Tingkat Dua/District). Dukuh is part of Desa Praja, it is the livelihood of community and is usually called *dusun, dukuh, kampung* and others.
2.	Law No. 5 of 1979 on Rural Government	Region that consists of unified orderly community, has an organization structure under a *Camat* (head of subdistrict) and has the authority to manage its own needs under the Unitary State of the Republic of Indonesia.
3.	Law No. 22 of 1999 on Local Government	A unit of orderly society that has the rights to manage its own needs following the origin and tradition of its community, that is acknowledged by the national government and is under a district (*kabupaten*).
4.	Law No. 32 of 2004 on Local Government	A unit of orderly society that has the rights to manage its own needs following the origin and tradition of its community, that is acknowledged and respected by the Unitary State of the Republic of Indonesia.
5.	Law No. 6 of 2014 on Rural	Rural and custom rural or other name is a unified orderly society that has regional boundary, has the authority to manage its own governance, pursue community interests based on its own efforts, origin of rights, and/or traditional rights that is acknowledged and respected by the Unitary State of the Republic of Indonesia. There are two types of rural: rural and custom rural. The formation of new rural is based on several criteria, such as: (i) at least five years part of mother rural; (ii) having minimum population size and number of households in the community, for example at least about 6,000 people or 1,200 households in Java and at least about 500 people or 100 households in Papua and Papua Barat; (iii) having transportation access inter and intra region; (iv) socially and culturally in harmony; (v) having resources (natural, human and other supporting resources); (vi) having rural boundaries that have been declared by head of district or city regulation.

KUD, as well as the Rural Electricity Cooperatives (*Koperasi Listrik Perdesaan*/KLP) have been developed but have not been successfully implemented. This was due to three major problems (PLN 1995): (i) high cost; (ii) uniform electric power tariff; and (iii) limited availability of investment fund for the rural electrification programme.

Similarly, McCawley (1978) was sceptical about the rural electrification programme for two reasons. Firstly, based on economic valuation, rural electrification seems a doubtful priority in Indonesia. He also argued that at present, electricity is a luxury goods and the rural electrification programme mostly benefitted the wealthier people in rural areas who usually use electricity for consumption purposes. Secondly, the programme was disorganized, fragmented and poorly coordinated. Three agencies which have direct responsibilities for the rural electrification programme are: (i) PLN; (ii) Department of Cooperatives and Small Enterprises Development; and (iii) Technology Assessment and Application Agency (*Badan Pengkajian dan Penerapan Teknologi*/BPPT). However, there is no single government department with an overall integrated view of the situation.

THE CURRENT DEVELOPMENT OF THE RURAL ELECTRIFICATION PROGRAMME

In 2003, the Indonesian government launched the Energy Self-Sufficient Village programme [*Desa Mandiri Energi*/DME]. The DME programme was based on two pillars: (i) non-oil, such as micro hydro, wind power, solar photovoltaic (PV), and biomass; and (ii) non-fossil oil, such as biofuel and bioethanol. Micro/mini-grid is one of the possible solutions to improve electrification ratio especially in rural and remote areas. Increasing electricity access is one of the basic services. According to the Ministry of Energy and Mineral Resources (MEMR) Regulation No. 3/2013, based on the technical guide in utilizing specific allocation fund in rural energy for financial budget 2013, there are four types of renewable energy that can be developed to increase rural electrification ratio (see Table 7.8).

The government through the PLN aims to increase the electrification ratio. PLN has prepared thirty-one units of work that support the rural electrification programme. The units of work are responsible

Table 7.8
Types of Renewable Energy following MEMR Regulation No. 3/2013

No.	Type	Note
1.	Microhydro	Small scale with capacity below 1 MW
2.	Solar-concentrated	Using photovoltaic technologies, electricity is distributed on-grid to end users. The number of users in one community is at least 30 members. The equipment that needs to be included are array module, solar charge controller, inverter, battery bank, module array support, distribution panel, house installation, power house, security system, and distribution network.
3.	Solar-dispersed	Using photovoltaic technologies, electricity is distributed off-grid or directly to end users. The number of users in one community should be less than 30 members. The equipment that needs to be included are array module, battery control unit, battery, lamp and box contact, inverter (if needed), and module array support (if needed).
4.	Biogas	Main component or 40–70 per cent of methane with carbon oxide.

for installing electricity networks (transmissions and distribution infrastructure). The central government budget has financed these tasks since 2011. The Ministry of Finance has provided a special allocation fund (*Dana Alokasi Khusus*/DAK) to support the programme. The fund is used for developing new microhydro projects (less than 1 MW), repairing microhydro plants, and expanding and improving services of microhydro (off-grid), developing solar panel (concentrate and disperse),[14] and home-based installation of biogas.[15] The government has also expanded the programme. Before 2011, DAK only mentioned rural infrastructure without any specific purpose. In 2011, the government allocated Rp 150 billion to support the rural electrification programme and in 2012, the fund was increased to about Rp 190,64 billion. Since 2013, the name of the programme has changed from rural electrification to rural energy. This indicates that the scope of energy services has expanded to include the broad energy area. As a result, the total allocation fund has increased substantially to about Rp 497,94 billion in 2013.

In addition to DAK in the electricity sector, the Ministry of Energy and Mineral Resources (MEMR) has implemented the rural electrification programme. According to the 2013 budget, MEMR allocated Rp 2.9 trillion for the extension of the grid connection (4,452 km for medium voltage network and 4,791 km for low voltage connection) and preparing the home distribution (3.431 units) with a capacity of 216.75 MVA. The Indonesian government also acknowledges increasing access to electricity as one of the main solutions for poverty alleviation. It started a programme called "cheap electricity and power saving" (*listrik murah dan hemat*) which is targeted at poor households and fishermen.[16] In 2013, the number of targeted households was about 94,140 (see Table 7.9). In 2014, the budget for rural electrification increased to Rp 64.5 billion and the number of targeted households increased to about 95,100. The unit cost increased from about Rp 1.6 million in 2012 to about Rp 2.2 million in 2015, or an increase of 36 per cent.

However, a high connection fee still remains the main obstacle for grid connection, especially among the poor. In September 2014, the number of poor people was about 27.7 million and about 63 per cent of them lived in the rural areas with a per capita monthly expenditure of about Rp 296,681 compared to Rp 326,853 in urban areas. Dealing with more than 60 million people without electricity access and with

Table 7.9

Number of Targeted Families and Budget for "Listrik Murah dan Hemat"

Year	Number of Targeted Families	Budget (in billion Rupiah)	Budget per Family (in Rupiah)
2012	60,702	100.7	1,658,928
2013	94,140	149.48	1,587,829
2014	95,100	213.99	2,250,248
2015	121,399*	273.18	2,250,006

Note: * planned figure
Source: Author's calculation from the Ministry of Energy and Mineral Resources.

the assumption that each family consists of four members, we have about 15 million households without electricity access. If we assume that 30 per cent of them are poor, this means that the government needs to support about 4.5 million poor households. If the budget for installation is about Rp 2.25 million, this implies that the government needs to prepare about Rp 10.1 trillion or about 37 times the current budget, or about 14 per cent of electricity subsidy in 2015. Thus, it seems that the current problem is not due to a lack of investment funds, but in allocating electricity subsidy to the targeted group.

Further, the budget for constructing medium voltage networks, low voltage networks, and distribution stations between 2011 and 2015 ranged between Rp 2.16 trillion and Rp 3.1 trillion. This implies that even after including the expenditure of the *listrik murah dan hemat* programme and investment on the networks and distribution stations, the existing spending on the rural electrification programme still falls

Figure 7.10
Correlation between Electrification Ratio and Budget on Rural Electrification Programme (provincial data, 2011–14)

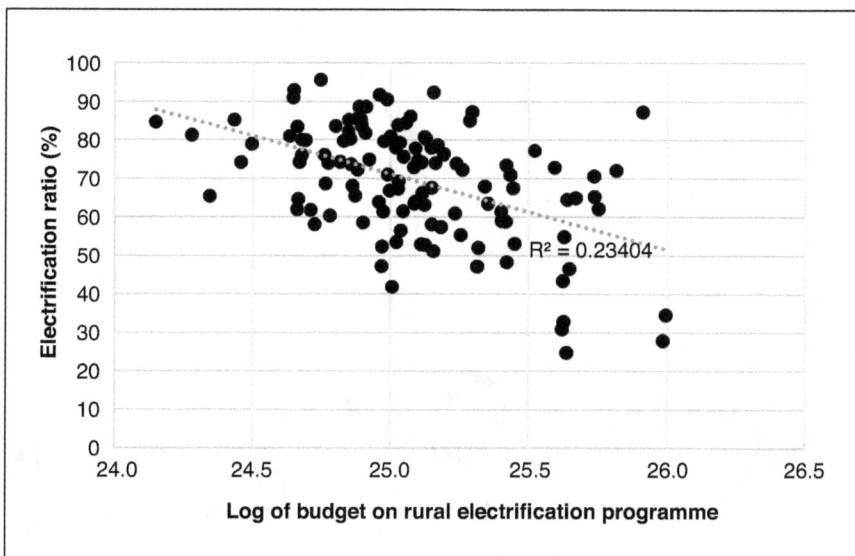

Source: Author's calculation.

below the electricity subsidy. This means that by reallocating electricity subsidy to support the rural electrification programme, the government can have better resources to improve the electrification ratio.

It seems that provinces with low electrification ratio correspond with a higher budget allocation on rural electrification programme (see Figure 7.10). However, the linear correlation between the two variables is relatively weak. A graphical depiction of the cumulative funds of the rural electrification programme and improvement in the electrification ratio at the province level can be used as a measure of the success rate of the rural electrification programme (see Figure 7.11). We expect that as more funds are allocated to the provinces, the electrification ratio will increase. However, there is a negative linear correlation between the total budget disbursements on the improvement of the electrification ratio. This implies that providing more budget

Figure 7.11
Correlation between Improvement in Electrification Ratio and Accumulation Fund on Rural Electrification Programme (provincial data, 2011–14)

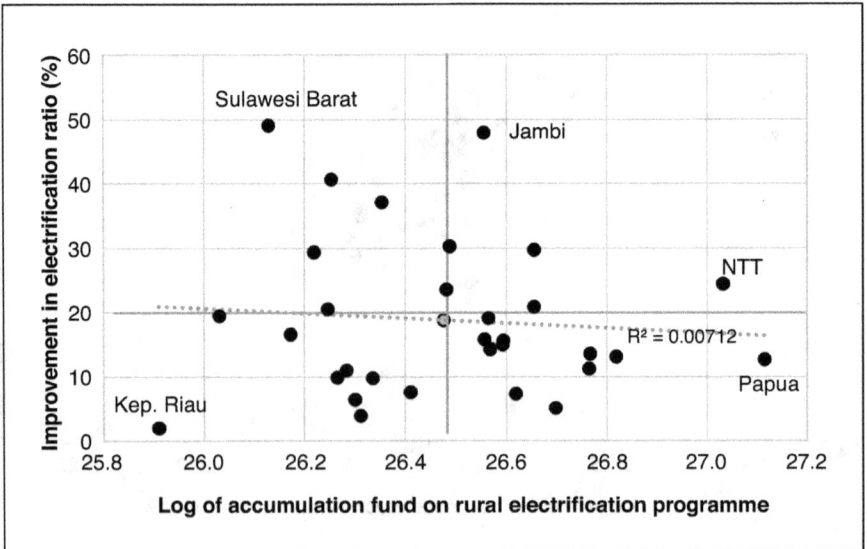

does not necessarily increase the electrification ratio. For example, Papua and East Nusa Tenggara (NTT) Province obtained the highest budget for the rural electrification programme, but the improvement in their electrification ratios were relatively lower compared to other provinces with a lower budget, such as Jambi and Sulawesi Barat Province. Kep. Riau (Riau Archipelagic) obtained the smallest budget and there was no substantial change in its electrification ratio.

To support the rural electrification programme, PLN adopts two approaches — extending the grid and off-grid connection. To extend the grid connection, PLN needs to develop network infrastructure, both for medium voltage and low voltage. It is estimated that by 2024, about 56,924 kmc (kilometre circuit) of JTM needs to be constructed and 57,851 kmc of JTR needs to be developed (PLN 2014). PLN foresees the total investment cost between 2015 and 2024 to be about Rp 41,093 billion (PLN 2014). The total investment cost of the rural electrification programme is about 4.7 per cent of the total PLN investment cost between 2015 and 2024 (excluding the investment cost from independent power producers) (PLN 2014).

A massive on- and off-grid (micro grid) connection programme was announced in PLN's letter no. 1227.K/DIR/2011. The programme was called SEHEN, which stands for *Super Ekstra Hemat Energi* [Super Extra Energy Saving]. There are two types of supply and utilization of solar PV — communal PV and autonomous (*mandiri*) PV. Under communal PV, there are two further types — PV communal-autonomous and PV communal hybrid.[17] Table 7.10 indicates the characteristics of the two types of PV. In the case of autonomous SEHEN, the total electricity production per year is about 26.3 kWh.[18] This still falls below the standard set by AGECC (2010) for basic human needs.

LESSON LEARNED FROM THE SEHEN PROGRAMME IN THE NTT PROVINCE

NTT Province is one good example to learn about the rural electrification programme in Indonesia for two main reasons. First, previous analysis has indicated that NTT has relatively low electrification ratio and electricity consumption per capita. Second, NTT has the highest

Table 7.10
Communal PV and Autonomous PV

Communal PV	Autonomous PV-SEHEN
1. Connected capacity location is more than 5 km of PT PLN's grid	1. Location is more than 10 km of PT PLN's grid or is located near the sea or river chasm
2. Population density relatively high	2. Location needs to be close to customers
3. Customers have income to pay the electricity bills	3. Customers have income to pay the electricity bills
4. Total capacity of 220 VA	4. Only enough capacity for 3 LEDs with a total capacity of about 3 watt
5. PT PLN finances the programme	5. Total capacity of 12 watt power (Wp)
6. Manage and supervise by PT PLN	6. Technical lifespan is 15 years for solar PV
7. Property belongs to PT PLN (except electricity equipment after the energy limiter)	7. Technical lifespan is 10 years for LED
8. Tariff for autonomous communal is Rp 14,800 per month (plus connection fee). This follows Presidential Regulation No. 8/2011 (for S1 category).	8. LED belongs to PT PLN
9. Tariff for communal hybrid PV follows Presidential Regulation No. 8/2011 (plus connection fee)	9. PT PLN finances the programme.
	10. This is a transition programme before customers are connected to 450 VA.
	11. Manage and supervise by PT PLN
	12. Property belongs to PT PLN
	13. Total monthly payment of Rp 35,000 that consists of a monthly fee (subscription fee of Rp 14,800 per month) and rental cost of equipment at Rp 20,200 per month.

number of SEHEN's customers. According to PLN in February 2013, the total number of customers was more than 113,715. Currently, the total number of residential customers (on-grid) was about 487,941 (PT PLN 2012). This indicates that more than 23 per cent of PT PLN's customers in NTT were on off-grid connection. In February 2013, the total sale of SEHEN reached about Rp 1.68 billion. However, the amount of accounts receivable was also higher than total sales which reached Rp 1.92 billion, indicating that many customers did not or could not meet the monthly payment. Alternatively, we can also argue that PLN did not collect the monthly payment effectively.

There are two main reasons why the amount of accounts receivable tends to increase and since January 2013, it was higher than total sales. First, PLN faced difficulties in identifying customers that were included in the SEHEN programme. This was because their contractors not only worked on projects for SEHEN but also for other customers. Hence PLN needed to validate the data before it could collect the money. The whole process took several months to complete. Second, customers delayed or refused their payment to PLN for several reasons, such as: (i) difficulties in making payment due to the distance to the PLN office or local bank; (ii) malfunction of SEHEN equipment; (iii) lack of money due to an irregular income.

NTT Province not only has the SEHEN programme, but the local and central governments also allocate budgets to support rural electrification programmes, such as the solar home system (SHS). Both SEHEN and SHS aim to increase people's accessibility to electricity. In 2010 and 2011, the provincial government constructed about 182 and 194 units of SHS respectively (Distamben NTT 2010). The MEMR constructed about 1,843 units in 2008 and 3,582 units in 2009 (Distamben NTT 2010). The Ministry of Less Developed Areas (*Kementerian Pembangunan Daerah Tertinggal*/KPDT) constructed 1,175 units of SHS in 2008 (Distamben NTT 2010). The government also developed concentrate or communal PV.[19] Besides PV, there are six micro hydro projects that have been operating in NTT. The projects are financed by the local government, central government (MEMR), and KPDT.[20] Finally, there are sixteen units of biogas with funding from the local and central governments.

PLN is responsible for the maintenance and operating expenditure of SEHEN, while under the SHS programme, maintenance and operation are the responsibilities of the user or community. Thus, there is a monthly payment for SEHEN which can be made directly through the bank or through PLN's local offices. Under the SHS programme, most services are free of charge and even if there is payment to be made, the amount is determined by the user (bottom-up approach) and is cheaper than SEHEN's tariff.[21] In terms of technical specification, there are differences. Energy and Mineral Resources (*Energi dan Sumber daya Mineral*/ESDM) provides higher voltage than SEHEN, or about 50 Wp.

Next, the National Program on Community Empowerment of Rural Independency (*Program Nasional Pemberdayaan Masyarakat Mandiri Perdesaan*/PNMP-MP) also allocates fund for the rural electrification programme. This is a bottom-up programme. Between 2009 and 2011, in Timor Tengah Selatan (TTS) district, NTT province, the total units of SHS that had been constructed was about 4.657 (Distamben NTT 2010). According to evaluation from the local government, four major problems were identified in promoting the SHS programme. First, the specification of equipment could not meet the required contract terms. Second, there was a change in equipment specification while the project was still underway. Third, there was a lack of capacity knowledge and understanding in constructing the project. Fourth, the prepared documents were only for formality. The actual implementation was completely different from the planned specification.

Both the SEHEN and SHS programmes are clearly in competition with each other. It is possible that one programme can alienate the other. If both SEHEN and SHS programmes were to exist in the same village, most people would prefer the SHS programme as it is almost free of charge. This condition creates conflicts and causes people to refuse to pay for the SEHEN programme. Further, there is also a possibility of double benefits. This happened when people participate in both the SHS and SEHEN programmes. When the SHS programme cannot function properly due to technical errors and when these cannot be resolved, the people turn to the SEHEN programme.

In conclusion, reflecting the implementation of the off-grid programmes between SEHEN and SHS, it seems that there is still a lack in synergy across the programmes. Although the main objective of the programmes is to improve people's access to electricity, the benefits and costs are not comparable across the programmes. As a consequence, the sustainability of the rural electrification programme may face substantial challenges.

Notes

1. <http://www.kkp.go.id/index.php/arsip/c/9126/87-PULAU-DI-INDONESIA-TIDAK-BERPENGHUNI/?category_id=2> (accessed 28 February 2014).
2. Kepulauan Riau Province, Sulawesi Tengah Province, and Papua Barat Province are not included in the calculation because the number of islands is more than 1,000.
3. ASTAE stands for the Asia Sustainable and Alternative Energy Program and ESMAP stands for Energy Sector Management Assistance Program.
4. This is the latest data that can be obtained from *Statistics Indonesia*.
5. PLN is a state-owned electricity company while non-PLN means that households can obtain electricity by having their own electricity generator (usually oil generator), or they can buy electricity from private businesses or cooperatives.
6. The average percentage of respondents without electricity is about 9.3 per cent. Some provinces have a large number of respondents without electricity access, such as Papua (54 per cent), NTT (31.7 per cent), Maluku (23.7 per cent), Papua Barat (22.3 per cent), Sulawesi Barat (18 per cent), Kalimantan Tengah (14.6 per cent), Kalimantan Barat (14.4 per cent), Sulawesi Tengah (14.3 per cent), Maluku Utara (14.1 per cent), Gorontalo (12.5 per cent), and Sulawesi Tenggara (10.4 per cent).
7. Unprotected water spring source means the water comes from unprotected usage water, bath and washing purposes, and other usages; protected water spring source means the water is protected from usage water, bath and washing purposes, and other usages. Protected well indicates that the well is protected by a wall of at least 0.8 metres above the ground and 3 metres below the ground, and there is a cement floor of about 1 metre from the well; unprotected well does not have any wall or cement floor.
8. The capacity of microhydro ranged from 5 to 50 kW in villages with these three basic criteria (DPE 2000): (i) the number of households ranges between 100 and 400 families; (ii) supporting the household industry; (iii) having a water flow rate of 1 to 3 m^3/s and a height of 5 metres.
9. In 1983, the Ministry of Home Affairs classified villages into three categories: *swasembada* (modern), *swakarya* (transitional), and *swadaya* (traditional). At that time, the government identified 65,000 villages and the share of

modern, transitional, and traditional villages were 16 per cent, 41 per cent, and 43 per cent respectively.

10. These were in Lampung (Sinar Siwo Megu), Luwu (Somabotuna), and Lombok (Sinar Rinjani). The three projects were supported by the US government (USAID) for US$9,168,953 and the Government of Indonesia through the Investment Fund Account (*Rekening Dana Investasi*/RDI) for Rp 9,168.2 billion. Up to end 1991/92, the total installed power in three KLPs were 10,294 kW with 1,660 kmc distribution network facility.

11. Rural electrification rate is the share of households that obtain electricity to the total number of villages. This means that even if only one family in the village has access to electricity, the whole village is considered as an electrified village, even though many families do not have electricity access.

12. Badan Pusat Statistik, "Jumlah Desa Menurut Provinsi, 2004–2014" [Number of Villages Based on Province, 2004–2014], <http://www.bps. go.id/linkTableDinamis/view/id/858> (accessed 28 February 2014).

13. BPS defines three main indicators that are further divided into several sub-indicators to differentiate between urban and rural. The indicators are population density, percentage of households in the agricultural sector, and availability of urban facilities such as schools, market, cinemas/theaters, hospitals, hotels, percentage of households having telephones and electricity. BPS develops composite indicators for all the variables. If the total number of indicators is less than ten, the region is classified as rural. The contribution of electricity to the total score is 1 or 0, with 1 meaning that the percentage of households that use electricity is less than 90 per cent.

14. Concentrate means power is brought together and transmitted by cable to the end user while disperse means direct usage by the end user. The minimum output for concentrate module is 100 Wp per unit, while for disperse module, it is about 10 Wp.

15. According to the Ministry of Finance Regulation No. 201/PMK.07/2012 on 17 December 2012, there is a special allocated fund for rural energy in 2013. This fund is to be used to promote renewable energy at the local level. The government allocates Rp 432.5 billion or US$43.25 million for rural energy and this is about 1.7 per cent of the total special allocated fund.

16. This programme is almost similar to the Rural Electrification Credit, where the government provides free connection services, free vouchers, and even free basic installation at home.

17. PV communal-autonomous is communal PV that is operated by individuals; PV communal hybrid is communal PV that in terms of operation, it is combined with non-solar energy to improve the efficiency level.

18. This is calculated from: 12 watt × 6 hours × 365 days.
19. For example, in 2011, MEMR developed 8 kWh for 40 households in subdistrict Pantar Timur, Alor, NTT; while in 2010, KPDT constructed 5 kWh for 30 households in subdistrict Pantar, Alor, NTT (Distamben, NTT 2011).
20. The lowest capacity is about 15 Kw and the highest is about 35 Kw.
21. Interestingly, in Timor Tengah Selatan District, NTT, according to Local Regulation No. 4/2007 on retribution or management fee in utilizing local assets, including for any access from renewable energy such as micro hydro, PV, and hybrid. The monthly tariff is Rp 15,000 and it includes contribution to the district government (Rp 10,000) and maintenance cost (Rp 5,000). The maintenance cost is made up of a management fee of Rp 2,500 and a maintenance fee of Rp 2,500. The installation cost for micro hydro, PV and hybrid is Rp 150,000.

References

Advisory Group on Energy and Climate Change (AGECC). "Energy for a Sustainable Future". <http://www.un.org/wcm/webdav/site/climatechange/shared/Documents/AGECC%20summary%20report%5B1%5D.pdf> (accessed 19 June 2012).

Birol, Fatih. "Energy Economics: A Place for Energy Poverty in the Agenda". *The Energy Journal* 28 (2007): 1–6.

Commission on Sustainable Development (CSD). "Report on the Ninth Session: Economic and Social Council". <http://www.un.org/ga/search/view_doc.asp?symbol=E/CN.17/2001/19 (SUPP)&Lang=E> (accessed 20 March 2014).

Departemen Pertambangan dan Energi/DPE [Department of Energy and Mining]. *55 Years of Mining and Energy Development*. Jakarta: DPE, 2000.

Distamben (*Dinas Pertambangan dan Energi Provinsi Nusa Tenggara Timur*) [Local Government Agency on Mining and Energy, East Nusa Tenggara Province]. *Data Potensi dan Pengembangan Energi baru Terbarukan* [Potential Data and Development of Renewable Energy]. Kupang: Distamben, 2010.

International Energy Agency (IEA). *World Energy Outlook 2014*. Paris: OECD/IEA, 2014.

Institute of Strategic and International Studies (ISIS) Malaysia. *Reforming Peninsular Malaysia's Electricity Sector: Challenges and Prospects*. Kuala Lumpur: ISIS Malaysia, 2014.

Kementerian Kelautan dan Perikanan/KKP [Ministry of Marine Affairs and Fisheries]. *Kelautan dan Perikanan Dalam Angka* [Marine and Fisheries in Figure]. Jakarta: KKP, 2013.

Kristov, Lorenzo. "The Price of Electricity in Indonesia". *Bulletin of Indonesian Economic Studies* 31 (1995): 73–101.

McCawley, Peter. "The Indonesian Electric Supply Industry". PhD dissertation, Australian National University, 1971.

———. "Rural Electrification in Indonesia: Is It Time?" *Bulletin of Indonesia Economic Studies* 14 (1978): 34–69.

Mohsin, Anto. "Wiring the New Order: Indonesian Village Electrification and Patrimonial Technopolitics (1966–1998)". *Journal of Social Issues in Southeast Asia* 20 (2014): 63–95.

Munasinghe, Mohan. "Rural Electrification: International Experience and Policy in Indonesia". *Bulletin of Indonesia Economic Studies* 24 (1988): 87–105.

Nugroho, Hanan. *Energi Dalam Perencanaan Pembangunan* [Energy in Development Planning]. Bogor: IPB Press, 2012.

Patunru, Arianto A. "The Political Economy of Environmental Policy in Indonesia". In *The Environments of the Poor in Southeast Asia, East Asia and the Pacific*, edited by Aris Ananta, Armin Bauer, and Myo Thant. Singapore: Institute of Southeast Asian Studies, 2013.

PT PLN (Persero). *50 Years of PLN Dedication*. Jakarta: PT PLN (Persero), 1995.

———. *Statistik PLN* [Statistics PLN]. Jakarta: PT PLN (Persero), 2009.

———. *Statistik PLN* [Statistics PLN]. Jakarta: PT PLN (Persero), 2012.

———. *Statistik PLN* [Statistics PLN]. Jakarta: PT PLN (Persero), 2013.

———. *Statistik PLN* [Statistics PLN]. Jakarta: PT PLN (Persero), 2014*a*.

———. *Rencana Usaha Penyediaan Tenaga Listrik PT PLN (Persero)* 2015–2024 [PT PLN Business Plan for Electricity Utility 2015–2024]. Jakarta: PT PLN (Persero), 2014*b*.

Sahai, Dhruva. "Toward Universal Electricity Access: Renewable Energy-based Geospatial Least-Cost Electrification Planning". <http://documents.worldbank.org/curated/en/2013/11/18875440/toward-universal-electricity-access-renewable-energy-based-geospatial-least-cost-electrification-planning> (accessed 11 March 2014).

Sambodo, Maxensius Tri. "Kebijakan Sektor Kelistrikan" [Policy in Electricity Sector]. In *Pengaruh Kebijakan Bahan Bakar Minyak (BBM) dan Tarif Dasar Listrik (TDL) terhadap Kegiatan Ekonomi dan Kesejahteraan Masyarakat: Studi Kasus Sektor Industri* [The Impact of Gasoline and Electricity Policy on Economic Activities and People Welfare: Industrial Sector Case Study], edited by Maxensius Tri Sambodo. Jakarta: LIPI Press, 2009.

Soerawidjaja, T.H. "Beberapa Komentar terhadap Rencana Penyediaan Energi di Indonesia" [Several Comments on Energy Supply Planning in Indonesia]. Paper presented at Seminar Nasional Kebijakan Energi Nasiona Sebagai Fondasi Terwujudnya Kedaulatan Energi Nasional Menuju Kemandirian Bangsa [National Seminar on National Energy Policy as a Foundation toward National Energy Sovereignty and National Independence], Jakarta, 28 November 2011.

United Nations (UN). "Report of the World Summit on Sustainable Development". <http://www.un.org/jsummit/html/documents/summit_docs/131302_wssd_report_reissued.pdf> (accessed 8 October 2014).

United Nations Development Programme (UNDP). *Energizing the Millennium Development Goals: A Guide to Energy's Role in Reducing Poverty*. New York: UNDP, 2005.

CONCLUSION

Based on the energy security framework analysis, this book came to the conclusion that although the five dimensions (regulation and governance, availability, technology development and efficiency, environmental sustainability, and affordability) are interconnected, they need to be treated with different priorities. This book pointed out that regulation and governance needs to be at the centre of electricity sector discussion in Indonesia. This implies that scholars need to set different weights when assessing the ranks of the five dimensions in the case of Indonesia. The analysis suggested that regulation and governance needs to be placed as the core of improving energy security, followed by availability, technology development and efficiency, environmental sustainability, and affordability dimensions.

Reviews on the historical perspective indicated that since the first trading of electricity in Indonesia in May 1897, in terms of the regulation and governance dimension, Indonesia has not developed a mature and stable environment for electricity business. We need to highlight that the period of Japanese colonization, political struggle in the early independence period, the economic crisis at the end of the old order regime, internal conflict within PLN organization, the economic crisis in 1997/98, the collapse of the Soeharto regime, and increasing electricity subsidies have affected the development of the electricity sector in Indonesia. Lack in incorporating the national interest into a clear policy direction and lack in institutionalizing good policies had led to inefficiency and spread of rent-seeking behaviour. Good governance and good corporate governance need to move in the same direction, one needs to reinforce the other in a positive way. The future performance of the electricity sector depends on how regulation and governance can create business opportunities and economic stability.

Although the New Order period could have created a certain level of political and economic stability that was necessary for the development of the power sector, the strategies were constructed under two weak foundations. First, in order to improve the availability of power supply, the government has allowed the private sector to generate electricity and sell it to PLN. Unfortunately, improper contract agreements (a lack of transparency) and the strong involvement of Soeharto's cronies in some of the dealings caused PLN problems which later became complex and serious. Currently, the government has prepared regulations and standard procedures for independent power producer (IPP) procurement, but this will not automatically result in better outcomes. More efforts need to be devoted to create a competitive environment through transparency and competition. The involvement of the Supervisory Commissions on Business Competition (KPPU) and the Corruption Eradication Commission (KPK) are necessary to detect any possibility of conspiracy and bribery on goods and services procurement. The government can also set up a special task force that aims to monitor the progress on IPP procurement and to solve problems that affect the progress of the projects.

Developing good governance is necessary, but not sufficient. PLN also needs to develop good corporate governance. The 1997/98 economic crisis had placed PLN in a dire predicament. The depreciation of the Rupiah caused PLN's electricity tariff to be below the buying price from the private power generating companies. Similarly, the draft on energy sale contract also indicates that the price of electricity purchase is denominated in US dollars. Considering this situation, the government and PLN not only need to implement a currency hedge to deal with currency risks, but also to optimize the use of Rupiah for any transaction and encourage investment financing from national resources.

Second, the availability of power supply has increased, but the proportion of renewable energy to the total electricity production has declined. As a result, electricity production has become less environmentally friendly and the generating cost is mostly influenced by world energy price, especially that of oil, coal and gas. This implies that increasing the supply of electricity has been developed under the expense of the external environment. Due to a decline in oil production and a rapid depletion of coal and gas resources, Indonesia needs to develop an exit strategy to reduce its dependency on fossil fuel. This means that Indonesia needs to optimize renewable energy and move forward to greater energy conservation and efficiency.

Further, while the availability of power supply is increasing, it does not mean that there is no room for energy conservation. Education on the importance of electricity conservation needs to be promoted. Even in developed countries such as Japan and Singapore, awareness on the importance of energy saving can be observed in many public spaces. Availability of electricity supply and environmental sustainability are interconnected. Promoting technological development, efficiency, and renewable energy can improve the availability of energy. All three elements are the main pillars if Indonesia plans to pursue a green path power system. This can be realized if the government determines its targets on: (1) contribution of renewable energy to the total electricity production; (2) intensity target (kg CO_2/kWh); and (3) renewable energy consumption per capita (kWh/capita).

Expanding the availability of electricity may not necessarily ensure the affordability and equitability of electricity access. The Indonesian government also needs to electrify 60 million people who currently have no access to electricity. For combating electricity poverty, the government needs to cut and reallocate electricity subsidy to support the rural electrification programme. Then, electricity subsidy also needs to be reallocated to speed up power investment outside Java and for small islands. There is also an issue of fairness with regards to electricity consumption and installed capacity per capita across the provinces. People without electricity access also suffer from a lack of other basic infrastructures and social protection programmes. As a result, improvements in the accessibility to electricity will also need to be followed up by an improvement in other basic services.

Unfortunately, although Indonesia has made many attempts to enact successful rural electrification programmes, there has not been much improvement from past experiences. The programmes that had a better outcome in improving electricity access were not institutionalized. It seems that rural electrification is largely conducted by trial and error; that is, without proper planning. There is an absence of a systematic coordinating body that would enable the power sector to synchronize and to coordinate programmes on rural electrification; the coordination would need to be conducted at the ministerial level by the PLN and interested private sector groups. The lessons that can be learned from the East Nusa Tenggara case study is that SEHEN's capacity output cannot meet basic human needs. Due to uncoordinated efforts on the rural electrification programme and a lack in competency, the sustainability of the rural electrification programme is in doubt.

To ensure sustainability of the rural electrification programme, the government can adopt two approaches. First, according to Law No. 6/2014 on Village, the village government has the authority not only in managing local administrative matters but also in providing the basic needs of the people in the village. This includes access to electricity. To do this, the local government needs to set up a local business entity that can provide small scale energy access to the people. The village government can use the village fund from the central government to improve electricity access. According to Government Regulation No. 43/2014 on the Implementation of Village Fund, the government pointed out that 70 per cent of the village fund needs to be allocated for poverty eradication, education and health, infrastructure, and other programmes that support the agriculture sector. Second, it is necessary to pool all rural electrification programmes under the coordination of the Ministry of Energy and Mineral Resources. This strategy is important to ensure that all programmes have similar standard, quality, and are substainable.

INDEX

About the Author

Maxensius Tri SAMBODO is a researcher at the Indonesian Institute of Sciences (LIPI) — Economic Research Center. Between 2013 and 2015, he was a visiting fellow at the Institute of Southeast Asian Studies (ISEAS), Singapore. His research interests are on energy, environment, natural resources and economic development. He obtained a PhD from the National Graduate Institute for Policy Studies (GRIPS); a master's degree in International and Development Studies from the Australian National University; and a bachelor's degree in Economics and Development Studies from Padjadjaran University. His latest publications appeared in *ASEAN Energy Market Integration (AEMI): From Coordination to Integration* (2013); *Government and Communities: Sharing Indonesia's Common Goals* (2014); and *ISEAS Perspective: Watching the Indonesian Elections 2014* (co-author). He currently leads studies on the rural electrification programme in Indonesia, energy security, and small scale renewable energy in the context of the ASEAN Energy Market Integration.

www.ingramcontent.com/pod-product-compliance
Lightning Source LLC
Chambersburg PA
CBHW070242290326
41929CB00046B/2328